THE NATION
THAT NEVER WAS

The Nation That Never Was

RECONSTRUCTING
★ AMERICA'S STORY ★

Kermit Roosevelt III

THE UNIVERSITY OF CHICAGO PRESS

Chicago

The University of Chicago Press, Chicago 60637
© 2022 by The University of Chicago
Published 2022
Paperback edition 2023
Printed in the United States of America

32 31 30 29 28 27 26 25 24 23   1 2 3 4 5

ISBN-13: 978-0-226-81761-3 (cloth)
ISBN-13: 978-0-226-82951-7 (paper)
ISBN-13: 978-0-226-81762-0 (e-book)
DOI: https://doi.org/10.7208/chicago/9780226817620.001.0001

Library of Congress Cataloging-in-Publication Data

Names: Roosevelt, Kermit, 1971– author.
Title: The nation that never was : reconstructing America's story /
Kermit Roosevelt III.
Description: Chicago : The University of Chicago Press, 2022. |
Includes bibliographical references.
Identifiers: LCCN 2021046120 | ISBN 9780226817613 (cloth) |
ISBN 9780226817620 (ebook)
Subjects: LCSH: United States. Declaration of Independence. |
Constitutional history—United States. | Slavery—United
States. | Equality—United States.
Classification: LCC KF4541 .R66 2022 | DDC 342.7302/9—dc23
LC record available at https://lccn.loc.gov/2021046120

Contents

Introduction

★

IN 2014 PHILADELPHIA cheered as thirteen-year-old Mo'ne Davis, the first girl in Little League World Series history to pitch a winning game, took the Taney Dragons to the semifinals. Her story embodied everything America likes to believe about itself: here was the barrier-shattering underdog, leading an underfunded urban team, proving that for those with enough talent and drive, anything is possible.

And yet . . .

The Taney Dragons took their name from Taney Street, which runs to their home field by the Schuylkill River. Everyone pronounced the team's name "Tay-nee," but that isn't right. Law students learn in their first year that it's actually "Taw-nee." They learn that because it's the name of Roger Brooke Taney, fifth chief justice of the United States Supreme Court. Taney was the author of the *Dred Scott* decision, where he had something different to say about Mo'ne Davis and her fellow Black Americans. He said they had no rights that the white man was bound to respect, that they could never be citizens of the United States. Mo'ne Davis took the mound with that man's name written across her back.

The connection wasn't well known in 2014, and when it surfaced, some said the success of the Dragons redeemed the name.

"It means something else," a column in *Hidden City Philadelphia* proclaimed. "Taney is a word that has taken on its own meaning, a word that's become a symbol of hope."[1] But not everyone agreed. A group of citizens pushed to change the name of the street. On June 25, 2020, the Taney Youth Baseball Association declared that "the name 'Taney' has remained a source of divisiveness" and "we cannot ignore the very real negative feelings" that it provokes.[2] In October, they announced a new name: the Philadelphia Dragons. Was that the right choice? It was not our fault—not the fault of anyone now living—that Taney Street was named for Roger Taney. The name came to Philadelphia in 1858, one year after the *Dred Scott* decision. But it was our decision what to do about it now. Either keep the name and try to understand it in its best light—as something changed, as something now bearing a positive message—or make a break with the past and start over.

The same decision is playing out across the country, with monuments and statues (often those erected to honor the Confederacy), with buildings and schools. And something very similar plays out with American history more broadly. Repeatedly, Americans have faced the choice between maintaining and rejecting a connection with the past, between putting it in its best light as a way to move forward and burning it all down to start over. Neither answer is necessarily correct; neither will be the right choice in every circumstance. But there's one scenario that might always be wrong: What if you burned it all down and started over . . . and then pretended that you hadn't? What if you insisted on locating your ideals and your identity in an old order that you had already rejected—that, in fact, you had overthrown and destroyed by force? That should seem deeply odd. Yet this is what we do with the most fundamental question of American identity. We tell ourselves a story that links us to a past political regime—Founding America, the America of the Declaration of Independence and the Founders' Constitution—to which we are not the heirs. We are more properly the heirs of the people who destroyed that regime.

Why do we do this? Stories of national identity exist to fulfill a particular set of purposes: to bring people together in the name of shared ideals. The story that tells us we are the heirs of Founding America—what I call the standard story—once seemed like a good way to do this. But it is not, and it never was. When the standard story flourished, it encouraged a complacency that prevented progress toward its stated ideal. It allowed many of us to believe things about ourselves that aren't true. Once it came under attack, that standard story lost some of its power to unify and became a subject of profound disagreement instead. Less obviously, but more seriously, as we pushed forward a more accurate account, the standard story increasingly undermined itself. Whether people realized it or not, a story that was supposed to promote inclusive equality instead fed exclusive individualism.

By inclusive equality, I mean, generally, this belief: "Our political community is open. Those who are now outsiders are fundamentally similar to us and may become insiders. Political outcomes are legitimate if they are the product of an open and fair democratic process. Government can and should act to promote equality." By exclusive individualism, I mean more or less the opposite: "Our political community is closed. Outsiders are different and dangerous. Political outcomes are legitimate if they protect the rights and interests of insiders. Government has no business promoting equality and should not redistribute, especially not to outsiders." The contest between these two visions is shaking the nation today—but understanding how we got to this point will take most of this book to explain. Most of the book concerns different stories of America. I will criticize the standard story on several grounds and offer different versions of it that highlight its flaws. And I will propose an alternative. The standard story ties us to a problematic past, but we can escape that trap. We can cut the cord that linked Mo'ne Davis and Roger Taney—not by simply renaming a street, but by changing our understanding of who we are and where we come from.

The way we think about American history now—as a continual unfolding and realization of the principles enunciated in the Declaration of Independence—holds us back. Yet maybe that is not the right way to think about America. Maybe our relationship to the Declaration is different. Maybe our origins are not what we have been taught.

I CAME TO THE IDEAS in this book in the same manner as Hemingway described going bankrupt: gradually, and then suddenly. Gradually because as I taught constitutional law at the University of Pennsylvania over the past eighteen years, I encountered different areas of the subject that made little sense. Some of them were hot, newsy topics: the Supreme Court's treatment of affirmative action, for instance, or its invalidation of a key part of the Voting Rights Act. Some of them were relatively obscure: cases from the nineteenth century about interstate conveyances or the state action doctrine. But all of these peculiarities, I came to see, turned out to have a common root. They were all situations defined by aspects of constitutional doctrine that were helping to maintain racial hierarchy.

And then the subject overcame me suddenly. As I was working my way through the legal research, stories and videos of police killing Black people were coming out with horrifying frequency and regularity. Between 2014 and 2018, the stories of—among others—John Crawford III, Michael Brown, Tamir Rice, Freddie Gray, Philando Castile, Eric Garner, Stephon Clark, and Botham Jean hit the national news. I could imagine myself, as a twelve-year-old, playing with a toy gun—one Fourth of July I had shot a cap gun at passing cars. I could imagine myself in a store, chatting on the phone and carrying an air rifle I had taken off the shelf. What I could not imagine was police arriving on the scene and killing me within seconds. My writing was taking on a new and furious relevance—and then the George Floyd video came out. Protesters filled the streets and suddenly—finally—it seemed like everyone was paying attention.

One of these processes was gradual and scholarly; the other was immediate and visceral. But they carried the same insight. The official story does not hold together. Something else is going on. And race has a lot more to do with it than we were told. That's a white person's reaction, of course: the salience of race has always been far more obvious to Blacks. What breaks on one person like a wave of revelation is for someone else the tide that's been pulling at their ankles since birth. Still, I hope that what I have to offer here will be useful for many.

I wrote this book in part as a way of exploring things I felt I should understand. Michelle Alexander said in the foreword to her extraordinary book about mass incarceration, *The New Jim Crow*, that it was written for the person she was before she wrote it. So this book might be useful for the person I was before I spent so long learning about American constitutional history, about the original meaning of the Declaration of Independence, about the ways that race winds through our national story. And, as Alexander also said, it is for people who want to engage with others—people who want to tell their friends or their relatives or their coworkers that there is a different way to think about America. That is fundamentally what I offer. The point of this book isn't just to say that we've been lied to, or that American history isn't as glorious a tale of progress as many of us like to believe. I do argue that the standard account of American history isn't accurate—not because it leaves out unpleasant truths, although of course it does. It's because it tells us a fundamentally false story about *where* our values come from, and about *who* the heroes and villains of our national story are. Once we see that, we also see something else: There is another story that hasn't been told. There is a different, better way to understand America. It is more true, it is more inspiring, and it is more useful. It can bring us together in the way the standard story promised to.

I considered calling this book *America Again* because I was so struck by the Langston Hughes poem "Let America Be America Again," recommended to me by my friend Rebecca Tushnet. The poem starts with a voice proclaiming the title phrase and echoing the familiar tropes of American greatness: the land where "opportunity is real, and life is free, equality is in the air we breathe." A second voice, in parentheticals, challenges that story: "America

never was America to me . . . There's never been equality for me."
"Who are you?" demands the first voice: who is questioning America's greatness? The second answers that it is the voice of America's
downtrodden: "the poor white . . . the Negro . . . the red man . . . the
immigrant . . . the worker"—people who have been excluded from
America's promise. Yet it is they who believe in it the most. "I'm the
one who dreamt our basic dream." They are the ones who will make
it real: "We, the people, must redeem the land . . . and make America again!" Fundamentally, that is the argument of this book. Our
ideals were not handed down by the men who created the America of 1776. Instead, these ideals were articulated in reaction to the
oppression and exclusion of that America and fought for in large
part by the people who were excluded.

One final note: in this book I say "we" a lot. No matter who
you are, you will probably encounter at least one "we" to which
your reaction is "not me." And maybe that's true. But that reaction
illustrates a theme of the book, which is that the basic American
struggle is over who is an insider and who an outsider—who comes
within the most fundamental "we": *We the People*. I could have tried
to separate these—I could have carefully divided them into "I" and
"we" and "they" and "you"—but I believe that something is gained
by considering how well "we" works in different contexts. And I
believe that in the end, a real and inclusive *we* is what we strive for.

1

Stories of America

★

WHO ARE WE—as a nation, as a people? There's a simple answer to that question: We are Americans. However, the simple answer raises the harder question: What does it mean to be an American? What does America mean? And there are even more fundamental questions that sit behind those: Where do our answers come from? What form do they take? What tells us who we are?

The first point I want to make, one that explains the organization of this book, is that *stories* do all this. Stories organize the world for us; they put the stamp of meaning on the stuff of chaos. This is true, obviously, of individuals. When people think about their lives, they think about them in narrative form. They find themes, heroes, villains, and above all meaning. James Joyce said that this is the artist's task: "transmuting the daily bread of experience into the radiant body of everliving life." In this sense, we are *all* artists—we are all the authors of our own stories, not because we decide what happens but because we decide what it means: how it's interpreted. And usually we are the heroes of our own stories.

This is not just true for individuals. As Jill Lepore writes in *This America*, nations too need a story: "some kind of agreed-upon past." Stories about a nation's history give individuals a sense of national identity—of what it means to be a citizen of that nation, what the nation itself stands for. They tell us what our values and collective identity are. They are stories not just about the past but about the future: they give us a purpose, a mission, even a sense of destiny. Are these stories true? Not always. Some distortion of the past is probably inevitable. History always involves interpretation, and strict factual accuracy is not the sole or even primary criterion of a national story's success. A national story works if it unites. Stories knit the nation together. Or they should. When a national story no longer works, it creates a kind of identity crisis—just as when some personal revelation or change in circumstances forces us to reassess our individual stories. When our stories stop making sense, who are we?

That is the plight of America now. There is a story we have told ourselves for generations—the standard story. Like most national stories, it was never completely true, but it was true enough. It brought Americans together—or at least, it brought together enough Americans to form a governing coalition. It told us reassuring things about ourselves—that we were good, that we always succeeded, that our history was a steady progress toward the realization of deep and noble founding ideals. It looked like it was working—at least, it looked that way to the people in power. But no longer. We are going through a national identity crisis. Like a person questioning the story of their life, America is struggling to make sense of who it is. The standard story is no longer viable.

A new version is emerging—a more honest, less triumphalist one. But this version is equally problematic. It still clings to the central feature of the standard story: the idea that modern American ideals have their source in the Declaration of Independence, and that the story of America is the story of a nation struggling to realize those ideals. This new version of the standard story is less false. Yet it is still, fundamentally, backward. In both versions, the story is actually harmful to the values it purports to champion. It misidentifies both the heroes and the villains; it holds at its heart a terrible contradiction that divides us, creating irreconcilable visions of America. We'll get to what that contradiction is shortly. For now, the point is that we need to abandon the standard story in all its versions. But we cannot abandon stories entirely. We have to replace the standard story with one that can do the same nation-building, identity-forming work. That better story can be more accurate, and it can also be more powerful because—as I will spell out—it affirms the same values that the standard story claims to, and more effectively. Like our standard story, this new story can exhort us to love our country, to appreciate its virtues, and to believe in our Constitution. It can be at once more truthful, more optimistic, more inclusive, and more just. It can be more American.

But first let's hear the standard story.

THE HISTORY OF AMERICA *as a nation starts with the Declaration of Independence. Back in 1776, our great Founders wrote down some wonderful principles. They called them self-evident truths. All men are created equal. They are endowed by their creator with inalienable rights, including life, liberty, and the pursuit of happiness. Our Founders fought a war for those principles, and they built a society around them. They codified those principles in the Constitution.*

The Constitution sets out our fundamental values: liberty and equality—the keys to what it means to be an American. It tells us who we are. For more than two hundred years, our Constitution has served us well, because of the wisdom of the Founders. Our task as Americans is to be true to those principles.

We haven't always done that. We had slavery, of course, which is in direct conflict with the Declaration's principles of liberty and equality. But we fought a second war for those principles—the Civil War was fought in the name of the principles of the Declaration. Abraham Lincoln said so in the Gettysburg Address in 1863, when he looked back fourscore and seven years to 1776 and said the nation was conceived in liberty and dedicated to the proposition that all men are created equal. So the Civil War was a test of a nation so conceived and dedicated—but it was also an opportunity for Americans to move forward, to realize the promise of the Declaration more fully.

Even after the Civil War, that promise wasn't fully realized. Racism and discrimination persisted. Eventually, the civil rights movement rose up to challenge them, marching on Washington in the name of the Declaration. In 1963, from the steps of the Lincoln Memorial, Martin Luther King talked about the Founders, the "architects of our Republic," the people "who wrote the magnificent words of the Constitution and the Declaration of Independence." They promised, he said, that all men, Black as well as white, "would be guaranteed the unalienable rights of life, liberty, and the pursuit of happiness." He pointed to segregation, to race-based denial of the right to vote, as breaches of the promise made by the Declaration, and he dreamed of a day when we would "rise up and live out the true meaning" of "all men are created equal."

Maybe that day still hasn't come, but it's getting closer. The story of America is a story of living up to the ideals of our Founders, the ideals that started us on this journey. We move forward, but we're guided by the past, by the spirit of 1776. We remember, as President John F. Kennedy said, that we are the heirs of that first Revolution, and we still carry that banner—the flag of freedom, of equality. We march in the name of the Declaration of Independence.

THAT IS OUR STANDARD STORY. It is what many of us tell ourselves to explain who we are: the heirs of the first Revolution, the descendants of the signers of the Declaration of Independence, of the drafters of the Constitution. American history starts with the high note of the Declaration, and we're trying to sustain it. We're following the Founders' wisdom, which for nearly 250 years has pointed the way to a better America and a more perfect union.

The standard story means to be relatively nonpartisan. One of the reasons for its durability and popularity is that it has both progressive and conservative versions. Conservatives tend to focus on individual liberty, while progressives focus more on equality. All presidents in the twentieth century appealed to the Declaration of Independence, though for different purposes.[1] Calvin Coolidge quoted the Declaration to argue that "the fundamental conception of American institutions is regard for the individual," while Franklin Delano Roosevelt invoked the pursuit of happiness to defend the New Deal. Conservatives look to the past mostly as a source of authority, and they often conclude that the Constitution should be understood in the same way the drafters and ratifiers understood it. Progressives look to the past for justice, identifying ways we have fallen short. Conservatives are more likely to celebrate Americans for living up to the ideals of the Founders, while progressives are more likely to suggest that there is still work to be done. Yet both versions hold that the ideals of the Declaration lead us forward. Gerald Ford said, "To be an American is to subscribe to those principles which the Declaration of Independence proclaims and the Constitution protects." Barack Obama, in his first inaugural address, said that "America has carried on . . . because we, the people, have remained faithful to the ideals of our forebears and true to our founding documents."

So the idea that our values were set out in the Declaration of Independence, fought for in the Revolution, made law by the Constitution, and gradually realized through our history is deeply embedded in our modern identity. There are many things to say about this story. Before evaluating it, let's start by describing. What should stand out to us about this idea of American identity?

The first thing to note is that it is a backward-looking story. Our ideals have their origin in the past—at our very beginning. The Declaration is the central document in this story, maybe more important, maybe more truly American, than even the Constitution. But the Constitution is important too. The Constitution has the answers to our current problems. If America seems adrift, we should go back to the wisdom of the Founders. Focus on the Constitution, the original understanding of it. Live up to the ideals of the Founders, be more like them. The way forward is by recovering past greatness.

The second thing about this story is that it's a success story. Yes, we've had our difficulties, but America always succeeds. We always triumph—because of the wisdom of the Founders and the ideals of the Declaration. The Civil War is probably the best example of that: it was a terrible war, but the ideals of the Declaration triumphed and we took a big step toward realizing them.

And the third thing is that it's a story of continuity. There's a line that goes from the signers of the Declaration of Independence, through the drafters of the Constitution, to us today. The continuity of the standard story is related to the fact that it's a success story: we're the same people we've always been, the same nation. The signers of the Declaration, the drafters of the Constitution, they got it right. We're living in the world they designed; we're fighting for the ideals they championed.

So this is a nice story in a lot of ways. You can see why it appeals to people. It tells us that we're good, we Americans. We started out with good ideals, which we haven't always lived up to, but we're getting better. We're succeeding. When things look dark, answers exist if we look back. There's authority in the past, in this moment of unity that everyone can rally around, everyone can share in. Everyone can feel a connection to the Declaration and the Founding.

I'm going to question these claims, but more important, I'm going to show that there is a better story—and it rejects all three of these features. This story looks forward, not back. It is a story of failure, not success. And it is a story of ruptures and breaks with the past, not a story of continuity. Given those differences, what is perhaps most amazing about the better story is how closely it tracks the standard one. It starts with a bang. A shot heard round the world. A war to throw off an unjust system and replace it with a better one. A determination to take into our own hands the decision who the American people are, to forge a new national identity. There's a short document expressing these ideals and a longer one giving them the force of law. There are soldiers who died for our rights and lawmakers who wrote them into our Constitution. All of this is true . . . but none of it in the way we have so often been taught. It's a different shot, a different war, different documents, different people. And we, like a child stolen from its parents and raised by impostors, we, too, are not the people we thought we were.

Again, that better story must wait. The standard story has persisted for a long time, and we need to look more closely at how and why it consolidated its hold on our national identity. Almost no one now actually argues *against* the standard story. Instead, we see arguments *within* its framework. But there have been other understandings of America's founding documents and ideals, expressed by dissenters from the triumphal narrative. There is a lot to learn from those perspectives. Not because we necessarily want the same things these dissenters did, but because their interpretations might be right. And, most important, embracing their views now might lead us down very different paths than it would have hundreds of years ago.

2

Questioning the Standard Story

Dissenters

★

THE STANDARD STORY as I have set it out is relatively straight-forward. It focuses on a few foundational documents, and only parts of them. It tells us that our ideals were stated in the preamble to the Declaration of Independence, fought for in the Revolution, and codified in the Constitution. Less explicitly, it venerates the Found-ers as great men, worthy of our admiration and emulation.

How has the story held up over time? Each of these elements has faced notable challenges. Overall, there have been two main developments. First, the triumphalist aspect of the standard story has diminished. Academics and activists have complicated our understanding of the Revolution, the Founders' Constitution, and the Founders themselves. These revisionist views have, to greater and lesser degrees, made their way into our politics and our culture. Some are still controversial; others are becoming conventional wis-dom. That has shifted the standard story in a slightly more progres-sive direction but has not altered its fundamental character.

The second development, which is more important, is that the standard story has become dominant. I do not mean the triumphal-ist version, which in fact has eroded. What has become dominant is the idea that the Declaration of Independence states our val-ues, and that American history has progressed—in fits and starts, with steps forward and back—toward a greater realization of those ideals. While there were meaningful challenges to that view in the past, today it is now largely unquestioned, even by those regarded as radicals. Indeed, as the luster of other parts of the standard story dims, one response has been to place more weight on the Declaration of Independence. This is a time-honored strategy—we will see it employed by the opponents of slavery and the champions of civil rights. But however well it may have worked in the past, it is a fundamental mistake in the world we live in now. The Declaration cannot do the work that we ask of it. Explaining why starts with an analysis of the key historical figures and arguments.

LINCOLN AND HIS FOILS

Abraham Lincoln is probably the most important single figure in the promotion of the standard story. He gives a strong statement of every element: the Declaration, the Revolution, the Constitution, and the great men. Lincoln's reading of the Declaration was relatively simple and consistent. In pronouncing that all men (by which he understood all people) were created equal, Lincoln argued, the Declaration set out a principle about their proper status in society and how they should be treated by government. In his 1858 debates with Stephen Douglas, he claimed that the "central idea" of America "at the beginning was, and until recently had continued to be, 'the equality of men'"—not equality in "size, intellect, moral development or social capacity" but equality of their inalienable rights. The authors of the Declaration

> meant to set up a standard maxim for free society, which should be familiar to all, and revered by all; constantly looked to, constantly labored for, and even though never perfectly attained, constantly approximated, and thereby constantly spreading and deepening its influence and augmenting the happiness and value of life to all people of all colors everywhere.

For Lincoln, equality is an *aspiration*, something that society works toward. The drafters of the Declaration "did not mean to assert the obvious untruth that all were then actually enjoying that equality, nor yet that they were about to confer it immediately upon them. . . . They meant simply to declare the right, so that enforcement of it might follow as fast as circumstances should permit." Lincoln's equality is conferred by the government, in the form of legal rights. Making people equal, not in their circumstances but in their rights, was for Lincoln a main purpose of government. The maxim of equality was placed in the Declaration, he said, not as part of its argument for independence but for future use. The Founders expected that Americans would pursue its perfection.

Lincoln's view finds its greatest expression in his 1863 Gettysburg Address, where he proclaimed that America was a nation "conceived in liberty and dedicated to the proposition that all men are created equal." The Gettysburg Address was transformative in important ways, but its understanding of the Declaration was by then relatively conventional. The interpretive victory had largely been won before the Civil War. (Briefly, people seeking to promote equality—notably Black and white abolitionists and enslaved people—fastened on the language about liberty and equality because the Declaration was the only federal document to offer those words.) To see how complete the victory of Lincoln's interpretation was, we can look at two of his best-known antagonists, Stephen Douglas and Roger Taney.

Douglas and Taney both contested Lincoln's reading of "all men are created equal," but each of them *accepted* Lincoln's understanding that equality referred to legal rights in society. Because they opposed equality—because they were trying to support slavery—they argued that "all men" did not really mean all people. "No man," Douglas proclaimed in 1858, "can vindicate the character, motives, and conduct of the signers of the Declaration of Independence, except upon the hypothesis that they referred to the white race alone, and not to the African, when they declared all men to have been created equal. . . ." Indeed, they did not even mean all whites.

They simply meant that "British subjects on this continent [were] equal to British subjects born and residing in Great Britain; that they were entitled to the same inalienable rights, and among them were enumerated life, liberty, and the pursuit of happiness."

Taney—joined by six other justices—said the same thing, and for the same reason. The "general words" of the Declaration did not include Black people. If they had, "the conduct of the distinguished men who framed the Declaration of Independence would have been utterly and flagrantly inconsistent with the principles they asserted; and instead of the sympathy of mankind, to which they so confidently appealed, they would have deserved and received universal rebuke and reprobation." Such hypocrisy was inconceivable, Taney argued because "the men who framed this declaration were great men—high in literary acquirements—high in their sense of honor, and incapable of asserting principles inconsistent with those on which they were acting." From a modern perspective, this argument is ludicrous. "All men" is a strange way to say "all British subjects," and one hardly vindicates the character of the signers by arguing that they were racists instead of hypocrites. The important point here, though, is that Douglas and Taney were forced into their absurd positions because they accepted Lincoln's understanding of equality. To find someone who did not, we have to go back further—and we will, in the next chapter. For the moment, though, let's turn to the other elements of the standard story.

The Revolution itself played less of a role in Lincoln's political thought and rhetoric, but he treated it as sacred, charging his listeners at the Young Men's Lyceum in 1838 to "swear by the blood of the Revolution" like "the patriots of seventy-six did to the support of the Declaration of Independence." (Oddly, the principle he sought to consecrate in the blood of the Revolution was "never to violate in the least particular, the laws of the country; and never to tolerate their violation by others"—about the least revolutionary principle you can imagine.) He not only praised the Founders; according to Gordon Wood, it was Lincoln who *made* Washington, Jefferson, Madison, and the rest into our Founders. Before Lincoln, "when most Americans referred to the 'founders' they meant John Smith, William Penn, William Bradford, John Winthrop and so on, the founders of the seventeenth century."[1]

Noted abolitionist speaker Frederick Douglass agreed with Lincoln on these points. In his famous 1852 speech, "What to the Slave Is the Fourth of July?," he gave a standard account of the Declaration and the Revolution. The Declaration, he said, "is the ring-bolt to the chain of your nation's destiny. . . . The principles contained in that instrument are saving principles." The signers of the Declaration, he went on, "were brave men. They were great men, too." So did the abolitionist William Lloyd Garrison. In the 1833 Declaration of Sentiments of the American Anti-Slavery Society, Garrison quoted the preamble as "[t]he corner stone" upon which a "band of patriots . . . founded the Temple of Freedom." Garrison and Douglass, we will see, did not agree with Lincoln about all elements of the standard story, and they may have been behaving strategically here, since criticizing the Declaration or the Revolution was unlikely to be effective. Condemning those aspects of the Founding would leave them no place to stand. But by venerating the Founding, they could use the exalted past as a fulcrum for criticism of the degraded present. Lincoln took this tack in his debates with Stephen Douglas, arguing that we had fallen away from the Declaration's principle of equality and must return to it. Frederick Douglass made the same point with a sharper tone. The America of 1852 was betraying its founding ideals, he charged. "Whether we turn to the declarations of the past or to the professions of the present, the conduct of the nation seems equally hideous and revolting. America is false to the past, false to the present, and solemnly binds herself to be false to the future." He also declared, "For revolting barbarity and shameless hypocrisy, America reigns without a rival."

The Founders' Constitution, the last piece of the story, presented a different issue. Reject the Declaration and the Revolution in the 1830s and you have very little left of America, no real way to argue that American values are on your side. However, with the Founders' Constitution, there was a choice. Foes of slavery could read it in its best light, trying to work with what they had, or they could reject it and try to build something new—the two options that face anyone born into an imperfect world. Lincoln and the Republican Party took the first one. The 1856 Republican platform committed itself to "the principles promulgated in the Declaration of Independence, and embodied in the Federal Constitution" and argued that the Constitution prohibited Congress from allowing slavery (a "relic[] of barbarism") in the territories. Douglass similarly ended "What to the Slave Is the Fourth of July?" by calling the Constitution "a glorious liberty document." As the election of 1860 approached, he told a Glasgow audience that "the way to abolish slavery in America is to vote such men into power as will use their powers for the abolition of slavery" and concluded that the Constitution "will afford slavery no protection when it shall cease to be administered by slaveholders."[2] Some radicals went even further and argued (implausibly) that the Constitution prohibited slavery.

Trying to claim the Constitution for your side makes some obvious sense. The Constitution is binding law and very difficult to change. (Amending the Constitution requires approval by two-thirds supermajorities in both houses of Congress and then three-quarters of states.) Still, not everyone chose this path. On July 4, 1854—two years after Douglass's excoriation of American hypocrisy and praise for the anti-slavery Constitution—William Lloyd Garrison took the stage at an anti-slavery rally and struck a match. He lauded the Declaration of Independence as announcing "equality of rights" but asked what there was to celebrate on its seventy-eighth anniversary. He produced a copy of the 1850 Fugitive Slave Act and set it on fire. And did the same to a copy of a judge's decision ordering the return of fugitive slave Anthony Burns. Then a judge's instructions to a jury considering charges against those who had tried to free Burns. Finally, he raised a copy of the US Constitution, "the source and parent of all the other atrocities—a covenant with death and an agreement with hell." As the flames consumed it, his voice rang out again. "So perish all compromises with tyranny!"

Garrison's interpretation of the Founders' Constitution as pro-slavery was consistent with his abolitionism. It was shared by the early Frederick Douglass, who in 1849 pronounced that the Constitution "was made in view of the existence of slavery, and in a manner well calculated to aid and strengthen that heaven-daring crime." It was also, of course, shared by supporters of slavery like Roger Taney. In *Dred Scott v. Sandford*, Taney announced his limited view of the Declaration's promised equality, and extrapolated from that a strongly pro-slavery reading of the Constitution. Congress lacked the power to ban slavery, Taney said—not just within states but in territories. And Black people could never be US citizens.

We'll return to the disagreement between Lincoln and his foils, both the pro-slavery Taney/Douglas and the abolitionist Garrison/Douglass camps, and see how those past disputes translate into the present day. (That turns out to be complicated—what was a pro-slavery position centuries ago is not necessarily one today.) For now, we can rest with this observation: In the period before the Civil War, there were interpretations of the Declaration that took it to condemn slavery and those that took it to be consistent with or even to protect slavery. Similarly, there were interpretations of the Founders' Constitution as both anti-slavery and pro-slavery. But here the interpretations did not line up so neatly with political positions: among those who read the Constitution as pro-slavery were the abolitionists Garrison and Douglass. The reason for this difference between the Declaration and the Founders' Constitution is simple. Rejecting the Founders' Constitution in favor of the Declaration was a possible anti-slavery political strategy; rejecting the Declaration led nowhere. The question to keep in mind is whether this is still true, or whether our current circumstances might support a different choice.

MARTIN LUTHER KING AND MALCOLM X

On August 28, 1963, nearly a quarter of a million people gathered at the Washington Monument and marched peacefully down the Mall to the Lincoln Memorial. The marchers—perhaps a quarter of them white—linked arms and sang "We Shall Overcome." They wore buttons showing a white hand and a Black hand grasped in fellowship. At the Lincoln Memorial, speakers addressed the crowd: director of the march, A. Philip Randolph, Walter Reuther of the United Auto Workers, Roy Wilkins of the NAACP, future congressman John Lewis of the Student Nonviolent Coordinating Committee, and others. Tenth and last came Martin Luther King Jr. King is, after Lincoln, probably the most significant champion of the ideals of the Declaration as a force for social transformation. Like Lincoln, King argued that the Declaration stated principles that had never been completely realized, but toward which American society should work.

Standing, literally and figuratively, in Lincoln's shadow, King started by echoing the Gettysburg Address: "Five score years ago . . ." Lincoln had counted back to 1776 and the Declaration; King's first stop was 1863 and the Emancipation Proclamation. But then he went back further, to the Constitution, the Declaration, and the rights they promised. What the Declaration was to Black Americans in the 1960s, King argued, was a guaranty of equality, of equal treatment by the government, of protection of unalienable rights. King was adopting Lincoln's vision of equality: equality is an end, a goal of government, something created and promoted by society but perhaps never fully realized. To Lincoln and King, equality was the destiny of America, the end of the march the Founders had started us on. You might think of the famous painting by Archibald McNeal Willard, *The Spirit of '76*, with its three Patriots marching across the Revolutionary battlefield. Guided by the ideals of the Declaration of Independence, America moves forward together. ("We cannot walk alone," said King.)

That's the aspiration, anyway. Like Lincoln and Douglass, King offered a jeremiad, a criticism of American society as falling short of the ideals of the Declaration. "We've come to our nation's capital to cash a check," he said, the "promissory note to which every American was to fall heir." But "instead of honoring this sacred obligation, America has given the Negro people a bad check, a check which has come back marked 'insufficient funds.'" Like Lincoln, King believed that America could make good on its founding promise. "We refuse to believe that the bank of justice is bankrupt." And, in the well-known peroration, he concluded by invoking his dream. "I have a dream," he said, "that one day this nation will rise up and live out the true meaning of its creed: 'We hold these truths to be self-evident, that all men are created equal.'"

King's dream was of a future of unity and justice. The speech, like the March on Washington in general, is conciliatory and optimistic. There is a mention of "vicious racists" in Alabama and "whirlwinds of revolt" that will "shake the foundations of our nation," but they are framed by warnings against "wrongful deeds" and "drinking from the cup of bitterness and hatred." "We must not allow our creative protest to degenerate into physical violence," King warned, nor "a distrust of all white people." For King, living out the full meaning of all men are created equal meant enacting and enforcing laws that give us an equal society. All of this fits with the standard story. It invokes the Declaration as a statement of ideals and the Founders' Constitution as a codification of those ideals; it sets the Founders up as great men. (Consistent with his pacific tone, King did not mention the Revolution or any other war.) It is no surprise that mainstream history has been kind to the March on Washington generally and this speech in particular: this was the version of the civil rights movement that much of white America could be comfortable with.

However, as we will see, it is not at all clear that King believed what he was saying. Specifically, it seems unlikely that he thought the Declaration and the Founders' Constitution were really the source of equal rights. He may instead, like the later Frederick Douglass, have been making a strategic choice. And among his listeners, not everyone was convinced. Walking around the Mall as an "uninvited observer" was a slim, six-foot-three man in glasses: Malcolm X, who later ridiculed the March on Washington. The white man "tricked you," he said, "had you marching back and forth between the feet of a dead man named Lincoln and another dead man named George Washington, singing 'We shall overcome.' . . . He made you think you were going somewhere and you end up going nowhere but between Lincoln and Washington."[3]

Where King dreamed of a future of interracial brotherhood, Malcolm X's dream was very different. He did not invoke the Declaration of Independence as explicitly as King did, but he echoed it. Blacks in America, he claimed repeatedly, were a distinct people, "a nation within a nation." Because they were denied their rights— not merely civil rights, but human rights—the government had lost whatever legitimacy it might have had. The remedy was separation: "Twenty million so-called Negroes in America today number a nation within a nation and are crying for freedom. We must be freed. We must be born. We must be separated . . . or cause the destruction of both! Separation is the only solution today."[4] This, Malcolm X said, is what the Declaration is about, the justification for one people to dissolve the political bands that have connected them with another. Far less pacific than King, he made the connection to the Revolution several times. "When this country here was first being founded there were 13 colonies," he said. "The whites were colonized. They were fed up with this taxation without representation, so some of them stood up and said 'liberty or death.'"[5] In current times, he continued, "America is a colonial power. She has colonized 22 million Afro-Americans by depriving us of first-class citizenship, by depriving us of civil rights, actually by depriving us of human rights." And so "you've got 22 million black people in this country today, 1964, who are fed up with taxation without representation and will do the same thing. Who are ready, willing and justified to do the same thing today to bring about independence for our people that your forefathers did to bring about independence for your people."[6]

Malcolm X evidently felt that his position was more in tune with the Declaration than King's was. "How in the world," he asked, "can a negro talk about the Declaration of Independence and he's still singing 'We Shall Overcome.'"[7] The Declaration, he believed, was about revolution. "Don't change the white man's mind," he said in "The Ballot or the Bullet." "You can't change his mind, and that whole thing about appealing to the moral conscience of America—America's conscience is bankrupt. She lost all conscience a long time ago. Uncle Sam has no conscience."[8] Malcolm X was a dissenter, then, but not in the Douglas/Taney vein. He read the Declaration not as a document that promised legal rights to everyone, or to a certain set of people, but rather as one that entitled people denied their natural rights to declare independence. The Black Panther Party, formed in 1966, did too. Their Ten-Point Program starts with an assertion of the right of self-determination—what I consider the central value of the Declaration: "We believe that Black people will not be free until we are able to determine our destiny." At the end it quotes the Declaration explicitly, starting with the self-evident truths of the preamble but going further.

> Prudence, indeed, will dictate that governments long established should not be changed for light and transient causes; and, accordingly, all experience hath shown that mankind are more disposed to suffer, while evils are sufferable, than to right themselves by abolishing the forms to which they are accustomed. But, when a long train of abuses and usurpations, pursuing invariably the same object, evinces a design to reduce them under absolute despotism, it is their right, it is their duty, to throw off such government, and to provide new guards for their future security.

For the Panthers, like Malcolm X, the Declaration was not just a statement of what government should do. It was also an account of what *people* could do when their government failed them.

In the 1960s, then, there were two very different readings of the Declaration. Martin Luther King, like Lincoln, saw it as an aspirational statement of principles, something that entitled people to demand equal rights from the government, something that condemned slavery, segregation, and racial discrimination in voting. Malcolm X and the Panthers, by contrast, saw it as a theory of revolution. Finding people who reject Lincoln's and King's understanding of equality is difficult. It takes us on a strange journey, from pre–Civil War apologists for slavery to 1960s Black radicals. While they did not do so for the same reasons, might they have been advancing the same reading of the Declaration? Is there something the various dissenters actually have in common, an interpretation that makes sense of all their positions?

There is. In fact, their common interpretation is vastly more plausible than that of Lincoln and King. Even more, it is more successful in leading us to a better America, because by urging us to turn *away* from the Declaration as a source of equality and democratic ideals, it allows us to see what we should long have been turning *toward*. Before digging into that, though, let's briefly consider today's debates about the standard story.

CONTEMPORARY CRITICS

The most important element of the standard story is the idea that our modern values of liberty and equality are stated in the Declaration. As the triumphalist version of the standard story is increasingly challenged, one response has been to place *increasing* weight on the Declaration, rather than turning away from it. The people who do this tend to read it as Lincoln did, or even to push further. Danielle Allen's *Our Declaration: A Reading of the Declaration of Independence in Defense of Equality* is perhaps the best recent example: from the words of the Declaration, she builds an argument for a thick notion of political equality within society.[9] Even those who do not see themselves as advancing a version of the standard story share something like this understanding of the Declaration—even those who think of themselves as offering a very different perspective, even those who are perceived as a threat to America's self-understanding. The most radical recent attempt to reinterpret America still holds fast to the Declaration.

On August 18, 2019, the *New York Times Magazine* cover showed a dark and empty sea. "In August of 1619," the cover text reads, "a ship appeared on this horizon. . . . It carried more than 20 enslaved Africans. . . ." What the paper called the 1619 Project announced a bold goal: to "reframe American history by considering what it would mean to regard 1619 as our nation's birth year. Doing so requires us to place the consequences of slavery and the contributions of Black Americans at the very center of the story we tell ourselves about who we are as a country."[10] The introductory essay—"The Idea of America," by Nikole Hannah-Jones—provides "the intellectual framework" for the project. Other essays, as well as poems, fiction, art, and photography, explore how familiar aspects of modern life trace their origins to slavery. Slavery, the *New York Times Magazine's* editor in chief explains, "is sometimes referred to as the country's original sin, but it is more than that: It is the country's very origin. Out of slavery—and the anti-Black racism it required—grew nearly everything that has truly made America exceptional."[11]

The 1619 Project is a bold challenge to the triumphalist version of the standard story. Of the four key elements—the Declaration as a statement of ideals, the Revolution as a war for those ideals, the Founders' Constitution as their codification, and the Founders as great men—it disputes three of them. The Founders' Constitution was pro-slavery, Hannah-Jones argues, the Revolution was fought in part to protect slavery, the Founders were not as great as we think—and neither was Lincoln.

The project was not limited to a single issue of a glossy magazine. Plans were announced to publish the 1619 Project as a book, to make a podcast, and to develop a curriculum based on it. The reaction was enthusiastic among the public and the elite alike. People lined up on the street to receive copies of the magazine, something the *New York Times* had not seen since the election of Barack Obama.[12] Nikole Hannah-Jones won a Pulitzer Prize for her piece. But there was also a backlash. On Twitter, conservative pundit Ben Shapiro called the project "divisive, erroneous, and terrible for the country." "No country can continue to exist as a functioning polity without a shared philosophy, culture, and history," he continued. "The 1619 Project is a dagger aimed at the heart of all three." Columnist George Will described it as "filled with slovenliness and ideological ax-grinding."[13] A group of mostly Black public intellectuals formed a response project called 1776 Unites to "uphold our country's authentic founding virtues and values and challenge those who assert America is forever defined by its past failures, such as slavery." President Donald Trump created the 1776 Commission, which published a report intended as a rebuttal on January 18, 2021, Martin Luther King Day. (On January 20, 2021, President Joe Biden dissolved the commission and pulled the report, which had been widely criticized by historians, from the White House website.) Most recently, states have enacted laws forbidding schools from teaching the project.

The critics with the most intellectual heft, however, were a group of mostly liberal history professors (Victoria Bynum, James McPherson, James Oakes, Sean Wilentz, and Gordon Wood), who accused the project of "factual errors" that "suggest a displacement of historical understanding by ideology." These historians did not contest the 1619 Project's story in its broad outlines. Indeed, they claimed that they "applaud all efforts to address the enduring centrality of slavery and racism to our history." Nonetheless, they identified specific "factual errors" in the project's treatment of elements of the standard story. On the Revolution, they took issue with Hannah-Jones's statement that "one of the primary reasons the colonists decided to declare their independence from Britain was because they wanted to protect the institution of slavery." (Alex Lichtenstein, charitably, suggested that these historians would oppose with equal vigor a categorical statement that preserving slavery was *not* a reason for declaring independence, but the tenor of the letter suggests otherwise.)[14] On the Founders' Constitution, they complained that "the project ignores [Lincoln's] agreement with Frederick Douglass that the Constitution was, in Douglass's words, 'a GLORIOUS LIBERTY DOCUMENT.'" Later, Wilentz rebuked the 1619 Project for its "cynicism."[15] He called the view that the Founders' Constitution was pro-slavery "one of the most destructive falsehoods in American history."

What explains the intensity of this reaction? While it is an overstatement to say that protecting slavery was a motivating factor for all, or even most, of the Patriots, the story of slavery and the Revolution is nonetheless considerably more complex than triumphalist versions have suggested. With respect to the Founders' Constitution, the 1619 Project's interpretation is shared by the majority of historians and constitutional law scholars. To say that these claims are outside the realm of responsible history—that they are ideology—is a wild overreaction. More than that, it is a projection. Professional historians generally understand that history requires interpretation. They do not need to claim truth for their perspectives, and they do not need to damn other interpretations as false. What declares itself truth and brands alternatives falsehood is not history. It is ideology.

What is the ideological opposition to the 1619 Project? Fundamentally, the concern seems to be that it may undermine people's faith in America or undermine American unity. This is not so much an argument that the standard story is true as that it is valuable. We will see that this claim is wrong on its own terms—the standard story is actually very harmful, and we would be a much better nation if we rejected it. As applied to the 1619 Project, it rests on a fundamental misunderstanding. It is true that the 1619 Project is divisive. That truth is self-evident: the angry reaction to it, even among self-professed liberals, is division. And it is true that by increasing the salience of race, the 1619 Project does threaten a sort of unity that the more triumphalist versions of the standard story promote. But the idea that letting people know how deeply rooted racism has been will make them lose faith in America is both patronizing and implausible. Patronizing because it suggests that some Americans can't handle the truth, and implausible because the people most likely to lose faith—Black Americans—know the problem of racism all too well already. It is one of the miracles of American history, as Hannah-Jones points out, that they have maintained their patriotism and dedication to America. The 1619 Project itself is a demonstration of this, because the project is not an attack on the standard story but a revision.

The 1619 Project does reject, or seriously question, three out of the four elements of the standard story. Unlike Malcolm X, however, it holds fast to the Declaration as a statement of American ideals. "Our founding ideals were false when they were written," Hannah-Jones argues—false because the ideals of equality and protection of natural rights were not extended to all people—but "Black Americans fought to make them true." What the 1619 Project is, really, is the extreme progressive version of the standard story: it tells us that we have fallen further short of our ideals, more frequently, more consistently, and more deliberately than we realize. Yet it still tells us that "our founding ideals" were written in 1776—and it is still a profession of faith in them, of faith in an America we can work to perfect.

"The Idea of America" opens and closes with a meditation on the American flag. It starts with Hannah-Jones describing her father's patriotic reverence for the flag and her childhood feeling that the flag was not really hers, that she was not really American, that honoring the flag meant accepting subordination. It ends with her wishing that she could tell her younger self that "her people's ancestry started here," that America's flag and its values were hers, and that Black people, once told "by virtue of our bondage, that we could never be American," in fact "by virtue of our bondage . . . became the most American of all." In its basic outlines, that is the argument made by Abraham Lincoln and Martin Luther King: America has not lived up to its ideals in the past but has come closer over time and may do better in the future. In its specifics, it attributes American improvement in large part to the efforts of those who were excluded from the promise of those ideals—but that is also relatively standard fare. Langston Hughes's 1935 poem "Let America Be America Again" makes the same point. It is the oppressed, Hughes says, "who dreamt our basic dream," and it is they who will make America what it should be, "the land that never has been yet."

That some people read this as an attack on the standard story is dismaying. It suggests an inability to recognize a story that foregrounds the efforts and achievements of Black Americans as a story of America. It suggests a belief that American ideals are tainted by including Black people as participants in the fight for those ideals. And it suggests that for some people, it is an essential element of the standard story that the Founders should be presented as great men with whom we should identify—the greatness of the Founders is probably the element of the standard story that the 1619 Project hits hardest. (Insistence on the greatness of the Founders is one of the ways in which the conservative standard story differs most starkly from the progressive one.)

Although the 1619 Project is widely seen as a challenge to the standard story, it is still working within that framework. It is deeply and conventionally patriotic. It accepts the Declaration as a source of ideals, as a set of aspirations toward which the best in American history strive. This is not anomalous. Those who want to promote equality—Danielle Allen being another example—tend to be those who lean hardest on the Declaration. They are the ones who read it as promising political equality within society, as stating a fundamentally democratic vision of government. I understand the impulse. I, too, want to promote equality; I, too, say that democracy is the principle that makes our government legitimate. And yet, if those are the values we want to promote, that view of the Declaration is exactly what we must let go.

3

The Exclusive Declaration

★

WHAT I HAVE DONE so far is to set out the standard story and to consider some of the people who have questioned it. The standard story tells us that the Declaration is fundamentally about human rights and that its central meaning is that all people are entitled to some kind of equal rights or equal treatment by the government. (The government should not, for instance, enslave some people or deny them the right to vote or to have equal access to public accommodations.) It tells us that the Revolution was a war for those principles, that the Founders' Constitution made them law, and that our Founders were great men. The next three chapters examine these elements of the standard story. Not the greatness of the Founders, although I will have some things to say about them, but the narrative that finds our ideals in the Declaration and follows them to the Revolution, through the Founders' Constitution, and to us in the present day. Not one of these components really stands up to scrutiny—in large part because the story actually goes off the rails with the very first one.

What does the Declaration of Independence mean? Answering that question requires us first to settle what it means to be right about what the Declaration means. In some sense, the meaning of a document is settled by practice. If everyone acts as though the

Declaration has the meaning assigned to it by the standard story, which generally they do, then that is what it means (or means to us, anyway). But people did not always accept it. If all we are interested in is accuracy, it isn't hard to argue that a different, and older, understanding is more persuasive. Admittedly, accuracy is not the sole consideration. As we've seen, some argue that the standard story is good for us as a country, even if it isn't accurate. For politicians and Americans more broadly, accuracy surely ranks behind consequences. In fact, we understand the Declaration the way we do now precisely because people turned away from the original understanding in search of good consequences, such as the abolition of slavery. That was a good strategy in the past, but today, we would be a better nation if our agreed-upon understanding changed again. Dislodging the standard story is not a threat to American unity or to faith in our country; instead, it offers the possibility of a dramatic improvement of both.

One central aspect of the standard story today is that it tells us that its understanding of the Declaration is also the original one. It tells us that the idea that the government should treat people equally is what the Declaration *always* meant. The standard story thus tries to connect modern Americans—all of us—to the Founding. It sets out the Declaration as, in Lincoln's words, the electric cord that links us to the founding ideal, though that connection is valued more by some of us than others. But if the standard story's claim of continuity turns out to be false—if it turns out that the original understanding of "all men are created equal" was *not* that the government should treat all people equally—that should be a powerful point against the standard story.

This historical claim about the original understanding of the Declaration can be judged by criteria other than success. We can ask what Jefferson and other drafters might reasonably have said, given their circumstances and goals. We can ask what would cohere with the other things they said in the Declaration and elsewhere, what would cohere with commonly accepted principles of political philosophy. We can ask what people said about the Declaration at the time. Considering these questions will show us that the view now widely accepted is almost certainly not what the Declaration meant when it was written. Modern Americans do not know the Declaration well. They tend to confuse it with the Constitution, a confusion the standard story encourages. (Perhaps most strikingly, a third of Americans believe the Declaration was written after the Civil War.) And they tend to know only a few phrases—most notably, the second sentence of the preamble, and specifically the phrase "all men are created equal."[1] That is an important phrase, to be sure, but to understand what it meant to Jefferson, it helps to pull back a moment to consider the context of the entire document.

The Declaration of Independence was not a statement about human rights in the abstract; it was not a declaration of concrete human rights, either. As the title tells us, it is not about rights at all; it is about independence. It was written at a specific moment and for a specific purpose, designed to do two things: to announce that the American colonists were throwing off allegiance to the British Crown and to justify that act.[2] With this task confronting him, what would make sense for Jefferson to put in the preamble? The standard story suggests that it is Lincoln's and King's understanding of "all men are created equal": the principle that the government must treat all people equally. That condemns slavery. It suggests an expansion of voting rights and the invalidation of many sorts of discriminatory treatment.[3] But this is wildly inconsistent with the practice not only of the American colonists but with that of every government that had, at that point, ever existed in the world.

It is almost literally inconceivable that Jefferson would have written such a thing, much less put it forward as a self-evident truth. To do so would have been—there is no other way to put it—incredibly stupid. The idea that the government must treat all people equally is, according to Lincoln and the standard story, an aspiration toward which we must continually strive, while recognizing that we will never fully achieve it. That is about the furthest thing imaginable from a self-evident truth. To proclaim as self-evident truth something that was universally denied would not start the argument for independence off on a strong footing. (Jefferson himself later noted that he had sought "not to find out new principles, or new arguments never before thought of, not merely to say things which had never been said before; but to place before mankind the common sense of the subject."[4] That is not the account of someone setting forth a new and radical proposition.[5])

Jefferson might, perhaps, have done such a thing if there had been no other way to make his argument work. (We will see that necessity can make people deny or invert obvious truths—as in Lincoln's use of the Declaration.) But far from being essential, the idea that the government must treat all people equally is irrelevant to the argument of the Declaration. The grievances set forth do not primarily allege that King George is treating the colonists *unequally* but rather that he is treating them *wrongly*—that he has undertaken "the establishment of an absolute Tyranny over these States." (It would not legitimize the oppression of the colonists, according to the theory of the Declaration, if he wrongfully oppressed residents of England as well.) And the colonists, as British subjects, are not just any people but insiders, members of the relevant political community, the people whose consent formed the government. So a claim that the government must treat all people equally is both broader than the concerns of the Declaration and somewhat wide of the mark. Lincoln himself said so: "The assertion that all men are created equal was of no practical use in effecting our separation from Great Britain; and it was placed in the Declaration, not for that, but for future use."[6]

In fact, a principle of universal equality in legal rights is not just irrelevant to the argument of the Declaration. It is counterproductive: it would demonstrate that the colonists are acting wrongfully, which is hardly the impression they sought to create. (One of the primary goals of the Declaration was to enlist foreign support for the Revolution.) If we think about an oppressive relationship between the government and outsiders that existed in 1776, what comes naturally to mind is not the relationship between the colonists and the king but slavery—practiced in the colonies but not recognized in England after the 1772 decision in the *Somerset* case.

Is it likely that Jefferson started the Declaration with a novel, useless, and radical claim that, in fact, offered better grounds for condemning the slaveholding colonists than the king? No—not because he was incapable of hypocrisy, as Roger Taney suggested, but because he was engaged in a deadly serious task. Americans today tend to forget that the Declaration was treason. When the signers pledged their lives, their fortunes, and their sacred honor in its support, all those things were really at stake. Had the Revolution failed, they would likely have been executed, expropriated, attainted. The Declaration of Independence was not the place for counterproductive and counterfactual speculative philosophy.

Perhaps more telling, we know what would have happened if Jefferson had written a passage of the Declaration that sounded critical of slavery—because he did. In an early draft, he charged that King George had introduced slavery to America and blocked colonial attempts to restrain the slave trade. He "has waged cruel war against human nature itself, violating its most sacred rights of life and liberty in the persons of a distant people who never offended him, captivating and carrying them into slavery in another hemisphere, or to incur miserable death in their transportation thither . . . [and] prostituted his negative for suppressing every legislative attempt to prohibit or restrain this execrable commerce." This was not, it is important to understand, an attack on the practice of slavery in America—Jefferson considered that quite different, and what survived in the final version of the Declaration was a complaint that King George was encouraging American slaves to rebel. But even criticism of the slave trade was removed by Congress "in complaisance," Jefferson later wrote, "to South Carolina and Georgia."[7] Even if Jefferson had wanted to write something critical of American slavery (and there is no evidence he did), it would not have survived congressional review.

So it is wildly implausible that Jefferson meant by the phrase "all men are created equal" anything close to what Lincoln and King understood it to mean. And the reaction of Jefferson's contemporaries suggests that almost no one understood it that way at the time.[8] If Jefferson did not mean that the government should give equal rights to everyone, what did he mean? That the government should treat all white men equally, as Stephen Douglas and Taney argued? This isn't right, either. "All men" really does mean all people. The mistake that the standard story makes—and it is perhaps less a mistake than a sleight of hand—is to overread the significance of "created equal." To say that all men are created equal does not come close to meaning that they are entitled to equal treatment by the government.

To see this, we need to remind ourselves of two fundamental distinctions—between natural rights and positive rights, and between the state of nature and political society. Once we do this, we will see that the principle that all men are created equal is in fact crucial to the argument for independence (Lincoln was wrong). We will see that it does extend to all people without contradicting the practice of the slaveholding colonists (Taney and Douglas were wrong, too) and that it was sufficiently widely accepted to count as something like a self-evident truth. In short, we will discover that there is a reading that succeeds in making sense of the Declaration in every way that the standard story's reading fails.

JEFFERSON'S EQUALITY

To understand what Jefferson meant by the claim that all men are created equal, we need to return to the context of the Declaration, to ask two fundamental questions. First, what is it trying to do? Second, how will it do so?

We have answered the first question already based on the historical setting and Jefferson's other writings: The Declaration is going to announce and justify the colonists' separation from Britain. But we can also answer it based on its own opening sentence. "When in the Course of human events, it becomes necessary for one people to dissolve the political bands which have connected them with another, and to assume among the powers of the earth, the separate and equal station to which the Laws of Nature and of Nature's God entitle them, a decent respect to the opinions of mankind requires that they should declare the causes which impel them to the separation."

This sentence tells us several things. It tells us explicitly what the Declaration is about: not the rights of individuals to enjoy liberty and equality, but the right of one people to separate from another. It tells us, implicitly, that the colonists are declaring independence, and hence must declare the causes. More important, though again implicitly, this sentence answers the second question. It describes the separate-and-equal station the colonists are assuming as one "to which the Laws of Nature and of Nature's God entitle them." That means that the justification is going to be based not on positive law—the law of some human government such as the British Empire—but on natural law, the laws of nature and of nature's God. It is going to be an argument of political philosophy based on natural law. How will that argument proceed? Jefferson aims to show that the colonists are justified in rejecting the authority of the Crown. He thus needs a theory about when political authority can be rejected and a demonstration that the colonists' case fits that theory. This, in short, is what the Declaration is. It first explains the origin and nature of legitimate political authority. It then explains when the exercise of political authority ceases to be legitimate. And then it endeavors to show that the situation of the American colonists fits the criteria that justify rebellion.

The first question the Declaration tackles is thus where legitimate political authority comes from. What entitles one person to demand obedience from another? This was not a novel question; it was a central concern of Enlightenment political philosophy, examined in great detail by Hobbes, Locke, and Rousseau, among others. One answer might be that political authority comes from birth, or from God. Some people are born to rule. That is the claim inherent in the characterization of the monarch as king "by the grace of

God"—which is, in fact, the style of the British sovereign. If this is so, it may be that rebellion against the king is never justified. It is, in fact, a sin. The divine right of kings was, at one point, a significant theory of political authority, as Jefferson knew. But by 1776, the argument was a bit of a straw man. John Milton had attacked it following the execution of Charles I in 1649, John Locke after the Glorious Revolution of 1688, and Thomas Paine in colonial America. In rejecting the idea that some people were simply born to wield absolute power, Jefferson was indeed stating a truth that was sufficiently widely accepted that he could call it self-evident. That is what the second sentence of the Declaration tells us. No one is born to rule. People are born, or created, equal. Jefferson's equality, we could say, is the principle that there are no kings. This should be taken as a statement of simple fact, just like a statement that there are no vampires, or there is no Santa Claus. There is no such thing as a king, where a king is someone who is legitimately entitled by birth alone to demand obedience of others.

"By birth alone" is a crucial qualification here. The Declaration is not necessarily anti-monarchical.[9] It sets out two criteria for a legitimate government: It must be formed by consent, and it must protect the natural rights of the people who formed it. People could consent to a monarchy, and even a hereditary one, and that government would be legitimate if it protected their rights. But it would be their consent, not God's will, that legitimated the monarch—and that consent could be withdrawn. That, in fact, was the situation of the colonists—the Declaration does not say that George's authority is illegitimate simply because he is a king, but rather that it is illegitimate because he is a tyrant. Jefferson reaffirmed this idea in a letter written on the fiftieth anniversary of the Declaration, stating that "the mass of mankind has not been born with saddles on their backs, nor a favored few booted and spurred, ready to ride them legitimately, by the grace of God."[10] Here, perhaps more explicitly than in the highly compressed Declaration, he makes clear that he is concerned with concept of the divine right of kings. That letter called this a "palpable truth"—a clear echo of his earlier description of it as self-evident.

So the first self-evident truth of the Declaration rejects legitimate authority on the basis of birth. Yet if some people are not entitled to demand obedience from others by virtue of their birth, how does the obligation to obey arise?

THE POLITICAL PHILOSOPHY OF THE DECLARATION

In answering this question, Enlightenment political philosophers typically began by imagining the state of nature. The state of nature is a world without society or government: people are on their own. (Whether such a state of nature ever existed is unlikely at best, but analogues do exist: independent nations, for instance, exist in a state of nature vis-à-vis one another—and, we will see, individuals outside a political community exist in a state of nature with respect to that government.) In this state, the philosophers generally agreed, people are free and equal. There are no governments to create laws that could bind them, and no one has a right to demand obedience from anyone else. What people have are their natural rights—to life and liberty, everyone agreed, perhaps to property, though philosophers differed about that.

The state of nature is free and equal in theory, but it would probably not be very happy in practice: with no government and no laws, people have no protection from others. They have their natural rights, but no way to secure them. The state of nature is the war of all against all, as Hobbes famously wrote, where life is solitary, poor, nasty, brutish, and short. People therefore would (naturally!) emerge from the state of nature by banding together to protect one another's rights through collective action—that is, by creating a government. This—following the principles of equality in the state of nature and the existence of natural rights—is the third self-evident truth proclaimed by the Declaration: governments are instituted "to secure these rights." Now we know the purpose of government: protecting people's natural rights. This sentence also tells us, very briefly, how a legitimate government is formed: Governments derive their "just powers" from the consent of the governed. (The question of consent is a knotty one, but not one we will explore here.)

If governments derive their just powers from the consent of the governed, it might seem that their authority can be rejected at will, simply by withdrawing consent. (Whether an individual can do this, or only a "people," would remain a question.) But Jefferson does not go so far: echoing Locke, he uses the purpose of government to measure when it has gone so drastically astray that it may be thrown off. This, too, is presented as a self-evident truth: "whenever any Form of Government becomes destructive of these ends, it is the Right of the People to alter or to abolish it, and to institute new Government."[11] That is the Declaration's political philosophy. People start out equal, endowed with natural rights but lacking the means to protect them. They create governments to secure those rights, and the government's legitimate authority comes from their consent. If the government fails to do its job, the people may reject it and start anew. This was a very standard statement of social contract theory. People differ about where Jefferson got particular ideas or phrases—the "long train of abuses" seems to come from Locke; the "pursuit of happiness" echoes George Mason; "manly firmness" was used by the editors of Jefferson's *Summary View of the Rights of British America*—but on the whole it "seemed commonplace, even a kind of 'boilerplate'" to the colonists of 1776.[12]

THE DECLARATION AND SLAVERY

If that is the Declaration's political philosophy, what are the implications? Here my account begins to move away from the widely shared understanding of the Declaration. Jefferson's Declaration, simply put, does not contain our modern values of liberty and equality. It is not even inconsistent with slavery. This is, I realize, a radical claim. Even Pauline Maier, who deeply studied the original understanding of the Declaration and sets out a version of Jefferson's equality similar to mine, nevertheless concludes: "The inconsistency between that idea and slavery was hard to deny."[13] But it is not hard to deny—not if we remember what the Declaration's argument is in fact about. I am not saying that the Declaration supports slavery, though that argument was adopted by the Supreme Court. And I am not claiming that the premises of the Declaration could not be used to generate an argument against slavery. My claim is simply that the argument the Declaration makes has no direct relevance to the practice of slavery. That is because Jefferson's equality is a precise and limited concept. So, too, with his concept of inalienable liberty: there is a precise meaning there, which does specific work in the argument of the Declaration, but it is not relevant to slavery.

The point of this analysis is not to question what our modern values are. There is no doubt that we are committed to liberty and equality. There is no doubt that slavery is contrary to American ideals: opposition to slavery is probably the most central element of our national identity. And there is no doubt that, nowadays, we find those ideals in the Declaration. But it matters what the Declaration's words actually meant to the generation that wrote and read them, and it matters what its argument actually was. Because if our modern American ideals of liberty and equality were not originally present in the Declaration, they must have come from somewhere else. And if the signers of the Declaration did not share those ideals, it may be that our relationship to them is different from what we have supposed it was. It may be that modern Americans are not the heirs of the signers after all. We, too, come from somewhere else.

There are two crucial points to understand. The first is that Jefferson's equality exists in the state of nature. That is a hypothetical starting point that never existed in the real world and, even if it did, would not survive the transition into political society. People start out equal, but they do not stay that way. They cannot—the division between those who govern and those who are governed is a necessary feature of political society. Far from being an entitlement to equal treatment by the government, Jefferson's equality is inconsistent with the very existence of positive law. Where Lincoln thought equality was the end of government (meaning its goal), we could say, Jefferson thinks government is the end of equality— meaning its termination. The Virginia Declaration of Rights makes this point explicitly: it talks about people's natural rights and then about what happens to those rights "when they enter into a state of society." This language was added by Edmund Pendleton to make it clear that freedom and equality were enjoyed by all men in the state of nature—not by enslaved people in the state of Virginia. The Massachusetts Constitution of 1780 had no such qualifier; it simply stated: "All men are born free and equal . . ." Within a few years, that language was used in freedom suits by enslaved people to invalidate slavery in Massachusetts.

That Jefferson's equality cannot exist in political society does not make it consistent with all kinds of slavery, of course. People form governments to protect their natural rights, and the government should therefore not violate those rights any more than is necessary. (People who form societies do accept some restraints on their natural liberty—the duty to obey legitimate authority and valid laws is such a restraint, and governments can take the life, liberty, or property of lawbreakers without losing legitimacy.) A government that tried to enslave its citizens would be going against its very purpose, and the people would, under the theory of the Declaration, be justified in rebelling. This is, of course, exactly the argument that the colonists repeatedly made: that the British were attempting to make them into slaves. But notice how this argument goes. A government that tries to make *its own citizens* into slaves is going against its purpose, because people form governments to protect *their own* rights. The second crucial point is that the whole concern of the Declaration is relationships within a political community, between the governors and the governed. The question the Declaration answers is when some insiders can reject the authority of other insiders.

How governments should treat outsiders is a totally different question. People who are not members of the same political community relate to one another, more or less, as if they were still in the state of nature. Different philosophers have different theories about how individuals should treat one another in the state of nature, and the Declaration does not endorse any particular one of them—it is simply not concerned with that question.

What about how to decide whether someone is an insider or an outsider? This turns out to be perhaps the central question of American constitutional history. But the Declaration says very little about it. It describes a relevant political community as "one people." That could be taken to have some sort of racial or ethnic element. Roger Taney argued in *Dred Scott* that the Constitution imposed just such a rule: the American political community is bounded by a racial line. Yet the "one people" whose independence the Declaration announces were ethnically similar to the other people whose authority it rejects, so "people" is not solely a racial construct. It seems more likely that the Declaration assumes that each political community controls its own membership, by whatever rules it chooses. And indeed, one of the Declaration's complaints against King George was that he was interfering with the colonies' ability to constitute themselves: "He has endeavoured to prevent the population of these States; for that purpose obstructing the Laws for Naturalization of Foreigners."

Slaves, because they were outsiders to colonial political communities, were also outside the argument of the Declaration. The fact that many enslaved people were the children of free colonists complicated this point, but the colonists were aware of that difficulty. In 1656 Elizabeth Grinstead won a freedom suit because her father, a member of the House of Burgesses, acknowledged her and she had been baptized a Christian. Virginia responded with a law enacted in 1662 providing that status as slave or free was determined by the status of the mother. This departed from British law and was clearly designed to allow free men to enslave their children: the preamble to the Virginia slavery law explained without embarrassment that "some doubts have arisen whether children got by any Englishman upon a negro woman would be slave or free." Later laws in the colonies provided that Christian baptism or conversion would not liberate enslaved people.

Jefferson's deleted passage about the slave trade confirms this political framework. He refers to Africans as "a distant people." They are not the "one people" referred to in the preamble to the Declaration, who are dissolving the "political bands which have connected them with another," but a separate people. They have no political connection to the British Empire at all. They do have natural rights to life and liberty, which are being violated without their consent. It follows that the authority exercised over them is not legitimate political authority. But no one argued that it was. Everyone knew that slaves were held by force. The pro-slavery arguments were not that slaves had consented or that they had formed the governments that enslaved them. Instead, slavery's supporters contended that the deprivation of natural rights was justified by alleged inherent racial differences or the supposed benefits that slavery conferred.

Claims of racial differences—made by, among others, Jefferson himself—were used to support arguments that enslaved people were incapable of caring for themselves if free, and also that slavery was in everyone's best interest. People were equally free in the state of nature, Harvard student Theodore Parsons admitted in a 1773 debate, but "such is the nature of society that it requires various degrees of authority and subordination." Relationships between people should be based on their quality, Parsons argued, and it was for the good of all if those who excelled in "wisdom and benevolence" (white people) exercised authority over their inferiors. Enslaved people in the Americas, supporters of slavery claimed, were better off than poor whites in England, and better off than they would have been in Africa, since their enslavement offered them not just Western civilization but Christianity and eternal salvation.

These are terrible arguments, of course: no one nowadays would take them seriously. But they were taken seriously at the time, seriously enough that an attack on slavery could not simply ignore them. (Anti-slavery activists engaged them at length.) The Declaration does ignore these arguments, not because it accepts them but because it ignores the whole issue of how a government should relate to outsiders.

On this issue, there are several different possible positions, each of which is consistent with the Declaration. One might argue that in the state of nature, it is always wrong to violate another person's natural rights, and that governments must therefore always honor the natural rights of outsiders. That would condemn slavery, although with the odd consequence of giving outsiders greater rights against the government than insiders. (All versions of social contract theory recognize that people tolerate some abridgment of their natural rights when they enter society and subject themselves to positive law.)

One might also argue the opposite: governments have no duty at all to respect the natural rights of outsiders. In that case, slavery is not wrong, at least not on the grounds that it violates natural liberty or equality. This, too, is consistent with the Declaration, which states explicitly that people form governments to secure their rights—not the rights of outsiders.

Or, more plausibly, one might argue that in the state of nature, violation of another person's natural rights requires some justification. Then the question comes down to whether the justifications offered for slavery are adequate—a matter on which the Declaration takes no position, and with regard to which one might distinguish between the questions of instituting slavery and of abolishing it. One might also distinguish between the enslavement of particular people—like defeated enemies—and the hereditary, race-based slavery practiced in America. Victory in war and enemy status provide a justification for slavery that is lacking for race-based hereditary slavery. The latter thus requires the support of something else, typically racism or religion.

Jefferson, in fact, drew precisely this distinction, believing that abducting people from their political community and enslaving them was wrong. We can see this in the deleted passage, which criticizes the international slave trade as a violation of the rights of a people who have committed no offense. Jefferson was a strong and consistent opponent of the trade, and as president he signed a bill prohibiting it. But he felt differently about the institution of slavery in America. People born into slavery were never a part of any political community. Abolishing slavery would pose practical problems, he thought, and endanger the safety of white Americans. As he wrote to John Adams in 1821, "Are our slaves to be presented with freedom and a dagger?"[14] He thus believed (or at least maintained) that slavery should never have been brought to America, but since it had, it should not be immediately abolished.

INALIENABLE LIBERTY

So Jefferson's equality does not condemn slavery. Might another Revolutionary principle do so? The Declaration also announces as a self-evident truth that people have an inalienable right to liberty. Does calling liberty "inalienable" mean that it should not be interfered with?[15] No. For one thing, it is a commonplace that when people enter society, they accept curbs on their liberty: natural rights and positive rights will never be coextensive. More significantly, "inalienable" does not mean sacred, important, or inviolable. It has a precise legal meaning, and Jefferson used it very deliberately. To call something "inalienable" means that the person who owns it must retain it—a person cannot give it away.[16] This matters to the argument of the Declaration because in one version of social contract theory, people start out with natural rights but surrender them irrevocably to a sovereign in exchange for protection.[17] If that were true, there would be no right to complain against an unjust sovereign and no right to revolution. The colonists could not charge that King George was violating their right to liberty, for they would have already surrendered that right.

Calling liberty inalienable responds to this potential difficulty, in a very compressed fashion: it tells us that while the colonists might have accepted certain restraints on their liberty, they did not irrevocably surrender the right.[18] For a more elaborate statement that confirms this reading, we can look to the Virginia Declaration of Rights, in which George Mason wrote that people "cannot, by any compact, deprive or divest their posterity" of natural rights. Mason's concern is the same as Jefferson's: he wants to rebut the argument that an initial (and presumably hypothetical) consent to the social compact binds a people's posterity to accept government authority.

What does this mean for slavery? Like the concept of natural equality, the idea of inalienable liberty turns out to mean much less than one might suppose. To call the right to liberty inalienable means it cannot be surrendered voluntarily. But no one thought that enslaved people had voluntarily surrendered their liberty; they were, obviously, held in bondage by force. The relevant question was whether the justifications put forward for violently depriving them of their liberty were adequate. That takes us back to the pro- and anti-slavery arguments canvassed above, a debate in which the Declaration simply does not participate.

The fact that "inalienable," far from meaning "sacred" or "important," turns out to be a highly compressed and technical method of picking among different strands of social contract theory should show us how far from our modern conceptions of liberty and equality the Declaration's concepts are. And it shows us something else important. When the Declaration needs to get more specific about what the social contract does and does not entail—which it does here in order to preserve the right to revolution—it does so. When specificity is not necessary to the argument—as it is not with respect to the question of the obligation of governments to respect the rights of outsiders, or with whether a natural right to property exists—the Declaration takes no position.

THE EXCLUSIVE DECLARATION

So what do the self-evident truths of natural equality and inalienable liberty amount to? Do they tell us that people should be treated equally by the government, that the government must respect all people's liberty? Do they state our modern understandings of liberty and equality, the values preached by Abraham Lincoln and Martin Luther King? Not as they were understood by Jefferson, not as they were intended to function in the argument of the Declaration. That much is pretty clear. What rights the government gives to people is a question about the operation of positive law within political society. The Declaration's statements about liberty and equality are about natural rights in the state of nature. These are simply not the same thing.

This means that the wrongness of slavery is not one of the self-evident truths the Declaration announces. Is it wrong, then, to take inspiration from the Declaration? Not necessarily. If you are launching a revolution against an oppressive government, it is perfectly appropriate to invoke the political theory of the Declaration. (Ho Chi Minh, for instance, quoted the Declaration to condemn French colonialism.) And if you are an insider arguing for rights you have been denied, it is appropriate, too. Elizabeth Cady Stanton and Lucretia Mott mirrored Jefferson's form in the Declaration of Sentiments, arguing that "the history of mankind is a history of repeated injuries and usurpations on the part of man toward woman, having in direct object the establishment of an absolute tyranny over her."

Abolitionists, though, find no support in the political theory of the Declaration. This point is hard to accept today. But the contemporaneous understanding of the Declaration was pretty clearly that it was about national independence, not individual liberty, and certainly not the liberty of political outsiders. Even more: the Declaration can be mustered to make an argument about slavery—but it is an argument against abolition. We will see this argument prevail in the Supreme Court with the *Dred Scott* decision, but it arose even earlier. In 1820, as Congress debated the admission of Missouri to the Union, Representative Alexander Smyth of Virginia argued that requiring Missouri to ban slavery would not only violate the Constitution but be inconsistent with the Declaration of Independence:

[The Congress of 1776] asserted that man cannot alienate his liberty, nor by compact deprive his posterity of liberty. Slaves are not held as having alienated their liberty by compact. They are held under the law and usage of nations. . . . We agree with the Congress of 1776 that men, on entering into society, cannot alienate their right to liberty and property, and that they cannot, by compact, bind their posterity. And, therefore, we claim that the people of Missouri cannot alienate their rights or bind their posterity by a compact with Congress.[19]

In 1848, John C. Calhoun said something similar. He described the phrase "all men are created equal" as a "hypothetical truism" about the state of nature. What about rights within society? Governments are made for particular purposes, he argued, "and no government under our system, federal or State, has the right to do anything inconsistent with the nature of the powers entrusted to it, or the objects for which it was entrusted." Can the federal government then interfere with the rights that people held under state law when the Constitution was ratified by banning slavery in a territory? Calhoun said no; that would be giving an unjustifiable preference to some states over others. This is an argument about the government's duty to equally respect the rights of insiders, and it is not an absurd reading of the Declaration—though we will discuss later why it fails.

The Declaration that I have described is an exclusive individualist document. It shows great solicitude for the rights and interests of insiders (though it does not promise them democracy), but really none at all for those of outsiders. Outsiders are present in the Declaration—there are references to enslaved people, Native Americans, and Hessian mercenaries—but all of these outsiders are seen as threats. Two of those groups—the enslaved people threatening "domestic insurrections" and the Native Americans referred to as "merciless . . . Savages"—are threats because the colonists have been mistreating them, violating their natural rights. The Declaration suggests that a government must protect insiders from outsiders, but not the reverse. It could plausibly be read, in fact, to imply that the government may not infringe on the rights of insiders in order to protect outsiders. The government should not take the property of insiders to benefit outsiders—even if that "property" consists of the outsiders themselves.

The Declaration surely looks much less attractive in this interpretation, but it is an accurate reading. What about the consequences? Once we accept that Jefferson's Declaration did not contain the values we now find in it, two other points follow. First, those values came from somewhere else. Second, we, who invoke those values, may not really be the heirs of the signers of the Declaration. We may be the heirs of a very different group of people. We may be the heirs of the enslaved people and the abolitionists who read the Declaration differently from its author; of Abraham Lincoln, who advanced that vision in national politics; of the US Army that fought for it; of the Reconstruction Congress that wrote it into law; of the civil rights marchers who brought those words back to life in the 1960s. Conversely, the real heirs of the signers may be the Confederates who declared their independence to protect the rights they thought they were due under the government they had created. Our America may have come into being not because we fought a war in the name of the ideals of the Declaration and more fully realized them in the Reconstruction Amendments but because we fought a war *against* the ideals of the Declaration and rejected them.

And if you think about it that way, losing the Declaration may be the best way to find ourselves.

4

The Ambiguous
Revolution

★

IN THE BACKLASH to the 1619 Project, one of its specific claims got the most attention. It was Nikole Hannah-Jones's assertion that "one of the primary reasons the colonists decided to declare their independence from Britain was because they wanted to protect the institution of slavery." If you interpret that to mean that all of the colonists declared independence to protect slavery, it is wrong. Some of the Revolutionaries were abolitionists. (Not that many—thirty-four of the forty-seven signers of the Declaration of Independence owned slaves.[1]) Hannah-Jones later acknowledged as much and said that curricula based on the project and the book version would "make sure the claims are properly contextualized." What if we temper the overstatement and suggest that for some of the Patriots, a desire to preserve slavery was one reason—and maybe a strong one—to declare independence? On its face, this is pretty plausible. Just as it seems unlikely that northern Patriots had slavery at the front of their minds, it is unlikely the southern ones didn't have it at least at the back of theirs. Maybe there would be no quarrel with this proposition. But it does not sit well with the triumphalist account of the Revolution. We do not usually tell ourselves that the Revolution was a war fought by slave-owning states against a nation that had partially banned the practice, that it had the effect of protecting slavery from the only power that could have abolished it, and that it was fought even in part for that reason.[2]

The triumphalist story wants to tell us the opposite: The Revolution was a glorious war for liberty, not just for the slave-owning Patriots, but for the world. And that is what the historians who attacked the 1619 Project say. Slavery "existed . . . without substantial criticism" until "the American Revolution [made] it a problem for the world."[3] The Revolution "unleashed antislavery sentiments that led to the first abolition movements in the history of the world." What originated in America was not massive plantation slavery but "organized anti-slavery politics."[4] Really, if you squint at it right, the Revolution freed the slaves.

What to make of this? One thing to say—though it's a little snarky—is that you don't need to squint at all. It's just a fact that the Revolution brought freedom to a lot of enslaved people, tens of thousands of them. Except those people weren't generally freed by the Revolution itself. Mostly, they escaped from the Patriots and found freedom with the British, often joining the royal forces to fight against their enslavers. (Sometimes the Patriots freed them in exchange for military service, but far less often. South Carolina, faced with a shortfall of manpower, took a different tack and promised to reward those who joined the fight for freedom . . . by giving them slaves.) In the Treaty of Paris, which ended the war, one of the American demands was that the British surrender those people as they withdrew. But the Americans did not call them people: Article VII of the treaty provided that the British forces would depart "without . . . carrying away any Negroes or other Property of the American inhabitants." To their credit, the British defied that treaty obligation.

Of course, the triumphalist story is trying to tell us something different—not that the British freed thousands of slaves in the Revolution, while Patriots tried to re-enslave them, but that the ideals of the Revolution spread around the world, eradicating slavery wherever they went. This is a rather heavy lift. (About American celebrations of the Declaration's liberty, Frederick Douglass said in

1852, "scorching irony, not convincing argument, is needed.") Does it seem likely that the British, defeated by slaveholding rebels they mocked as hypocrites, but holding true to the freedom they had promised escaped slaves, were then inspired by the ideals of the Revolution to end slavery in their remaining colonies? Not really.

If the British were looking for intellectual inspiration, they could have gotten stronger egalitarianism without hypocrisy from Revolutionary France, which abolished slavery in its colonies in 1794, consistent with the 1789 Declaration of the Rights of Man and of the Citizen, which announced: "Men are born and remain free and equal in rights." As to slavery, that document is everything the Declaration of Independence is not. It is a statement about real people, not hypothetical ones, as the use of "born" rather than "created" indicates. It is about rights within society, not the state of nature, as the use of "remain" indicates. It makes clear the distinction between insiders and outsiders (citizens as opposed to "men" generally). And it goes on to say something about the government's obligation to treat people equally: "Social distinctions may be founded only upon the general good." The fact that Jefferson participated in the drafting suggests that the differences from the Declaration of Independence are no accident. When he wanted to write principles that condemned slavery, Jefferson knew how to do it. Or, of course, the British could have looked to their own abolitionists, like Granville Sharp, or the philosophers the American rebels borrowed from, like John Locke or Algernon Sidney. When the British banned slavery in their remaining colonies in 1833, they were certainly not following the United States, which had not yet banned it.

So what is the truth about the Revolution and slavery? The record is not clear. Different people sought independence for different reasons, and likely they sometimes said what they thought would advance their cause rather than what they truly believed. History requires interpretation, and a claim to possession of the one singular truth is a hallmark of ideology. Still, the facts make it hard to argue with a straight face either that slavery existed everywhere without substantial criticism or that the American Revolution made it a problem for the world. As to the first, it's true that slavery existed, in some form, in virtually every society the world had ever known. But to say that it existed without substantial criticism obscures some important distinctions. It is true that enslaving outsiders, with justification, was often considered relatively unproblematic. One of the common forms of slavery—the practice of enslaving defeated enemies—was defended by John Locke, who elsewhere called slavery vile. The theory was that enemies could justifiably be killed, and enslaving them was more merciful. (Enemies are outsiders, but similar reasoning could be applied to anyone who committed a crime punishable by death, which for much of human history was many crimes.) However, enslaving insiders, or enslaving anyone without justification, was usually considered a bad thing—very similar, in fact, to killing without justification. This is why so many historical figures condemned it and why the colonists found it effective to charge that King George sought to make them slaves.

The colonists' practice of slavery was not a practice of enslaving individuals who had done something to invite their fate. It was the practice of kidnapping people who, as Jefferson himself said, had committed no offense, or, perhaps even worse, breeding people for the sole purpose of enslavement. "Let us be entirely clear," writes David Brion Davis, "on the essential point. No slave system in history was quite like that of the West Indies and the Southern states of America."[5] Similar things had been done before—the children of slaves were often enslaved, and racial differences are a classic means of identifying outsiders—but the scale of the slave labor force and the attempts to maintain and increase it through a systematic program of breeding and mass rape make it stand out. That kind of slavery did not exist everywhere without substantial criticism.

Did the American Revolution make it a problem for the world? It is hard to see how. While some of the Patriots did oppose slavery as part of the same set of principles that justified revolution, this was not an innovation on their part; those principles came largely from Enlightenment thinkers like Locke and English Whigs like Algernon Sidney. Most of these thinkers condemned at least the kind of slavery practiced in the colonies. The Declaration's preamble merely borrowed Enlightenment political philosophy—and, deliberately, enough to support independence but not to undermine slavery. Some Patriots had an understanding of the Revolution that did not condemn slavery. And in practical terms, what the Revolution most obviously did was to place American slavery beyond the reach of the only national government that had the power to end it. (If the ideals of the Revolution ended slavery, it seems a little odd that they did so in Britain before they did in America.)

So if the standard story—that the Revolution somehow ended slavery—is not entirely convincing, what about the argument that some Patriots were motivated by a desire to protect it? It is true, and the colonists knew it, that as colonies they were subject to British decisions about slavery, and their power was quite limited. In 1774 slave states represented about 10% of the population and 14% of the wealth of the British Empire. And of course they lacked representation in Parliament entirely. In the new United States, however, whatever national government emerged would not have the power to end slavery, and the slaveholding states would likely control that government: they constituted more than half the population and wealth.[6]

Independence thus protected slave states from British abolitionism. It also protected them from American abolitionism, to the extent that might have affected British policy. A mostly Quaker abolitionist society formed in Philadelphia in 1775. If America had remained part of the British Empire, that society would have sent its petitions to Parliament, which had the power to ban the slave trade and slavery in the colonies. English Quakers did just that, and the flood of petitions that Parliament received in the 1780s and '90s was a significant part of the movement against the slave trade. Because of the Revolution, however, the Philadelphia society's petition, written by Benjamin Franklin in 1790, went instead to the US Congress. The committee to which it was referred concluded (correctly) that under the Founders' Constitution, Congress lacked the power to abolish slavery or ban the international slave trade. Congress took no action.

So in some sense, independence clearly protected slavery. In order to estimate how significant the transfer of authority from the British Empire to independent states was, we would have to know how substantial and powerful the abolitionist movement was in England. And then, to answer the ultimate question about the motive for declaring independence, we would have to know how threatened colonial slave owners felt. Answering these questions is not easy, but a fair look at the evidence suggests that a concern to protect slavery probably deserves some place among the reasons for revolution.

Abolitionism in England was gathering strength as the Revolution approached. This is not a coincidence—the natural rights philosophy of the Enlightenment can indeed generate an argument against slavery; it is just one that the Declaration does not make. Thomas Clarkson's 1808 history of the movement includes a "map," showing how different "springs or rivulets" came together to form the "torrent which swept away the Slave-trade." From 1650 to 1700, he writes, "we find but few labourers in this case." Between 1700 and 1750, "we find them considerably increased, or nearly doubled." And between 1750 and 1787, "we find their increase beyond all expectation."[7] Clarkson lists dozens of abolitionists active in 1776. Perhaps he had a motive to overstate their numbers, and admittedly most "abolitionism" in Britain took as its target the slave trade and not slavery in the colonies. However, abolitionism was there, and it was growing.

Was this abolitionism a threat? For evidence of the success of British abolitionism, people generally point to the *Somerset* case, the 1772 decision by Lord Mansfield that proclaimed slavery "odious." The precise meaning of the decision is disputed and unclear, but it was generally read to abolish slavery in England, in the absence of positive law authorizing it. As to that law, supporters of slavery had petitioned Parliament, while the case was pending, to authorize slavery in England. Parliament refused, which suggests that the pro-slavery side was not politically dominant.

Did the colonists perceive a threat? They definitely knew of the decision, which was widely reported in colonial papers.[8] (The slave it freed was from Virginia and had been brought to England by a Scottish merchant.) It was not met by an enormous amount of protest in the colonies, which might tend to suggest that slave owners did not see it as a significant threat. On the other hand, slave owners in the West Indies did react strongly, which might suggest that the North American silence had something to do with the fact that the growing movement for independence was coming together around different themes. "No taxation without representation" could unite the colonies and perhaps win foreign support; "Hands off our slaves" could not. (Benjamin Franklin, for complex reasons, wrote an essay before Mansfield's decision expressing the hope that it could lead to abolition of the trade in slaves and even to "procuring Liberty for those that remain in our Colonies.")

So the evidence here is equivocal, and unsurprisingly scholars disagree. Matthew Mason reports that "something of a default position in the literature coheres around the idea that American slaveholders saw *Somerset* as a fundamental denial of their property rights and their political control over their slaves within an increasingly hostile, antislavery empire."[9] The statement of a widely held scholarly opinion is generally not greeted by other scholars with demands for retraction and charges that it is "astounding," "false," "simply untrue," or "an error of verifiable fact"—but again, what this shows is that the response reflects an ideology that is threatened.

What is more clear is that the drive for independence created a conflict over slavery, and in that conflict the Patriots were the pro-slavery side. As the struggle for independence grew, the British both discussed and implemented plans to free slaves as a method of fighting or ending the rebellion. Samuel Johnson—who asked acidly, "How is it that we hear the loudest yelps for liberty among the drivers of Negroes?"—went on to suggest "that the slaves should be set free, an act, which, surely, the lovers of liberty cannot but commend." "If they are furnished with firearms for defence, and utensils for husbandry, and settled in some simple form of government within the country," he continued, "they may be more grateful and honest than their masters." Abolitionist Member of Parliament David Hartley proposed—privately in correspondence with Benjamin Franklin and publicly in the House of Commons—a plan of reconciliation whereby the British would repeal all of the remaining post-1763 acts in exchange for the colonists agreeing to extend to slaves the right to trial by jury. Hartley called slavery "a vice which has spread through the continent of North America, contrary to the laws of God and man, and to the fundamental principles of [the British] constitution" and explained his proposal as a first step "to extirpate slavery from the face of the earth."[10]

The British did not just talk about freeing slaves. They did it, too: as a military measure, they issued emancipation proclamations. In 1775 Virginia governor Lord Dunmore's Proclamation offered freedom to slaves of Patriots who would join the British army. Dunmore's "Ethiopian Regiment" wore sashes embroidered with the words "Liberty to Slaves." In 1779 Henry Clinton's Philipsburg Proclamation went further and declared all Patriot slaves free. "Few Scotch excepted," said Richard Henry Lee, Dunmore "united every man in the Colony [of Virginia]" against the British.[11] Jefferson wrote that the proclamation "raised the country into a perfect phrensy."[12] This is not saying that a desire to protect slavery *started* the Revolution, which after all kindled in New England, but it does seem to have been a reason why many southerners joined the Patriot cause.[13] The colonists admitted this, or rather declared it. Inciting slave rebellions is one of the accusations that the Declaration levies against King George: he has "excited domestic insurrections amongst us." Let that sink in: the Patriots are fighting a war that the standard story tells us made slavery a problem for the world. Why? Because their enemies are interfering with slavery. In fact, this charge comes last in the list of grievances, which scholars believe was organized to end with the most severe.[14] It is also present in many state and local independence resolutions.

The Revolution certainly was an important moment for slavery. What its impact was and how it was achieved, however, are difficult questions. It is probably true, for instance, that the Revolution contributed to British abolitionism by reducing the value of slavery to the British Empire. It may also be that the Revolution made British abolition easier by eliminating the political power that American slaveholding interests might have exerted within the empire.[15] But this is a far cry from the triumphant march of the Declaration the standard story imagines.

Getting closer to the triumphalist story, there were indeed strong connections between British and American abolitionism. Yet that was mostly a consequence of the connection between the Quakers in England and those in America. Quaker abolitionism predated the Revolution, and Quakers were not Revolutionaries. Clarkson's survey of the sources of abolitionism credits the Quakers and notably excludes the Revolutionaries: "We see then this great truth first apparent, that the abolition of the Slave Trade took its rise, not from persons who set up a cry for liberty, when they were oppressors themselves."[16] Christopher Leslie Brown, in *Moral Capital: Foundations of British Abolitionism*, concludes that "the American Revolution did not cause abolitionism in Britain. It neither moved men and women to act nor indicated what, specifically, they should do."[17] Indeed not, because the American Revolutionaries generally *did not free their slaves* and in fact *demanded the right to re-enslave those who had escaped.*

The view of the Revolution as a war for the liberty of all is a perspective, not a capital-*T* Truth. Some participants seem to have felt that way; there is support for it in the historical record. There is also support for a quite different view: that the Revolutionaries were focused on supposed injustices inflicted on them and rather blind to the injustices they inflicted on others; that they fought, in some cases, for the right to continue those injustices. (And not just against the people they enslaved, but also the other outsiders— Native Americans—listed as a threat in the Declaration. Another motive for revolution came from resentment of British constraints on westward expansion into Native American lands.) Each perspective counts as history.

What does not count as history is maintaining that one of these perspectives is the Truth and everything else is ideological falsification. What we see with the letter from the prominent historians complaining about the 1619 Project is an ideology trying to shut out a different perspective. One reason for this has to do with history as an academic field, and the fight over the 1619 Project is in part a generational conflict within the discipline. Historians have consistently been moving away from triumphalism over the past decades, fueled by two major revisionary insights: that slavery was more central to the story of America, and that Black agency was more important, in both abolition and subsequent civil rights struggles, than previous generations acknowledged. The argument about the Revolution and slavery is an element of that debate, too. More triumphalist versions of the standard story are losing out to what Ibram X. Kendi called on Twitter a "tidal wave of revisionist racial history over the last five decades . . . largely written by women, by historians of color, by younger historians, by antiracist white historians." When you cannot win by persuasion, there is a temptation to declare victory by fiat.

But another reason, and maybe even a stronger one, has to do with America. The idea of American history as continuity—one of the key features of the standard story—attaches us to the past in two senses of the word. It links us and, as a consequence, makes us emotionally invested. Attacks on the past feel like attacks on us in the present; a condemnation of our historical forebears echoes down the generations. This is a mistake, for two reasons. The first is that it misinterprets the 1619 Project, which is not an attack on the standard story but simply a different version of it. If you cannot see the project as telling a familiar story of how our heroic predecessors fought to make founding ideals a reality, it may be because you have trouble with a story in which so many of those heroic predecessors are Black people. For some people, the whiteness of a triumphalist version is essential to the standard story. Indeed, there is a maximally triumphalist version in which the only bad guys are outsiders (the British) and the Americans are all freedom-loving Patriots. However, that version is no longer taken seriously even outside the academy. Everyone understands that some Americans have been on the wrong side of history, and once you grant that, the 1619 Project differs only in emphasis and degree.

The second reason is more important: it is that we have made confronting the flaws of the past harder than it should be. If we understand our story as one of rupture, rather than continuity, judgments of Americans in the past are not implicit judgments of Americans in the present. And if we understand our task as not to live up to founding ideals but to be better than the past, flaws and limits in those ideals do not imperil the project of American progress. Downplaying the flaws and preserving the idea of continuity is a strategy—it is the strategy of making the best of what we have, the strategy of Lincoln, of the later Douglass, and of Martin Luther King's "I Have a Dream" speech. But it confronts serious difficulties. First, there are undeniable but arguably marginal flaws that historians and activists bring out. These complicate the story, and our political culture tends to understand them as negatives and tries to minimize them. The Declaration's complaints about domestic insurrections and merciless savages are an example: those sound bad, and you don't hear much about them in conventional politics. With the Revolution, something similar happens with the British emancipation proclamations and the Patriot demand for the return of the formerly enslaved.

In each case, though, there are also central features that cannot be minimized. Instead, we celebrate them, without much thought as to their implications. In the Declaration, the colonists say that the duty of the government is to protect their natural rights. They complain of infringements and assert that they will judge when those infringements justify revolt. We present these elements as though they are good things, but they lead in alarming directions. With the Revolution, the heroes are the mostly white paramilitary organizations like the Sons of Liberty and the Minutemen; the tyrannical general government is the villain. The Patriots complain of being oppressed, deprived of their freedom, and taxed unfairly; they violently reject government authority. Again, we celebrate these features, but how do they translate into the modern world? (Or the world of the 1860s?) Do we want modern Americans to think that distrust of the national government is their founding principle, to view all government with suspicion? Do we want them to see white paramilitaries as heroes and taxes as cause for revolution?

In *The Whites of Their Eyes: The Tea Party's Revolution and the Battle over American History*, Jill Lepore examines the links between modern extremist ideology and misreadings of founding history. The truth is, of course, much more complicated than the Tea Party's ideological version. Yet there is no denying that our standard story makes the construction of that ideology possible. We can try to tell the standard story differently—we could emphasize that the complaint was about taxation without representation; we could try, as the 1619 Project does, to acknowledge Black agency and the role of Black people in the development of American ideals. But that only gets you so far. The Founding is an era of white supremacy; the author of the Declaration enslaved his children; the Revolution is a war against the national government justified by perceived infringements on the rebels' own rights. As long as we tell a story of continuity, we cannot eliminate those facts from the American identity we construct . . . and we give support to people who do not want to eliminate them, who want to make them more central.

Making the best of what you have is a strategy, and sometimes it's the right one. But we are not making the best of what we have, because we have much more than we know. If we let go of the idea of continuity, things look very different. Lincoln appealed to the Founding and the Declaration because he had nothing else. Rather than vindicating its ideals, however, he and other Republicans ended up as revolutionaries destroying the existing political order. Because of them, we do have something else, and we don't need a revolution to grasp it. All we need to do is to see that the revolution has already happened, and to embrace the different America it made for us.

5

The Geostrategic
Constitution

★

IT IS TIME NOW to turn to the third element of the standard story. The story gives pride of place to the Declaration as the source of American values, but it also points us to the Founders' Constitution, the document written in Philadelphia in 1787. Abraham Lincoln focused much more on the Declaration, but he connected the two. The Declaration, he said, was an "apple of gold" framed in a "picture of silver"—the Constitution. "The picture," he continued, "was made for the apple, not the apple for the picture."[1] The Declaration is primary, in this view, but the Constitution exists to effectuate its principles. Martin Luther King linked them as well, invoking in "I Have a Dream" the memory of the "architects of our Republic," the people "who wrote the magnificent words of the Constitution and the Declaration of Independence." Those two documents, he said, constitute a promissory note that that all men, Black as well as white, "would be guaranteed the unalienable rights of life, liberty, and the pursuit of happiness." It is fairly conventional to argue that the Constitution was written to fulfill the promises of the Declaration, to make real its values and give natural rights the protection of positive law. As Jack Balkin puts it in *Constitutional Redemption*, "The Constitution is a body of law; but the promises contained in the Declaration are its soul."[2] In political discourse, people often do not even distinguish between the two.

The Declaration invoked here is of course the Declaration of the standard story—the Declaration that claims the government should treat all people equally and not infringe on their liberty. And so the argument is that the Founders' Constitution likewise embodies our modern principles of liberty and equality. But as we have seen, our American values of liberty and equality are not in the Declaration. Consequently, it would be surprising to find them in the Founders' Constitution, and indeed we will not. However, there is another way in which the standard story gets the Founders' Constitution wrong. There is no reason to expect *any* values to be stated in the Declaration and codified in the Founders' Constitution, because there is very little connection between the two.

Much as it does with the Declaration, the standard story fundamentally misunderstands the purpose, and consequently the nature, of the Founders' Constitution. As we have seen, the Declaration does not make bold new claims about human rights. Instead, it starts with widely accepted principles of political philosophy in order to develop an account of when legitimate political authority can be rejected. Likewise, the point of the Founders' Constitution was not to create a government that would protect the natural rights of individuals, which was the purpose of the governments described in the Declaration. It was something else entirely.

THE PURPOSE OF THE FOUNDERS' CONSTITUTION

What was the Constitution supposed to do? As with the Declaration, we can answer this question by looking at the words of the document with an awareness of the historical context. The preamble tells us its aims: "to form a more perfect Union, establish Justice, insure domestic Tranquility, provide for the common defence, promote the general Welfare and secure the Blessings of Liberty to ourselves and our Posterity." To some extent, this language is consistent with the idea that the Constitution aims to fulfill the purpose of government described in the Declaration. Most strikingly, it is supposed to secure the blessings of liberty, which sounds like a nod to the inalienable right. (Note, too, the echo of the Declaration in limiting the set of people who are supposed to benefit from this government: We the People create the government to secure the blessings of liberty "to ourselves and our Posterity.")

But how is the Constitution going to secure the blessings of liberty? Now we need to think about the context, and about some of the goals the preamble puts before liberty—"a more perfect Union," "domestic Tranquility," and "the common defence." The basic point here is that the government the Constitution created was radically different from the governments described in the Declaration. It came into being in a very different situation. It consequently set out to deal with a very different set of problems and, unsurprisingly, took a very different form. What do I mean by this? Recall that the Declaration describes governments as the creation of individuals in the state of nature. The task for those governments, it says, is to protect individuals from other individuals. But the Constitution did not bring individuals together out of the state of nature. The Declaration announced that the colonies were independent states. They were in the state of nature vis-à-vis the British Empire, since that is how independent states relate to one another. The colonies all had governments, however, and during the Revolutionary period they drafted constitutions. The colonists were all members of particular political communities—they were citizens of their states, a citizenship that they took very seriously.

Consequently, the task of the federal government created by the Founders' Constitution was not to protect the natural rights of individuals from other individuals. State governments were presumed to be doing that. State constitutions typically began with declarations of rights that resembled the Declaration of Independence. The Massachusetts Constitution of 1780, for instance, pronounced in its preamble that "the end . . . of government, is . . . to furnish the individuals who compose it with the power of enjoying in safety and tranquility their natural rights." Like the Declaration, these constitutions often went on to affirm the right to revolution as well. Massachusetts again: "Whenever these great objects are not obtained, the people have a right to alter the government, and to take measures necessary for their safety, prosperity and happiness."

What the federal government did was thus not to bring the American people out of the state of nature but to bring the *states* out of the state of nature—or, more precisely, out of the Articles of Confederation. The Declaration had announced that the thirteen colonies were "Free and Independent States"—free and independent as nations or individuals are in the state of nature. They were, "among the powers of the earth," "separate and equal," endowed with full authority "to levy War, conclude Peace, contract Alliances, establish Commerce, and to do all other Acts and Things which Independent States may of right do." They stood, as independent nations do, in the state of nature as to each other and the rest of the world.

Just as the state of nature proved perilous for individuals, it was perilous for the newborn states. They needed to act in concert to defeat the British, and thereafter they needed to cooperate to survive in the face of potentially predatory European powers. The first American attempt at self-governance was the Articles of Confederation—essentially a treaty among independent states. They created a national Congress, but not a national judiciary or executive branch. The powers of Congress were quite limited: it could request money and cooperation from the states, but it could not tax or compel obedience. It could not enact laws that regulated private individuals at all, so it clearly could not protect their natural rights from each other. To use the most extreme example, it could not prohibit one American from killing another.

The drafters created such a weak national government because they were thinking of it not as the protector of natural rights but as a necessary means of facilitating cooperation among the states—and as a means by which the states could band together to protect themselves from other nations, as individuals did in leaving the state of nature: "common defence" is the first of the purposes of the Confederation listed in Article III. As far as individual people were concerned, though, the national government was seen more as a threat to rights than as their defender. This was the lesson of the Revolution, the political model built into the Articles of Confederation: a distant general government (think King George) may threaten the rights of individuals, and if that happens, the states will stand up to protect those rights.

So the drafters of the Articles set out to create a government that was too weak to become a tyrant. They succeeded in that—brilliantly—but the government they created was also too weak to govern effectively. It could not keep the peace between the states—Maryland and Virginia warred over oysters; as the Constitutional Convention gathered in 1787, New Jersey and Connecticut were considering an attack on New York. And it could not after all guarantee the safety of the states against external threats: Congress could not reliably field a national fighting force because it had no ability to compel the states to contribute or cooperate.

To confirm that these were the problems the Constitution sought to resolve, we can look at James Madison's 1787 pamphlet "Vices of the Political System of the United States." First on his list is the "failure of the States to comply with the Constitutional requisitions"—to pull their weight in the confederacy. Second is the "encroachments of the States on the federal authority"; third is violations of the treaties entered into by Congress; and fourth is the "trespasses of the States on the rights of each other." Not until the eleventh ("Injustice of the laws of States") do we get anything suggesting a concern for individual rights. A similar theme is evident in the *Federalist Papers*, written by Madison, John Jay, and Alexander Hamilton to win support for the Constitution. The first papers, where one would expect the most powerful justification of the new Constitution, focus on what Akhil Reed Amar calls "geostrategic" considerations.[3] After a general introduction in *Federalist* no. 1, *Federalist* nos. 2–5 discuss "Dangers from Foreign Force and Influence," before moving on to "Dangers from Dissensions Between the States" (nos. 6–7) and "Consequences of Hostilities Between the States" (no. 8). Not until *Federalist* no. 10 do we get a discussion of how a national government might make better domestic policy. *Federalist* no. 10 is much discussed now, precisely because of what Amar calls its "prophetic sketch of the federal government's eventual role in protecting minority rights." But not then. As Amar writes, "Scholars have shown that this essay and its ideas had remarkably little impact on Madison's contemporaries."[4]

The main goal of the Constitution, then, was the first goal listed in the preamble: to form a more perfect union, to meld the separate states into one nation. It sought to do this primarily for reasons of interstate and international relations. A single nation on the American landmass would resist dismemberment by the European powers in war. It would be able to negotiate more effectively in peace. A single nation would not require a standing army, which the Framers saw as a dangerous tool for would-be tyrants. And a single economic union would benefit the states via free internal trade.

In all of this, we can see a parallel to the Declaration's theory of government. However, the entities whose rights and existence are being protected and harmonized are the states, not individuals. The rights of states to free commerce are being protected. They are promised protection from invasion and domestic violence, and they are guaranteed a republican form of government. They are protected from each other, as well: domestic tranquility means a lack of interstate conflict. The states are even guaranteed some kinds of equality—equal suffrage in the Senate, for instance. Yet the Founders' Constitution has almost nothing to say about the liberty and equality of individuals. Its ban on titles of nobility is probably the strongest pro-equality statement. That is concerned with stopping individuals from being placed above others, not with preventing them from being pushed below—"there are no kings" is nice, but it is probably less important than "there are no slaves," which the Declaration and the Founders' Constitution could not say.

What about the Bill of Rights? The Bill of Rights was not part of the original Constitution in two ways—one literal, technical, and unimportant; the other figurative and crucially important. First, the technical point, the Constitution became effective, according to its terms, when it was ratified by New Hampshire in 1788. The Bill of Rights—the first ten amendments, adopted as a package—was ratified in 1791. But so what? It was understood during the ratification process that there would be amendments. Some states ratified the Constitution on the condition that amendments be added. For all intents and purposes, we can count the Bill of Rights as part of the Founders' Constitution.

Except that it wasn't the Bill of Rights.

The phrase "Bill of Rights" was known to the Founders, of course. It originates with the English Bill of Rights of 1689, Parliament's codification of the Declaration of Rights that followed the Glorious Revolution.[5] Many state constitutions had something similar, but these provisions looked much more like the Declaration of Independence than like the first ten amendments: they generally contained broad statements of political philosophy. And like the Declaration of Independence, they were typically inspired by the Virginia Declaration of Rights. Indeed, the Virginia Declaration became so influential that, as Gerard Magliocca writes, "most Americans came to believe that only a text like [it] could be a bill of rights."[6] The great Chief Justice John Marshall, writing in the early nineteenth century, used the phrase "bill of rights" a few times in his opinions, but he was referring to the limits on the federal government and the states imposed by Article I, Sections 9 and 10, respectively.[7] The founding generation did not consider the first ten amendments a bill of rights.

Why not? Probably because they did not seem as important then as they do now. Nowadays, Americans tend to think of the federal Constitution as the source and protector of their most important rights, but that was not the founding vision. (Modern Americans also often think of the Bill of Rights as the source of their constitutional rights against state governments, which is not just anachronistic but flatly wrong: as the Supreme Court held in *Barron v. Baltimore*, the Bill of Rights binds the federal government and not the states.) According to the founding vision, the federal government was actually the threat to liberty. The states were its protectors. As Amar has brilliantly shown, the Bill of Rights is in fact designed in several ways to protect individuals from federal oppression not by giving them rights but by strengthening state authority.[8] In this it mirrors the whole Founders' Constitution, which has the general aim of protecting and facilitating the operation of state governments—the geostrategic considerations—in order to make it easier for states to protect the rights of their citizens.

The Bill of Rights confirmed some individual rights against the federal government. But because the federal government was assumed to be largely concerned with interstate and international relations, its interaction with individuals was a lesser concern. (This was Hamilton's *Federalist* no. 84 argument against including a bill of rights at all: because the powers of the federal government are limited and enumerated, it lacks the ability to interfere significantly with individual liberty.)

If the Founders' Constitution were truly concerned with protecting the natural rights of individuals, it would have made more sense to look to the interaction of individuals with other individuals, or with their own state governments. This, strikingly, the Founders' Constitution does almost not at all. There is not a single provision in the Founders' Constitution, including the Bill of Rights, that can be violated by a private individual—they say nothing at all about what individuals can do to other individuals. The Congress created by the Founders' Constitution had legislative powers, and it could regulate individuals. But the powers are limited to certain contexts. Again, the most basic protection of natural rights—a law prohibiting one American from killing another—is beyond the power of Congress, absent special circumstances that make the killing an issue of federal concern.

With respect to the relationship between individuals and states, the Founders' Constitution does more, but not much. It tells states that they may not grant titles of nobility or pass bills of attainder, ex post facto laws, or laws impairing contracts. Madison, interestingly, wanted to go further: he wanted the federal government to guarantee the rights of conscience, freedom of the press, and trial by jury against state interference. He also wanted to restate the right of revolution: "That the people have an indubitable, unalienable, and indefeasible right to reform or change their Government, whenever it be found adverse or inadequate to the purposes of its institution." Neither proposal succeeded.

Nowadays, we do think of the Bill of Rights as protecting individuals from state governments—we think about cases such as *Miranda v. Arizona*, dealing with the right to remain silent; or *Gideon v. Wainwright*, dealing with the right to counsel; or *Texas v. Johnson*, dealing with flag burning and free speech, as Bill of Rights cases. But they are not. *Miranda* is not a Fifth Amendment case, *Gideon* is not a Sixth Amendment case, and *Johnson* is not a First Amendment case. The Bill of Rights restrains the federal government, not the states, and these famous cases do not deal with rights contained in the Founders' Constitution. All of those decisions involve the Fourteenth Amendment, which is most significant here for its absence from the Founders' Constitution.

The Founders' Constitution strips some authority from states—generally attributes of international sovereignty such as the ability to coin money or make treaties. Those are roles that the federal government takes over: it is the outward-looking sovereign of the American nation. The Founders' Constitution also places some limits on what states can do to citizens of other states. But as far as it is concerned, states can do just about anything they want to their own citizens.[9]

And their slaves.

THE FOUNDERS' CONSTITUTION AND SLAVERY

Almost no modern scholars agree with me that the Declaration of Independence is consistent with slavery. Yet most do recognize that the Founders' Constitution is not just consistent with slavery but actively supports it. Where the Declaration is agnostic about the institution, the Founders' Constitution is pro-slavery. But pro-slavery compared to what? (Compared to the Confederate Constitution, it looks pretty good!)

There are several possibilities, and they could yield different answers. One might be the Declaration: if the Constitution carries forward the values of the Declaration, as the standard story claims, is it different with respect to slavery? On this point, everyone agrees (though for somewhat different reasons): if you believe the Declaration is inconsistent with slavery, the Founders' Constitution clearly must be pro-slavery by comparison. Even if you believe, as I do, that the Declaration is at best neutral with respect to slavery, the Founders' Constitution is pro-slavery by comparison, for it interferes with both state and federal authority in a way that protects the institution.

Another might be the Articles of Confederation, which never mention slavery. (The Founders' Constitution never uses the word, but everyone knew that certain provisions were about slaves.) It was generally understood that Congress under the Articles of Confederation lacked the power to interfere with slavery, so the Articles were not anti-slavery in that sense.[10] However, states retained their power as sovereigns to determine the status of enslaved people who entered their borders: the Articles did not strip power from states to compel them to recognize slavery under certain circumstances, so neither were they pro-slavery in a way that the Founders' Constitution was. And perhaps most important, the Articles did not tilt the national government in favor of slaveholders. Each state had one representative in Congress.

One might also compare the Founders' Constitution to the range of what was possible at the time. Compared to other versions of the Constitution that might have been ratified, is this one pro-slavery? That is a complicated counterfactual question. It certainly seems true that a Constitution that immediately abolished slavery would not have been ratified. It is less clear that a Constitution that clearly set slavery on a path to extinction would not have been ratified. Present political actors are often willing to inflict costs on future generations. However we resolve that question—if indeed we can resolve it—it is obvious that slavery was a subject about which the states disagreed, and it raised several issues that required federal resolution. As we look at them, we will see that the Founders' Constitution generally resolved them in a pro-slavery way.[11]

THE THREE-FIFTHS COMPROMISE

What are the pro-slavery provisions of the Founders' Constitution? There are three obvious candidates. We encounter first the Three-Fifths Compromise, Article I, Section 2, which apportions representatives among the states according to their free populations and "three fifths of all other Persons"—meaning slaves.

Some people think that the Three-Fifths Clause is demeaning because it suggests that slaves are three-fifths of a person in some moral or dignitary sense. This is not quite true: the clause does not say that slaves should be regarded as three-fifths of a person; it tells us to use the number of free persons and three-fifths of the number of other persons for a specific calculation. Admittedly, Madison himself offered such a gloss in *Federalist* no. 54, describing the Constitution as "with great propriety" viewing enslaved people "in the mixt character of persons and of property . . . inhabitants, but as debased by servitude below the equal level of free inhabitants; which regards the slave as divested of two fifth of the man." In terms of how it works in the Constitution, though, the calculation does not measure the moral worth of these persons but rather determines how many representatives a state gets. Counting slaves at all enhances the power of slave states in the federal government. Using their whole number, in the manner of free persons, would enhance their power the most.

The strongest anti-slavery position, then, would replace three-fifths with zero; the strongest pro-slavery position would replace it with one. So what are we to make of three-fifths? Is it pro-slavery or anti-slavery? One theory holds that it would have made sense to count all people—including slaves, women, and children—in apportioning legislative power, for they are all people with interests deserving protection, and representatives in Congress, although not electorally accountable to them, will nonetheless represent their interests. This is a plausible thing to say about children, a more difficult argument to make with respect to women, and utterly preposterous with respect to slaves. Representatives from slave-holding states, elected by slaveholders, represented slaveholders and advanced slavery. They did not represent enslaved people.[12]

In consequence, the Three-Fifths Compromise represents what Amar calls "proslavery malapportionment"—a structural device that reliably and consistently overrepresented the interests of slave-holders in the national legislature.[13] As Frederick Douglass wrote in 1849, "One thing is certain about this clause of the Constitution. It is this—that under it, the slave system has enjoyed a large and domineering representation in Congress, which has given laws to the whole Union in regard to slavery, ever since the formation of the government."[14] Nor was its effect limited to Congress. Because the Electoral College allocates electors based on a state's number of representatives plus its senators, slaveholding states got extra clout in the selection of the president as well.[15] Four of the first five presidents hailed from the slave state of Virginia, and one of them, Thomas Jefferson, would have lost the election of 1800 to John Adams of Massachusetts without the edge provided by the Three-Fifths Compromise. Ten of the first twelve presidents owned slaves.

The Three-Fifths Compromise is a compromise, certainly, between the most and the least pro-slavery possibilities. But if our baseline is that slavery is wrong—if we think in terms of modern values—then anything above zero is pro-slavery. Was there any alternative? Amar suggests that perhaps a descending staircase would have been acceptable: count four-fifths of slaves in 1790, three-fifths in 1800, two-fifths in 1810, and down to zero in 1830. That might have sent the message that slavery was on a path to extinction—or at least that the slave power would not perpetually control the national government.[16] Instead, the Three-Fifths Compromise held out that prospect, and it was in fact losing control of the presidency with the election of Abraham Lincoln that precipitated southern secession.

THE INTERNATIONAL SLAVE TRADE

The second pro-slavery provision relates to the powers of Congress. Article I, Section 8, gives Congress the power to regulate commerce with foreign nations. That power might have been used to ban the international slave trade, but Article I, Section 9, carves that trade out of Congress's regulatory power: no restriction on "the Migration or Importation of such Persons as any of the States now existing shall think proper to admit" is allowed until 1808. So important was this provision to South Carolina's and Georgia's plans to replace the enslaved people who had escaped during the Revolution that it received an additional layer of protection. Article V sets out the procedures by with the Constitution may be amended, but it excludes two topics from the amendment power: "No state . . . shall be deprived of its Equal suffrage in the Senate" without its consent, and no amendment can affect the Article I, Section 9, protection of the international slave trade.

However, the protection lasted only until 1808. Could that be viewed as a compromise, as a recognition that slavery was in fact on a path to extinction? No. The overarching theme of the Founders' Constitution is, indeed, compromise. But this was a relatively unambiguous victory for the pro-slavery faction. First, opposition to the international trade was not the same thing as opposition to the domestic continuation of slavery—a distinction Jefferson made on both moral and prudential grounds. At the time, some slaveholders opposed the international slave trade for the simple economic reason that banning it would increase the value of the slaves they held.[17] The bloc that got its way in the protection of the international slave trade was not all the slave states together but really only the Carolinas and Georgia.[18]

Second, protecting the international slave trade until 1808

allowed it to last as long as even those states needed it. Madison said as much: "Twenty years will produce all the mischief that can be apprehended from the liberty to import slaves."[19] By 1808, the international trade of slaves was no longer necessary. According to the 1790 census, the United States, including its territories, had an enslaved population of 697,497. By 1810, shortly after Congress banned the international slave trade, the enslaved population stood at 1,191,362. The ban did not slow the growth of the enslaved population, which by 1860 reached almost four million.[20] The important slave trade was now intra-American, running from the upper South to the Deep South and transporting far more enslaved persons than the Middle Passage had.[21]

Again, there are baseline questions. Protecting the international slave trade until 1808 was probably not as pro-slavery as protecting it forever. But singling out one form of commerce for protection from congressional interference, enshrining that protection against amendment . . . there is no doubt that this is pro-slavery.

THE FUGITIVE SLAVE CLAUSE

Last, and most strikingly, Article IV, Section 2, provides that "No Person held to Service or Labour in one State, under the laws thereof, escaping into another, shall, in Consequence of any Law or Regulation therein, be discharged from such Service or Labour, but shall be delivered up on Claim of the Party to whom such Service or Labour may be due." This Fugitive Slave Clause represents a solution to one of the problems posed by the coexistence of slave and free states within a federal union.

The question that slavery posed was what would happen when a person with a status recognized by the law of one state—the status of slave—came within the territory of a state that did not recognize that status. Without the Constitution, the answer was whatever the state said. At one extreme, the slave might remain a slave no matter how she reached the free state or how long she remained there. At the other, the slave might be instantly freed, no matter how she arrived. (England, for instance, was widely understood after the *Somerset* case to maintain that rule, encapsulated in the maxim that English air was too pure for a slave to breathe.) Under the Constitution, free states retained the power to decide the status of slaves who entered their territory with the permission of their masters.[22] But that was no longer true with fugitives. The Constitution stripped states of their sovereign power to determine the status of persons within their territory in order to affirm that the bonds of slavery could not be broken by escape. That is pro-slavery, obviously, but, more important, it is anti-states' rights. Rather than simply allowing states to make their own decisions about slavery—which the Constitution generally did—the Fugitive Slave Clause curtailed their sovereign power in a pro-slavery way.

Again, this is in part a compromise. There was a stronger pro-slavery position available, which was that even slaves voluntarily brought into free states must remain slaves. But again, if the standard story is to make sense—if we are to point to the Founders' Constitution as the source of our modern American values—we must judge by modern standards. Stripping states of their sovereign authority and compelling even limited recognition of slavery under other states' laws is clearly pro-slavery. As South Carolina delegate Charles Cotesworth Pinckney boasted upon his return from the Constitutional Convention, "We have obtained a right to recover our slaves in whatever part of America they may take refuge, which is a right we had not before."

ANTI-SLAVERY READINGS OF THE FOUNDERS' CONSTITUTION

The Founders' Constitution clearly contains pro-slavery provisions. However, anti-slavery drafters had some influence. Opponents of slavery offered anti-slavery readings of the Constitution before the Civil War. Some historians do so today. So it is worth spending a little time to examine those readings and ask what their significance is.

Before the Civil War, the general view was that the Founders' Constitution was pro-slavery in the ways that I have described. Abraham Lincoln agreed. When the Corwin Amendment—a last-ditch attempt to preserve the Union by making explicit and entrenching against amendment the rule that Congress had no power to interfere with slavery within a state—was proposed, Lincoln responded in his first inaugural address that "holding such a provision now to be implied constitutional law, I have no objection to its being made express and irrevocable." The anti-slavery strategy of political abolitionists was not to work toward a federal ban on slavery. It was to prevent the expansion of slavery into federal territories and new states, to surround the slave states with a "cordon of freedom" in order to pressure them (somehow) into abolishing slavery via modification of their own state laws.

The abolitionist William Lloyd Garrison agreed with Lincoln about what the Constitution meant. But where Lincoln thought that working within the existing regime offered the possibility of ending slavery, Garrison preferred the more radical tack of secession by the free states. The difference between them was not about how to interpret the Constitution but about how to fight slavery. Frederick Douglass demonstrates the point well: When he believed that the national government was irrevocably committed to supporting slavery, he agreed with Garrison. When he saw the possibility of a national government opposed to slavery, he changed his mind.

There were some areas of disagreement. First, a radical group including such abolitionists as Lysander Spooner implausibly read the Founders' Constitution as prohibiting slavery. Spooner suggested that federal judges should hold slavery unconstitutional, but the 7–2 majority in *Dred Scott* showed the vanity of that hope. As Wendell Phillips wrote in a review of Spooner's book, "All that we have to do, *as Abolitionists*, with Mr. Spooner's argument is to consider its influence on the Anti-Slavery cause." From that perspective, it was a disappointment. "If merely *believing* the Constitution to be Anti-Slavery would really make it so, we would be the last to stir the question," Phillips continued. "But alas, the ostrich does not get rid of her enemy by hiding her head in the sand. Slavery is not abolished, although we have persuaded ourselves that it has no right to exist."[23]

There was a more significant dispute between Lincoln Republicans and pro-slavery advocates about the issues decided in the *Dred Scott* case: whether Congress could prohibit slavery in the territories and whether Black people could be citizens of the United States. But let us simply consider the Constitution that both sides agreed on. Is that pro- or anti-slavery? As with all such questions, the answer depends very much on whom you ask, and why, and when. People like John C. Calhoun, Roger Taney, or Stephen Douglas will tell you that it is pro-slavery, because they want to advance slavery. William Lloyd Garrison and the early Frederick Douglass will tell you it is pro-slavery because they think that dissolution of the Union is the best way to fight slavery: they want to reject the existing order and make another. Lincoln and the later Douglass will tell you it is anti-slavery because they believe that anti-slavery politics offers the best path to ending slavery: they want to work with what they have. And all these people, remember, *agree* about the legal effect of the Constitution. (Later Douglass is a limited exception because he slid into the Spooner camp in maintaining that the Fugitive Slave Clause wasn't about slaves.) What that shows is that this is a subjective question. So we need to think about why we are asking the question now, or why we might prefer one answer rather than the other. Why do people nowadays argue that the Founders' Constitution is anti-slavery?

Sean Wilentz is probably the leading modern proponent of the anti-slavery reading. Viewing the Founders' Constitution as pro-slavery is "destructive," Wilentz said; "one of the most destructive falsehoods in all of American history."[24] But destructive of what? He does not explain, but we could say it is destructive of continuity, of the triumphalist version of the standard story, of the idea of the Founders as our heroic forebears. Destructive, perhaps, of our unity and faith in America. If the Founders' Constitution was anti-slavery, then we can more easily tell a story of American values stated in the

Declaration, codified in the Constitution, and realized over time. If it was pro-slavery, the story becomes more complicated. We can still tell the standard story, but now there has to be a fall and redemption aspect to it. (The ideals of the Declaration and the Revolution, perhaps, were betrayed by the Founders' Constitution.[25] And then perhaps redeemed in the Civil War.)

There are, then, two elements to the argument: the falsity and the destructiveness. As far as destructiveness goes, we will see that it is the standard story that poses the threat to true unity. It is the standard story that damages our ideals and undermines our faith in America. But what about falsehood? It is surprisingly difficult to figure out what Wilentz thinks is false in the claim that the Founders' Constitution was pro-slavery. He does not, so far as I can tell, disagree with the conventional interpretation of the Three-Fifths Clause, the protection of the international slave trade, and the Fugitive Slave Clause. What he seems to focus on is the fact that the Constitution never uses the word "slave" or "slavery." That is true, and it is certainly true that this was a deliberate choice. The drafters of the Constitution, some of them, were embarrassed about slavery and did not want to name it explicitly. The supporters of slavery cared whether it was protected or not; there was no reason for them to care whether it was named.

Wilentz says, repeatedly but obscurely, that the choice not to use those words had substantive consequences. It "was a substantive matter, not a cosmetic one," which "had to do with ensuring that the Constitution contained nothing that could be construed as acknowledging and thereby endorsing property in man." The Framers avoided "naming and thereby legitimizing [slavery] in the Constitution."[26] However, Wilentz does not identify any legal issue or principle that naming slavery would have changed. That is not surprising, because the legal effect of constitutional provisions does not in fact depend on direct naming rather than circumlocution. The Fugitive Slave Clause, for instance, prevented free states from declaring escaped slaves free. Everyone—excepting outliers like Spooner and the later Douglass—understood that, and no one today seriously denies it. It was fully capable of achieving that goal without using the word "slave."

Did the circumlocution avoid some sort of recognition of property in man? Again, only in a cosmetic sense. By requiring that such persons be returned to those "to whom such Service or Labour may be due," the clause obviously recognized some kind of a right to another person's labor under slave-state law and privileged it over the contrasting rights created by free-state law. What kind of a right was that? Not a contract right, for there were no contracts with slaves. What it recognized was a property right. In fact, the principle that a person has the right to demand a thing's return is the essence of a property rule.[27]

Perhaps more striking, consider the ill-fated Corwin Amendment, which provided that "No amendment shall be made to the Constitution which will authorize or give to Congress the power to abolish or interfere, within any State, with the domestic institutions thereof, including that of persons held to labor or service by the laws of said State." Here again, the words "slave" and "slavery" are missing. But the clear effect is to enshrine slavery against federal interference; to argue that the use of "institution" has some substantive anti-slavery effect seems willfully blind.

So perhaps the point is that the Constitution did not contain any such explicit guarantee, that "the slaveholders failed to win the absolute protection for slavery they desired"?[28] This argument, too, is odd. Slavery was absolutely protected, in the sense that Congress lacked the power to ban it in states where it existed. Even the Lincoln Republicans conceded this, so textual confirmation would have made no difference to the Republican strategy or the course of history. Lincoln's first inaugural address said just this: that is why he did not object to the Corwin Amendment, which would only have made "express and irrevocable" what he believed the Constitution already provided.

The crucial disputed legal issue, as things turned out, was whether Congress could ban slavery in the territories and require new states to ban it as a condition of admission. That was the key to the Republican cordon of freedom strategy; that was what Taney claimed the Constitution prohibited in *Dred Scott*. But that is a purely legal question about the scope of congressional power and the restrictions imposed by the Fifth Amendment. It is not affected by whether the Constitution uses the word "slave" or not. Taney did claim that the Constitution recognized slaves as property, but his argument was not that the Constitution singled slaves out for special recognition (though in fact it does). It was that slaves were property like any other sort: "no word can be found in the Constitution which gives Congress a greater power over slave property, or which entitles property of that kind to less protection that property of any other description."[29] Change all the circumlocutions to explicit mentions of slavery and it neither makes Taney's arguments any stronger nor opens the door for others.

The Constitution does not explicitly mention most sorts of property. It says, for instance, nothing about horses, but that does not mean that it excludes the idea of property in equines. It simply means that the Constitution, then as now, recognized that property law was state law. John Quincy Adams distinguished types of property: "The property in horses was the gift of God to man at the creation of the world; the property in slaves is property held and acquired by crime, different in no moral aspect from the pillage of a freebooter, and to which no lapse of time can give a prescriptive right."[30] The Constitution does not draw this distinction, except to give special powers and special protection to slavery. Does that mean that Taney was right? No, and I will discuss the defects of his argument later. (Briefly, a legitimate government *can* ban possession of certain types of property.) But it does mean that the choice to use the word "slave" or not is more cosmetic than anything else.

It is true that the pro-slavery delegates did not get all they wanted. They would have preferred five-fifths to three-fifths, and a guarantee that slave owners could take their slaves to free states, and (possibly) an indefinite protection of the international slave trade, and (had they more foresight) a guarantee that Congress could not ban slavery in the territories. (The Confederate Constitution gave them all these things, except it actually banned the international slave trade.) But the fact that they did not get everything they wanted does not make the refusal to use the word "slave" any more substantive. Nor does it obviously make the Founders' Constitution a paradox, as Wilentz repeatedly terms it.[31] When both sides get part of what they want, we usually call that a compromise. The question we have to ask is whether it was a good compromise, worthy of our veneration, or whether the concessions to slavery went too far.

The Garrisonians and the Lincoln Republicans disagreed on that, but they did agree it was a compromise. (Garrison did not say that the Constitution was *written by* the devil, as he might have with the Confederate Constitution: he said that it was an *agreement with* hell—a deal with the devil.) The Garrisonians found it unacceptably morally compromised and rejected it; the Republicans sought to work with it. Yet whether to reject the Founders' Constitution is no longer the question for us; we need only decide what we should think about it.

You can ask that question in terms of what was possible, and maybe the Founders' Constitution doesn't look so bad from that perspective, if you think a constitution was necessary. The necessity argument has to confront the fact that the Founders' Constitution didn't actually work out very well, but it is an argument that we can make about the past. Slavery was the price of union, and perhaps a less pro-slavery constitution could not have been ratified. However, neither "necessary" nor "the best we could have done" is the same as "anti-slavery." If you are trying to tell a story of continuity, the appropriate question is whether the Founders' Constitution embodies our modern values. From the modern perspective, the answer is clear. The Founders' Constitution is pro-slavery, and its word choice does not save it. While the Declaration squarely says there are no kings, the Founders' Constitution does not even pretend that there are no slaves.

This was plain to Lincoln, and it is plain to us. So why do people react with such vehemence to suggestions that the Founders' Constitution was what it rather obviously was? The widespread attachment to triumphalist versions of the standard story, or to versions where the continuous development of American ideals proceeds through each element (the Declaration, the Revolution, the Founders' Constitution), is in part a product of its prevalence and familiarity. To some people, it feels neutral. In much the same way that for some people whiteness exists as a neutral category, with only non-whiteness racialized, the standard story feels like truth, and everything else is ideology. (When you're used to privilege, equality feels like oppression.)

But part of it is, I think, a little more reflective. I think that people genuinely believe that the standard story has good consequences. They genuinely believe that the standard story inspires us; it unites us; it includes everyone in a vision of America that gives us the best way to move forward together to realize our ideals (1776unites.com!).

They're wrong.

The standard story is not just less than objectively true and neutral; it is harmful. By telling the standard story, we are actually acting out a different story, a more sinister one. By giving the Declaration and the Founding pride of place in the construction of our national identity, we are repeating, in some ways, the sins of the past.

In the next two chapters, I will tell you two versions of the standard story that are a little more accurate than the one we are accustomed to. I'm going to tell you tell you the story of America as the consistent quest for a single value. And I'm going to show what happens if you try to trace the principles of the Declaration through American constitutional history.

Spoiler alert: Neither of these stories is going to be a very happy one.

6

The Story of Continuity

★

THE PRECEDING CHAPTERS have offered a critical examination of the three main elements of the standard story: the Declaration of Independence as a statement of American ideals of universal liberty and equality, the Revolution as a war for those ideals, and the Founders' Constitution as a codification or implementation. Not a single one of these elements is particularly plausible. The Declaration is concerned with independence, not universal human rights, and its political philosophy offers nothing to outsiders. The Revolution was fought for many reasons, by people who were primarily concerned with their own rights, not those of the outsiders they were oppressing. The Founders' Constitution is actually not the kind of government described in the Declaration—it is not designed to protect the natural rights of individuals at all.

I am not saying that the standard story is false. There are obviously many respected historians who advance it, and there is support for it in the historical record. More significantly, national stories are by nature interpretations of the past, and there is no single true interpretation. What I am saying is that if we look at the historical record and try to adopt the perspective of people at the time, the standard story seems to miss a lot of what was there and add things that were not. Ultimately, my argument is that the consequences of the standard story are bad. In its triumphalist versions, it encourages complacency. And in all versions, it brings along things we do not want in our national story. There are troubling elements to it that we cannot eliminate, no matter how we shade the past. I will now set out two more accurate versions of the standard story, which help us to see clearly what we are committing ourselves to when we adopt it.

History is complicated, of course, but there are two ways of describing the standard story that can help us create a more accurate version. First, the standard story tells us that American history is a story of continuity. It is the story of the realization of a single value—equality, the principle to which our nation was dedicated. Second, it tells us that the ideals of the Declaration have guided us on this path. This chapter and the next take those narrative structures seriously. Here, I ask what we find if we look through our history for a single lodestar value. And in the next chapter, I identify the influence the Declaration has had on our development as a nation.

UNITY AND (IN)EQUALITY

In some ways, it makes sense that the standard story tells us that our fundamental value is equality. America is—at least now, at least in the rhetoric of politicians—committed to equality. And since the point of a national story is to bring people together, equality is a convenient choice for a focal value. Equality includes everyone; equality is a way to unity. From another perspective, though, the idea that equality is our founding and guiding value is bizarre and ironic. It is bizarre because there is simply no reason to think that the people who came together at the key moments of the standard story would have been interested in equality in our modern sense. (Equality is a contested concept, but I assume that people who support slavery or racial hierarchy are not supporters of equality in this sense.) It is ironic because, historically, claims for equality have been about the most divisive thing there is. As we will see, inequality usually does a much better job of uniting Americans—some of them, at least, and often enough to take or hold power.

If you look at American history and try to discern a single value for which we constantly strive, equality is not at the front of the pack. The strongest contender is unity. Union and national security—getting enough people to act together to win domestically and to resist foreign aggression—are the basic American goals. It is possible to tell a story where this theme recurs, where it provides the central motif for the development of the nation. It is possible to tell a story of a distinctively American identity born with the Declaration and the Founding and enduring through the centuries. But this story is not a happy one. It is a story of the shadow of slavery hanging over the nation, of the poison of racial hierarchy working its way through the body politic. Union is pursued at the expense of other values, and the value that is sacrificed, most often and most consistently, is racial equality. This story, too, starts with the Declaration of Independence. Although the Declaration is about disunion with Great Britain, it has a subtext of unity: unity among the American colonists. It concludes not just with the declaration that the colonies are independent states, but also with a description of them as united and with a mutual pledge of support.

Unity was necessary. The colonies acting separately could not have defeated the British. Their choice was join or die, as Benjamin Franklin's political cartoon said. This meant bringing together supporters and opponents of slavery. (Not free and slave states: in 1776, every state recognized slavery. The Betsy Ross flag shows us thirteen stars in a circle, and every star represents a slave state.) Some of the colonists disliked slavery; others were very attached to it. In consequence, the Declaration adopts a political theory that has no direct implications for slavery: it is about the rights of insiders and focused on the question of when the governed may reject the legitimate political authority of their governors. Jefferson might have thought initially that he could bring the two sides together by offering something to each—his first draft balances the pro-slavery complaint about domestic insurrections with a relatively anti-slavery one about the introduction of slavery to America. But the pro-slavery side bristled at the criticism and the anti-slavery side did not fight for it. (The breadth and depth of opposition to slavery in the North should not be overestimated. Jefferson later suggested that his "Northern brethren also . . . felt a little tender under these censures; for tho' their people have very few slaves themselves, yet they had been pretty considerable carriers of them to others.") The result was that the criticism of the slave trade was removed while the complaint about rebellions remained. Accepting slavery was the price of independence. Perhaps it did not seem a high price: remember that at least three-quarters of the signers of the Declaration owned slaves.

What about the Revolution? We know, again, that there were both pro-slavery and anti-slavery people fighting on the Patriot side. So would it make sense that the war they fought would be a war for ideals inconsistent with slavery? Not really. We would expect that different people had different understandings of the ideals of the Revolution. Yet the understanding everyone could share was that if it succeeded, the states would be independent and free to make their own decisions. For some of them, this turned out to mean abolition, and some Patriots probably expected that. For others, it turned out to mean that slavery was safer than it had been, since it was removed from the reach of a national government with the power to abolish it. In those states, one consequence of the Revolution was probably a rise in racism, since the practice of slavery required a justification. (This suggests an important and more general point: Racism can produce inequality through discrimination, but inequality can also produce racism, as people who benefit from that inequality seek to justify it.)

We see the same thing with the Founders' Constitution. By 1787, abolitionism had made headway in the North. At the Constitutional Convention, there were four free states represented (Pennsylvania, New Hampshire, Massachusetts, and Connecticut) and one missing (Rhode Island). There were people who disliked slavery among the drafters, but there were also people who were very attached to it. It would be silly to expect an anti-slavery document to emerge from that drafting process. We would expect a compromise—with perhaps a pro-slavery tilt, since, as with the Declaration, the intensity of feeling seems to have been greater on the pro-slavery side. Repeatedly, southern delegates insisted that a less pro-slavery Constitution would sink the whole American enterprise. If southern states did not get at least three-fifths representation for their slaves, said William Davie of North Carolina, the Constitutional Convention's "business was at an end." As the Framers debated the international slave trade, John Rutledge of South Carolina pronounced that "the true question at present is, whether the Southern States shall or shall not be parties to the Union." When the compromises were done, Charles Pinckney told the South Carolina House of Representatives that "we have made the best terms for the security of this species of property it was in our power to make. We would have made better if we could; but on the whole, I do not think them bad."

So accepting slavery was also the price of union. The drafting of the Constitution was another "join or die" moment. If the colonies could not form one dominant nation on the North American landmass, France, Spain, and England might dismember the United States. Without a single nation, states would more likely have standing armies, threatening both intrastate tyranny and interstate wars. So the Founders' Constitution accepts slavery, protects it, and rewards slave states with extra power in the federal government. The preamble to the Constitution, the Reverend William Barber has observed, puts justice before tranquility in its list of goals. But it puts union before both, and union requires compromise.

These compromises work—at first. The Revolution succeeds; the Constitution wins ratification. And so we get America: a nation built upon compromises, chief among them the acceptance of slavery. (If we think about Indigenous peoples, we could also call America a nation built on genocide and theft, but that is a different story.) But they don't work forever. In my constitutional law class, I take the first few weeks to read through the Founders' Constitution, clause by clause, with my students. Then I ask them: What do you think? Is this a glorious statement of American principles that has served us well for over two hundred years? Or is it a covenant with death and an agreement with hell? Students usually laugh. They laugh because they're surprised, because of course they've been taught the standard story about how wonderful and successful the Constitution has been. Most of them haven't heard the phrase "a covenant with death and an agreement with hell." It originates, remember, from William Lloyd Garrison, who urged northern secession rather than union with slaveholders and burned a copy of the Constitution. "So perish all compromises with tyranny!" Of those two descriptions, it seems undeniable to me that Garrison's is closer to the mark. The Founders' Constitution is a deal. You get an American nation, but you must accept slavery. That's a bargain with evil, a deal with the devil. And like most deals with the devil, it doesn't work out very well. Because what happens? The Founders' Constitution is pro-slavery, but it does allow for some change—its protection of the international slave trade, for instance, explicitly expires in 1808. It doesn't make clear how far slavery will be allowed to spread—whether Congress can ban slavery in the territories, whether pro- or anti-slavery conditions can be placed on the admission of new states, how the balance of power in the national government will shift. On those questions, the Constitution kicks the can down the road. And that road leads straight to the battlefields of the Civil War.

The Civil War happened because the Founders' Constitution compromised and did not resolve the issue of slavery. I mean that first in the political sense. The Constitution could have taken a position one way or the other—it could have said, no limits on slavery. Maybe that Constitution would have been ratified. Or it could have said, slavery will end. Not immediately—that Constitution certainly wouldn't have been ratified—but in some number of years, perhaps set on a path to extinction by a descending staircase version of the Three-Fifths Compromise. That might have been acceptable. But it was easier to say nothing about it, and that's what the Founders did. The Constitution was structured to support slavery, and in the early years the slave states controlled the national government. Then things change. The North grows in population, supported by free states in the Midwest. Admission of new states threatens to upset the balance of power in the Senate. The careful preservation of equal numbers of free and slave states ends with the Compromise of 1850, when California comes in as a free state (though initially with one pro-slavery senator). The balance tips further with the admission of Minnesota (1858) and Oregon (1859). The North is increasingly controlling the federal government, and anti-slavery forces are increasingly controlling the North.

In the 1856 election, the anti-slavery Republican Party takes eleven northern states. The South goes entirely for James Buchanan, and he wins. In 1860, it's sectional again. The South votes for John Breckinridge, but he doesn't win. Abraham Lincoln wins. Lincoln is, to an extent it is very difficult to overstate, not the southern choice. In ten of the eleven states that are going to secede, Lincoln gets literally zero votes. That's because he's not on the ballot, because no one wants to face the consequences of publicly supporting him.[1] In the eleventh, Virginia, he gets 1.1% of the popular vote. So the South sees the national government falling into the hands of anti-slavery forces. They fear the national government will try to end slavery. And they secede.

At that moment, unity failed. The compromises that made America didn't last, because they weren't a well-thought-out resolution to the conflicts and tensions of the Founding. They were just postponements, and you can't put the reckoning off forever. So the Civil War comes about in part because of a political failure in the Founders' Constitution. But you could also see it as a consequence of a moral failure. Abraham Lincoln understood it that way. He said the Civil War was "the woe due" for slavery, that God might will it to continue "until every drop of blood drawn with the lash, shall be paid by another drawn with the sword." You could also say that the Founders' Constitution was doomed to fail, that when you put unity ahead of justice, the bill always comes due.

Unity and justice struggle against each other during the Civil War, too. We think of the Civil War as the war that ended slavery, and it was. However, it doesn't start out that way. Before the war, Republicans want to preserve the Union. They do want to end slavery, but they don't make arguments for direct abolition. They're willing to take their chances with the slow-moving cordon of freedom strategy: they intend to encircle the slave states with free states and territories, and then, somehow, slavery will die out. Lincoln says he has neither the power nor the inclination to interfere with slavery where it exists.

War comes anyway, and the rebel South makes it clear in their Confederate Constitution and secession documents that it's a war for slavery. On the part of the United States—because that's whom they're fighting: not the North but the United States—it is in the beginning a war for union. If he could save the Union by freeing all the slaves, Lincoln says in a famous letter to Horace Greeley, he would do it. But if he could save the Union by freeing none, he would do that, too.

When Lincoln wrote that letter, he had already drafted the preliminary Emancipation Proclamation that was released on September 22, 1862, after the Battle of Antietam. It is certainly plausible that one of his aims—maybe the dominant one—in the letter was to emphasize that emancipation was necessary as a military measure (therefore within his power as commander in chief) and not simply desirable as a matter of justice (but unconstitutional). Still, what he released on September 22 was the preliminary proclamation. That declared—in its very first sentence—that "hereafter, as heretofore, the war will be prosecuted for the object of practically restoring the constitutional relation between the United States, and each of the States, and the people thereof, in which States that relation is, or may be, suspended or disturbed." The stated goal was reunion, which was separable from abolition. The preliminary proclamation set an effective date for emancipation of January 1, 1863, offering the rebel states at least the theoretical possibility of accepting reunion without abolition. Perhaps more important, the preliminary proclamation says nothing about military service, which is crucially important in bringing Black people into the American political community. (Black military service, I will argue, is more or less responsible for the creation of modern America.) It talks instead about paying compensation for the abolition of slavery in loyal states, and colonization—which would *remove* Blacks from the American political community. So even if we believe that Lincoln was committed to emancipation as a condition of reunion by September 1862, something very important changed by January 1863.

With the 1863 Emancipation Proclamation, for the first time in American history, the nation actually sets itself against slavery. The war does become a war for freedom. And we try for a while to follow this new track. For just about the only time in American history, we put justice before unity. Before the unity of white people, in particular. You could also say that we tried to forge a real unity, not just unity among white people, even if it meant that some white people would end up on the outside. We do this with Reconstruction.

America's view of Reconstruction has changed over time. What I want to point out here is simply that Reconstruction accomplished amazing things—by military force. At the point of a bayonet, the Constitution was transformed by the Reconstruction Amendments. Former Confederate states wrote new constitutions that affirmed equality. Black men—former slaves—were elected to state and federal office. Hiram Revels and Blanche Bruce were elected US senators from Mississippi. Between 1870 and 1877, fourteen Black men were elected to Congress from former Confederate states. In Louisiana and across the South, integrated governments operated integrated schools and police forces. But again, this is not the product of unity. It is accomplished only through military force. The defeated Confederates do not accept this transformation of their society, and violence is common. In 1873, a white militia massacres Black people who attempt to defend Republican officeholders at the courthouse in Grant Parish, Louisiana. In 1874, a pitched battle rages through the streets of New Orleans, as the Crescent City White League defeats the integrated New Orleans police force and state militia and occupies the statehouse. President Grant sends federal troops, and the White League retreats before they arrive. The federal government is fighting for justice and an American political community that is open, even if that makes some whites feel like outsiders.

The will to maintain a military occupation of the South does not last. Pretty quickly, the national mission changes back to what it was with the Declaration, with the Constitution—back to unity. Rather than saving the Union by defeating the Confederates, we will obtain unity by bringing the North and South together, healing the wounds of the Civil War. How do we do that? In the same way the Declaration and the Constitution did, by sacrificing racial justice. With the Compromise of 1877, the federal government abandons, or at best largely scales back, the use of federal military power to support state governments. The integrated governments that were set up are overthrown by force, and southern whites take back control. Like Lincoln's unpopularity in the South, the extremism of this shift in power is something that is hard to overstate. The standard story doesn't have much to say about it, because it doesn't fit well with a story about the progress of equality. It has been underplayed in our history books. Most Americans don't know that military coups swept over half the country, with the acquiescence of the federal government. But that is what happened. The legitimate governments of southern states and cities were overthrown by force, by white supremacist paramilitary organizations. Black people and Republicans were disenfranchised and massacred. They call it the Redemption of the South, and what it means is we turn away from the idea of equality. We restore racial hierarchy. Redeemer governments write new constitutions; they put up monuments to Confederates and terrorists. In 1891, the Redeemer government of New Orleans erects a monument to the victors of the Battle of Liberty Place: the White League. In 1920, a committee erects a monument to honor the three white men who died in the attack on the Grant Parish courthouse as "heroes . . . fighting for White Supremacy."

And then, as nations do, we start creating a story that justifies what we are doing. This story is a southern version of history. Slavery was not so terrible, it tells us, and the Civil War was fought for states' rights. The real mistake was Reconstruction, which subjected the South to oppressive rule by the incompetent and corrupt until Redemption righted the ship. Redemption, this story tells us, is the real birth of America. (Redemption fits badly with a story of equality, where slavery is the aberration. But it fits very well with a story of unity, where Reconstruction is the aberration.) Many respectable historians, in what came to be known as the Dunning school (after Columbia professor William Dunning), endorsed this story as the truth. As Eric Foner writes, "Finding it impossible to believe that blacks could ever be independent actors on the stage of history, with their own aspirations and motivations, Dunning et al., portrayed African Americans either as 'children,' ignorant dupes manipulated by unscrupulous whites, or as savages, their primal passions unleashed by the end of slavery."[2]

Of course, this story existed not only, and not primarily, in academia. National stories are supposed to reach widely; they are supposed to inform the worldviews of ordinary citizens. This one spread through popular fiction and, maybe most notably, the moving picture. There's a movie about the Civil War and its aftermath that follows two families, one from the North and one from the South. They fight on opposite sides of the Civil War, but they're both American. When the war is over, the reunion of the nation is symbolized by two marriages between these families—the bonds of matrimony knit up the wounds of war. This movie is, as you might have guessed, *The Birth of a Nation*, from 1915. And it really is about the birth of the American nation. It's trying to tell us that Founding America broke apart—broke into two more or less equally legitimate sides, the North and the South—but then came back together in the moment of Redemption, and now we can all go forward happily together, because in the end we're all Americans.

The story is straightforward. Its rising action—the part of the movie where tensions are growing and things are getting worse—is about the oppression of Reconstruction, with the carpetbaggers and the scalawags and the corrupt and depraved freedmen. Its climax is a moment much like the Battle of Liberty Place: the Ku Klux Klan defeats the integrated militia and police force—the legitimate government of the South Carolina town where it's set. The falling action—the bit that shows you everything will be all right—is the day after that battle when the town holds new elections. The freed slaves turn out to vote; they're met by armed Klansmen standing in front of the polling booths, and they turn around and go home. The resolution is the weddings, which reaffirm that the nation can go forward unified—not so much because we're all Americans as because we're all white. The marriages show that regional lines could be crossed, but racial ones could not.

That is what I have referred to as exclusive unity. It is unity among a group defined largely by who is not allowed to become a member: American unity built on the exclusion or subordination of Black Americans. Like *Dred Scott*, it tells us that America's "we" is limited by race. *The Birth of a Nation* was very popular with some people, including President Woodrow Wilson, the first southerner to hold the presidency since the Civil War. (Wilson was a racist even by the standards of his time: he resegregated the federal government and defended the Klan.) It was less popular with others: it was the target of a campaign by the NAACP and W. E. B. Du Bois and was banned in some northern cities. Du Bois fought the national story embodied in the movie more broadly. In 1909, he argued for the value of Reconstruction accomplishments, including broader democracy, public schools, and social welfare programs. In 1935, he published *Black Reconstruction in America, 1860–1880*. The last chapter, "The Propaganda of History," confronts the Dunning school, charging: "Herein lies more than mere omission and difference of emphasis. . . . We have too often a deliberate attempt to so change the facts of history that the story will make pleasant reading for Americans."[3]

However, this opposition was in the minority. A false story of American history, which produced unity among whites through racial hierarchy, remained dominant until the 1960s, when scholars began to reevaluate Reconstruction.[4] They did this because of other social changes that made it harder to see Redemption as our founding moment. The civil rights movement gained momentum in the mid-twentieth century. The Supreme Court issued decisions like *Brown v. Board of Education*, banning segregation in public schools, and *Loving v. Virginia*, striking down bans on interracial marriage. Congress enacted laws banning racial discrimination and protecting Black voting rights. This period, often called the Second Reconstruction, shows us a different face of unity. It offers us the promise of the standard story: unity in the service of equality, achieved through civility, patience, moderation, and faith in America.

It doesn't work. Martin Luther King seeks unity and justice together, but in the end he gets neither. Opinion polls in 1964 find broad support for civil rights laws—equality in principle—but less support for vigorous enforcement of those laws—equality in practice.[5] Polls asking about King himself show opinion shifting against him, from a plus-six-point net positive rating in 1964 to minus thirty in 1966. The Second Reconstruction, like the first, is divisive. Equality movements always are. The 1960s and 1970s are a tumultuous period. People feel that their traditional way of life is under attack, that the America they understand—the America they see when they look back—is being taken from them. Inequality turns out to be a more powerful way of bringing people together. The Republican Party's "Southern Strategy" appeals to racial anxiety to win over formerly Democratic voters. Ronald Reagan promises to restore the original understanding of the Constitution—the vision of Founding America—and undo the distortions of the Warren Court. And it works. The Second Reconstruction is followed by the Second Redemption.

Reagan's presidency is notable because it brings so many people together—he wins two absolutely crushing electoral victories over Carter and Mondale—but it follows the pattern set in the Declaration and repeated thereafter: it brings the nation together at the cost of racial equality. The electoral maps demonstrate this. They seem to show a united country—Reagan wins 44 states and 489 electoral votes in 1980, then 49 states and 525 electoral votes in 1984—but Carter still wins 41% of the popular vote, Mondale 40.6%. Among Black voters, Carter wins 82% and Mondale 91%. The winner-take-all system of the Electoral College erases those votes, showing us a false unity.

So the pattern repeats itself. It's fading, I hope, and if you want to tell a story of progress you can tell it in that way. But if you look back to the Declaration and the Founding for the basic theme of the American story, it's not liberty and it's not equality. It's purchasing unity at the price of racial justice. If you listen closely, you can still hear that theme, even on the progressive side of American politics. You can hear it in the arguments that Democrats need to set aside identity politics, to empathize with working-class whites: that's how they can forge a winning coalition—unity. You hear it in the objections to Maine's adoption of a state song that glorifies a Maine Civil War regiment, because "we are not [the] Union, we are [the] United States."[6] (This is why we should not refer to Lincoln's side in the Civil War as the Union, and certainly not as the North: those terms suggest that it was something other than the United States.) And you can hear it in the argument that the Founders' Constitution was anti-slavery, that Thomas Jefferson's Declaration stated our ideals, and that we should move forward together by revering and emulating men who fought for their freedom while holding others in bondage.

If you look back with clear eyes, then, the story of America isn't so much a burst of idealism that casts its light into the present day as it is a primal sin—a betrayal that echoes down the ages. We purchase unity at the price of justice, and more specifically the value of racial equality.[7] We do it again and again. And while we do it less obviously now, it is still a theme of our political and constitutional discourse. It is a part not just of *Birth of a Nation* but also the standard story. The standard story tells us, quite literally, to embrace an American identity that includes slavery, to make that compromise in the name of unity. There is an attempt to downplay the significance of this by suggesting that slavery is actually inconsistent with the Declaration and the Founding, but I have come to suspect that the racial hierarchy of Founding America is not a bug but a feature of the standard story.

The reason for this is that the trade-off between unity and racial justice is not accidental. It is necessary in its first iterations. The states must act together in the Revolution; they must come together with the Constitution. After the Civil War, though, things could have gone differently. Congress agreed to recognize southern governments and seat their representatives once they ratified the Fourteenth Amendment, to release the Confederate states from the grasp of war that had protected the rights of the freedpeople. The southern governments had been remade, but they weren't stable without military support. The ballot promised by the Fifteenth Amendment could not replace the bullet—not when southern states used both force and law to stop Black men from voting. (When Malcolm X offered the choice between "The Ballot or the Bullet," the first had a track record of failure, and the second a record of success.)

The abandonment of Reconstruction, the Redemption of the South, the Southern Strategy—these were not necessary to the survival of the United States. They were choices to forge a dominant political coalition of whites by subjugating Blacks. Reagan did not simply ignore racial inequality, and the Southern Strategy did not set racial issues aside, in the way we might (ignoring the complaint about slave rebellions) say the Declaration does. It worked by foregrounding the concerns of whites who felt their privilege eroding. The exclusion of Black people is not incidental to the creation of unity; it is instrumental. Going back at least to 1976, the Democratic presidential candidate has never received less than 82% of the Black vote and has never won the white vote. When enough white voters joined together to get their way, that is, it was always against the will of Black voters.

The key to this kind of unity is not downplaying race but rather increasing its salience. (As Martin Luther King said in 1965, at the conclusion of the march from Selma to Montgomery: "The segregation of the races was really a political stratagem employed by the emerging Bourbon interests in the South to keep the southern masses divided and southern labor the cheapest in the land.") Increasing racial hierarchy gives poor whites something of psychological value.[8] Scapegoating Black people, as the Dunning school did, leads poor whites to blame them, not rich whites, for their hardships. With each tactic, racial solidarity among whites helps overcome their economic divisions, allying poor white people to white economic elites. Overall, the message is the same one we find with a careful reading of the Declaration: Black people are outsiders, and outsiders are dangerous.

The strategy of focusing on race creates unity—not among all Americans, certainly, because its whole point is to create and deepen racial divides. But it creates unity among a group sufficiently large and politically powerful to form a governing coalition. It gets enough people together to win. And we should remember that when we talk about unity, that is too often all we mean: unity among a group strong enough to get its own way.

What is the conclusion to draw? It is the point that I started with. Our constitutional history is hard to describe as a consistent development of founding principles of liberty and equality. Those were not the main concerns in the founding era, and even afterward, progress on racial equality has proved neither inevitable nor constant. Indeed, a recent analysis suggests that it is relatively anomalous: it occurs in meaningful ways only when three factors coincide: a large-scale war requiring military mobilization of Black men, a justification for the war couched in terms of American egalitarianism, and a domestic political movement able to demand that national leaders live up to those stated ideals.[9] These factors coexist during the Revolution, the Civil War, the Second World War, and the Cold War, but have otherwise been lacking. In their absence, we generally see whites banding together to create an exclusive unity. The story of continuity, it turns out, is an exclusive one.

7

The March of
the Declaration

★

SO FAR, I HAVE argued that the standard story is not fully convincing. The main justification for the standard story, however, is not so much that it is true as that it is useful. It is supposed to be a story everyone can feel good about; it should bring all Americans together in the shared pursuit of noble values. A focus on utility makes some sense: the criterion for a successful national story is indeed whether it unites a people around a shared identity. But the standard story fails here as well. It creates a false and partial unity, and it undermines the values it purports to promote. If we try to tell American history as a story of continuity, it takes a sinister turn. The call for unity has a long history in America—and not a particularly happy one.

Something similar happens with the Declaration of Independence more specifically. Most people, if pressed, will admit that it wouldn't have made that much sense for Jefferson to announce as self-evident a principle that condemned slavery, and that neither the colonists nor any other government in the world followed. Still, they might say, the Declaration has been an inspiring force for good. It has helped people fight for equality, even if that version of equality isn't quite in the document itself. Well, yes and no. It is certainly true that the Declaration has inspired people. It has inspired some people who actually do have valid arguments under the Declaration as it was understood by the Revolutionary generation—people like Ho Chi Minh and Elizabeth Cady Stanton. And it has inspired people who do not—enslaved people, early abolitionists, and Abraham Lincoln. But if we look at the effects of the Declaration on the American struggle for equality, the picture is mixed at best.

This chapter examines two aspects of the role of the Declaration in American life. First, there is its use in political argument. The Declaration has sometimes been used for good, particularly before the Civil War. It has supported bad causes too, however, and there is nothing good the Declaration does that could not now be done better by a different document. And, as with the standard story more generally, there are bad things that cling to the Declaration, which we cannot simply rub away. Embrace the desirable gloss we have placed on the Declaration, and we open our arms to its problematic features as well.

Second, there is its effect on the Supreme Court's interpretation of the Constitution, which has been nothing short of disastrous. The Declaration has been a powerful force *against* both liberty and equality. That's a strong claim, and perhaps a surprising one: How could a document that extols liberty and equality undermine those values? The answer lies in the fact that the Declaration's theory of natural rights is not necessarily an inclusive or egalitarian one. Protecting the natural rights of insiders can have harsh consequences for outsiders—and even for other insiders.

THE DECLARATION IN POLITICS

The founding generation paid little attention to the Declaration's preamble. They read it as a consensus version of widely accepted political philosophy that turned specific only at a few necessary moments. When did the preamble rise to prominence? Pauline Maier's article "The Strange History of 'All Men Are Created Equal'" is the best investigation I have found of this specific question. During the 1790s, Maier reports, the Declaration was "first rescued from the obscurity into which it had so quickly sunk." It was rescued because it was the only federal document that spoke about equality and inalienable rights. "As a result," Maier continues, "those who found those ideas useful in national politics had to cite the Declaration . . . they had no alternative."[1] Who were these people? Anyone who wanted to struggle against what they saw as tyranny, including feminists but, in particular, opponents of slavery. Early abolitionists, both Black and white, appealed to the Declaration as a condemnation of slavery; so did enslaved people suing for freedom. The practice grew. "It was during the antebellum debate over that 'peculiar institution,'" Maier writes, "that 'all men are created equal' took on its modern meaning."[2] Abolitionists such as William Lloyd Garrison and Frederick Douglass regularly appealed to the Declaration as a statement of anti-slavery ideals. They read Jefferson's equality in a new way: not as a pre-political state of nature but as an entitlement to equal treatment by the government.

In 1854, anti-slavery forces coalesced into the Republican Party, which incorporated the Declaration of Independence into its platforms of 1856 and 1860. The 1856 platform stated the now-conventional view, invoking in its first resolution "the principles promulgated in the Declaration of Independence, and embodied in the Federal Constitution." It went on not only to affirm congressional power to ban slavery in the territories but to deny that Congress has the power "to give legal existence to Slavery in any Territory of the United States." (Ironically, it relied for this claim on the Fifth Amendment's Due Process Clause, the same provision Taney would invoke to invalidate such a ban.) The 1860 platform continued in the same vein, this time quoting the Declaration's preamble explicitly. The Republicans lost in 1856, and John C. Frémont ("Free Soil, Free Labor, Free Speech, Free Men, Frémont!") faded from view. (During the Civil War, Frémont briefly commanded the Department of the West, but was removed by Lincoln for insubordination—which in large part consisted of precipitous emancipation.) But the victor of 1860 did more than anyone else to popularize the understanding of the Declaration embraced by the Republicans. That man was, of course, Abraham Lincoln. Lincoln invoked the Declaration routinely before the war, but most important he echoed it in his Gettysburg Address. After the Gettysburg Address, the practice of invoking the Declaration for equality continued. Members of Congress, debating a constitutional amendment to ban slavery, spoke of it as the means to bring into the Constitution the Declaration's "sublime creed of human equality."[3] They said similar things about the Civil Rights Act of 1866 and the Fourteenth and Fifteenth Amendments.

Later activists for equality also invoked the Declaration, often filtered through the Gettysburg Address. One hundred years after the Republican Party platform embraced the Declaration for equality, the Democrats followed suit. The "Civil Rights" plank of the 1952 Democratic platform paraphrased Lincoln: "Our country is founded on the proposition that all men are created equal. This means that all citizens are equal before the law."[4] In 1963, Martin Luther King's famous speech echoed Lincoln's rhetoric before appealing for equality in the words of the Declaration. Signing the Civil Rights Act of 1964, President Lyndon Johnson also counted back to the Declaration: "One hundred and eighty-eight years ago . . ." "We believe that all men are created equal," he continued. "Yet many are denied equal treatment."[5] A year later, in his Special Message to Congress in support of the Voting Rights Act of 1965, Johnson borrowed a different piece of the Gettysburg Address. "We are met here tonight as Americans," said Johnson, evoking Lincoln's "we are met on a great battlefield." Johnson went on to quote "all men are created equal" in support of the "right to be treated as a man equal in opportunity to all others."[6]

Now the idea that the Declaration contains our modern values of liberty and equality is part of our basic understanding of America. The Declaration is the heart of the story we tell ourselves to explain who we are and where we have come from. It is often referred to as "the American creed"—as Supreme Court Justice Arthur Goldberg did.[7] The National Archives website displays the Declaration and proclaims that it "states the principles on which our government, and our identity as Americans, are based."[8] Even the 1619 Project accepts it.

Stirring stuff. But supporters of slavery had a different reading. The government had an obligation to treat the people who had formed it equally, John C. Calhoun argued—and therefore it could not disadvantage the South by prohibiting slavery in the territories. A ban on slavery, Alexander Smyth claimed, would violate the natural rights of slave owners. When the southern states seceded, they consistently invoked the Declaration—not for the equality that abolitionists had found in it, but for the right to revolution that the Patriots did. Southern whites resisting Reconstruction argued that Congress was imposing on them a form of government to which they had not consented, and that it had repeated the abuses of King George by, among other things, dissolving southern legislatures.

So what can we take from this? It is true that the Declaration has been invoked for noble causes: for abolition, for women's rights, for Lincoln's side in the Civil War, for civil rights and equality generally. Yet it has been invoked for less noble causes, too: for slavery, and for the side of Jefferson Davis.[9] The abolitionists are just the ones who prevailed. And they prevailed not because of the strength of their interpretation but because of the strength of the US Army.

Still, you might think, the battle is over, and the Declaration has been cleansed. In our post–Civil War world, it stands for Lincoln's equality, not Jefferson's. It stands for the vision of Martin Luther King. This is partly true. In our political rhetoric, Lincoln's version has won—though that does not necessarily make relying on the Declaration a good idea. In the Supreme Court, though, something different seems to be going on.

THE DECLARATION AND THE
CONSTITUTION: CREATION

To grasp the influence of the Declaration on the Supreme Court, we need to better understand its relationship to the Founders' Constitution. The standard story tells us that the Declaration contains ideals of liberty and equality and that the Founders' Constitution was written to promote those ideals. This account is false, because the Declaration does not contain the ideals that Lincoln attributed to it, and even if it did, those values are not in the Founders' Constitution. The Declaration does contain a theory of natural rights and the role of governments in securing them. But the Founders' Constitution is not connected to that, either, because the Founders' Constitution did not create a government that brings individuals out of the state of nature and protects their natural rights against other individuals. The government it created serves geostrategic purposes, and the state of nature it abridges is one that existed between the states.

It is possible, however, to connect the Declaration to the Founders' Constitution in two ways. First, the Declaration is relevant to the origins of the Constitution, and in particular to the question of its legality. Second, the Declaration is relevant to the interpretation of the Founders' Constitution and the states' revolutionary constitutions, and in particular the powers people might be supposed to have delegated to those governments. On the first point, we often think of the Constitution as coming from nowhere. It might not be the document that created the United States—many people, including Lincoln, give that honor to the Declaration. But the Declaration creates in a negative way, by rejecting a prior legal order— that of the British Empire. The Constitution creates in a positive way, by making a new order. However, the Constitution operated negatively as well. Most people will admit that the Declaration was an act of treason under British law, a violation of the existing law. But they will be far less willing to accept that characterization of the Constitution.

We must remember, though, that the Constitution did not come from nowhere. There was an existing legal regime it displaced— the Articles of Confederation. Our standard story tends to neglect the Articles. One reason for the neglect may be that they were obviously not a government devoted to the liberty and equality of individuals but rather a league among sovereign states, and realizing that opens the possibility that the Founders' Constitution was not so different. Another, though, is that they show us failure and discontinuity in the American story: failure because they worked terribly and were set aside, and discontinuity because the process by which the Constitution replaced the Articles was inconsistent with the rules set out in the Articles themselves. Article VII of the Constitution provided that it would be effective upon ratification by nine of the states. Upon ratification, the government created by the Articles would cease to exist. (The Congress created by the Articles, for instance, would lose its powers.) Yet the Articles proclaimed themselves "perpetual" and provided that any amendment required unanimous consent.

The drafters had been charged by Congress with "the sole and express purpose of revising the Articles of Confederation," but the Constitution they came up with, in effect, destroyed the existing government—it was, you could say, treason. In practical terms, of course, it was low-stakes treason. Reject the authority of King George, and he will send Hessian mercenaries to remind you of his love. Reject the Articles of Confederation, and not much will happen. The problem with the Articles, after all, was that the national sovereign was not powerful enough. The sovereign most offended by the rejection of the Articles was probably Rhode Island, which as the smallest state highly valued its veto power over amendments. But Rhode Island was not about to use military force against the other states. Still, the legal question remains: Was the Constitution treason?

One response to the charge of treason is to embrace it. Treason is okay, it turns out, if it succeeds. (History is written by the winners, they say—although the Civil War turns out to be an important departure from this principle.) Traitors who win are revolutionaries, and if they reject the prior legal regime, the fact that they are traitors by its lights tends not to matter. Thus we can comfortably admit that the Founders were traitors under British law. We don't care because we are no longer British subjects. We are Americans, and under our law the Founders are Founders. However, this move is not available with the transition from the Articles of Confederation to the Founders' Constitution. The Constitution wants to suggest that we are the same nation—we have, perhaps, simply formed a "more perfect Union" than the one created by the Articles. You can see this by the treatment of debts incurred under the Articles: the Founders' Constitution expressly preserves them, suggesting that the new nation is in important ways a continuation of the old one. So the argument that we don't need to worry about a violation of the Articles because we have rejected that legal order is less satisfying.

A second response to the charge of treason is to deny it on legal grounds. The Articles of Confederation were a treaty, some people say, and the breach of a treaty by one or more parties releases all the others from their obligations. Because states were not living up to their obligations under the Articles (recall Madison's complaints in his "Vices" pamphlet), they ceased to be binding. In this view, the Articles fell apart on their own, and the Constitution did come from nothing: there was no legal order in place for it to supplant. This account, as well, is a little hard to square with the Constitution's adoption of debts incurred under the Articles. The Constitution doesn't seem to see itself as a repudiation of the Articles, just an alteration. The nation's governing charter changes, but the nation persists. Where could one turn for authority to change that charter through a process inconsistent with the charter itself? The answer, of course, is the Declaration of Independence. The Declaration was written upon the occasion of one people dissolving the political bands that had connected it to another, of one people abolishing—at least for themselves—the government to which they had owed allegiance. But "abolish" is only one of the options the Declaration sets out. If a government fails to fulfill the purposes for which it is created, the people may also "alter" it. The Declaration, then, legitimizes the Founders' Constitution despite its inconsistency with the Articles.

So far, so good, perhaps—legitimizing the Constitution probably doesn't seem like a bad thing. But if you accept this argument, you are committing yourself to something else as well. If we say the Declaration allows states to break out of the Articles, despite their unanimity requirement and self-proclaimed "perpetual" status, it surely allows the southern states to leave the Union created by the Founders' Constitution. That constitution said nothing about perpetuity or secession. The debate over the legality of the Constitution is a bit arcane, but it illustrates one of my larger points: We cannot pick and choose the more appealing elements of the Founding and claim a connection only to them. Embracing the Founding connects us to other things; using the Declaration to support the Constitution leads to supporting secession as well.

THE DECLARATION AND THE CONSTITUTION: INTERPRETATION

The second relationship between the Declaration and the Founders' Constitution is that the philosophy of the Declaration may help us interpret the Constitution. Knowing the purpose for which a government is created may help us decide what powers the people would or would not give to it. In particular, if people create governments to secure their natural rights, it seems likely that they would not give them the power to arbitrarily interfere with those rights. One can make this argument directly for state governments, which are Declaration-style governments. It is a little more complicated for the Founders' Constitution, which is instead geostrategic in its aims. But it is still plausible to argue that the Constitution was intended to secure natural rights indirectly, by protecting the state governments that were the direct guarantors. And this supports an inference that people would not give the federal government the power to arbitrarily interfere with their natural rights.

The theory of the Declaration suggests, then, that laws that infringe on the natural rights of insiders may go beyond the powers granted by the people. A series of such abuses can justify revolution, but judicial review can provide an alternative. If judges strike down these offending laws, revolution is unnecessary. The Supreme Court has accepted, at least on occasion, the idea that the purposes of government limit its power. Its first notable appearance is in *Calder v. Bull*, a case from 1798 about the powers of a state government. *Calder* presented a rather narrow dispute about ex post facto laws, but Justice Samuel Chase's opinion sweeps more broadly. He starts by announcing that there are some inherent limits on what a state legislature may do, even if those limits are not written down anywhere. "I cannot subscribe to the omnipotence of a State Legislature, or that it is absolute and without control; although its authority should not be expressly restrained by the Constitution, or fundamental law, of the State."

Where do the limits come from? Chase explains that "the people of the United States erected their Constitutions, or forms of government, to establish justice, to promote the general welfare, to secure the blessings of liberty; and to protect their persons and property from violence." Although this language echoes the preamble of the Constitution, "United States" here means not the nation but the states individually—Chase is talking about state governments. That is why he speaks of "Constitutions" in the plural, omits the federal Constitution's mentions of a more perfect union, domestic tranquility, and the common defense, and adds in the state-government goal of direct protection of natural rights. Knowing these purposes can tell us something important, Chase argues.

> The purposes for which men enter into society will determine the nature and terms of the social compact; and as they are the foundation of the legislative power, they will decide what are the proper objects of it: The nature, and ends of legislative power will limit the exercise of it. . . . There are acts which the Federal, or State, Legislature cannot do, without exceeding their authority. There are certain vital principles in our free Republican governments, which will determine and over-rule an apparent and flagrant abuse of legislative power; as to authorize manifest injustice by positive law; or to take away that security for personal liberty, or private property, for the protection whereof of the government was established. An

ACT of the Legislature (for I cannot call it a law) contrary to the great first principles of the social compact, cannot be considered a rightful exercise of legislative authority. The obligation of a law in governments established on express compact, and on republican principles, must be determined by the nature of the power, on which it is founded.

What sort of acts might violate these "great first principles"? Chase gives a list of examples and then explains the principle that unites them: certain things are so manifestly unfair—always and under all circumstances—that people creating a government would never give the government the power to do them.

A few instances will suffice to explain what I mean. A law that punished a citizen for an innocent action, or, in other words, for an act, which, when done, was in violation of no existing law; a law that destroys, or impairs, the lawful private contracts of citizens; a law that makes a man a Judge in his own cause; or a law that takes property from A. and gives it to B. It is against all reason and justice, for a people to entrust a Legislature with SUCH powers; and, therefore, it cannot be presumed that they have done it.

People sometimes describe Chase as saying that natural law trumps positive law, but that is a serious misunderstanding. All people have natural rights, but this argument does not suggest that anyone can invoke natural rights as a defense against state law. If it did, it would presumably allow slaves to assert their natural rights to liberty against state laws authorizing slavery. Instead, the argument is that natural law can be used as a guide to interpreting positive law, in particular the constitution that grants powers to the government. People create governments to secure their rights and would not give them the power to arbitrarily interfere with those rights. As with the Declaration, this is an argument that is available only to insiders—only to the people who created the government and gave it its powers. It is only their rights that the government is created to secure. People might well create a government with the power to violate the natural rights of outsiders—to conquer them or enslave them. That is why Chase repeatedly referred to citizens.

Another limit on the argument in *Calder v. Bull* is that Chase wrote only for himself, and other justices rejected his reliance on natural law. Fortunately for supporters of the Declaration-style argument, it would later win the support of a majority—indeed, a supermajority: seven justices would join the opinion.

Unfortunately for supporters, that opinion was *Dred Scott*.

It is well known that *Dred Scott* discussed the Declaration of Independence in the context of its holding that descendants of slaves could never be citizens of the United States. There, Taney rejected the idea that "all men" could mean all men, since that would (he thought) have made the slaveholding signers hypocrites. (Taney was wrong on this point because the proposition that all men are created equal is in fact consistent with slavery.) It is less well known that the second part of *Dred Scott*, the invalidation of the ban on slavery in federal territories, also relies on the Declaration. The form of the argument, however, is the same as that of Justice Chase's. To understand the argument, we need to understand the case in which it was presented.

Dred Scott was born into slavery in Virginia around 1799. His owner, Dr. John Emerson, was a surgeon in the US Army and during his service took Scott into the state of Illinois from 1834 to 1836 and into federal territory (what is now Minnesota) from 1836 to 1838. In both these places, slavery was prohibited. Scott later sued, arguing that the laws of Illinois and the federal territory made him a free man.

The conflict between the laws of free states and slave states was something that the Founders were well aware of. (This, remember, was the issue in the *Somerset* case, when an enslaved person from Virginia was brought into England.) The Fugitive Slave Clause resolved it in one context, in favor of slavery: slaves who escaped to free states could not become free on account of those states' laws.

Instead, they remained slaves and had to be returned. But what of slaves who were brought into free states voluntarily?

Here the free states had more authority, and they pushed back against slavery. Most states, at some point, allowed slaveholders at least a limited right of transit—they could bring slaves through the state without emancipation if they did not stay for too long. If they did exceed a prescribed limit, or if they became a resident of the free state, enslaved people would be free. A similar rule applied to free territories. Was that rule permissible? Taney said no. He relied on the Fifth Amendment to the Constitution, which prohibits the federal government from depriving people of life, liberty, or property without due process of law. "An act of Congress which deprives a citizen of the United States of his liberty or property, merely because he came himself or brought his property into a particular Territory of the United States," he said, "could hardly be dignified with the name due process of law."

How was due process of law lacking? Slaveholders were being deprived of property, yes—their state laws said that their slaves were their property, and federal law said they were not. But this deprivation was being accomplished in the conventional way. The legal rule came from the Missouri Compromise, a federal statute that provided in federal territory north of thirty-six degrees and thirty minutes north latitude, "slavery and involuntary servitude, otherwise than in the punishment of crimes . . . shall be, and is hereby, forever prohibited." The Missouri Compromise was enacted via the normal congressional lawmaking procedures, and any slave owner whose slaves claimed freedom under it would have his day in court. He could go all the way to the Supreme Court, as the *Dred Scott* case did. So there was no lack of process in any ordinary sense of the word.

In fact, what was lacking, in Taney's view, was not the process but the law. For Taney, a duly enacted federal statute wasn't enough to count as law—and here his reference to an "*act*" of Congress that "could hardly be dignified with the name of due process of *law*" is a telling echo of Chase. The Missouri Compromise, Taney believed, was one of the things that Justice Chase referred to as "an ACT of the Legislature (for I cannot call it a law)." It was beyond the powers granted to Congress, and therefore it was not a law.

How is a judge to decide whether what confronts him is a valid law or a mere act, outside the bounds of delegated power? The argument is a little more complicated with the federal government, but Taney ends up in the same place as Chase: knowing the purpose for which people create a government can help us identify powers that they would never give it. Like Chase, Taney's discussion of the Missouri Compromise echoes the Declaration's language about securing rights, referring to "the personal rights and rights of property of individual citizens as secured by the Constitution."

Chase, we saw, argued that people would never give the government the power to arbitrarily violate their natural rights, or to take acts that are always and clearly unfair. Ex post facto laws and bills of attainder are examples of government action that can be condemned independent of context. And, said Taney, so is a law providing that certain kinds of property cannot be brought into a territory.

Was Taney right? That *Dred Scott* was incorrectly decided is almost an article of faith among the legal community nowadays. That is so, I suggest, because the standard story, as a story of continuity, requires us to identify with the Founding and the Founders' Constitution. A Constitution that produced *Dred Scott* is so monstrously unjust that we cannot identify with it; thus *Dred Scott* must be wrong.

There are two important points to be made about this feature of our constitutional faith. First, it is not so clear that *Dred Scott* is wrong in holding that Black people could not become citizens of the United States. Before the Constitution, the states were essentially sovereign nations. When they joined the United States, they gave up some aspects of their sovereignty, among them the ability to exclude or discriminate against the citizens of other states. (This was part of the larger project of making the United States a single economic unit.) The Privileges and Immunities Clause of Article IV required the states to grant citizens visiting from other states the same rights they granted local citizens. This infringes on a fundamental aspect of sovereignty: the ability of a state to define its political community, to say who are the "people" for whom the government is established.

In the context of slavery, the question was pointed: What if the visitor was a person not entitled to citizenship under the laws of the state he was visiting? Southerners expressed alarm at the prospect that they would be forced to recognize the rights of visiting free Blacks to, among other things, bear arms. The Founders' Constitution did not give an explicit answer to this problem, but it is not unreasonable to suppose, as Taney did, that the concept of federal citizenship had some limits. The US Congress, in its 1790 Naturalization Act, offered the possibility of US citizenship only to "free white persons." That was the view of the national government. Would states be allowed to circumvent it and make Black people federal citizens through state law, against the will of other states? It is perfectly plausible to argue that the Founders' Constitution prevented this. If Taney was right, it did so by creating a class of outsiders who were born and lived among Americans but inherited their outsider status from their mothers under laws enacted to make sure that white fathers could enslave their Black children. (Is that inconsistent with the Declaration? Thomas Jefferson did it.)

The question of *Dred Scott*—who can become one of the people— is central to an understanding of what kind of a constitution we have. A constitution with a race-based barrier to entry, as *Dred Scott* declared the Founders' Constitution to be, is an exclusive constitution: the political community is closed. The racial prejudices of some states take away the power of more egalitarian states to admit people (free Blacks) to the American polity. A constitution with birthright citizenship is an inclusive constitution: the political community is open. That constitution takes away the power of anti-egalitarian states to exclude people from the nation. We have an inclusive constitution now, but whether we did before the Civil War is a question without a clear answer.

Even if *Dred Scott* is wrong, there is a second and more important point. It doesn't really matter if *Dred Scott* is right or wrong—the Founders' Constitution still produced it, directly or indirectly. Either the decision is correct, and the Founders' Constitution is directly responsible for it, or it is incorrect, and the Founders' Constitution is responsible for giving America seven justices who would vote for it anyway. The pro-slavery tilt of the antebellum Supreme Court is no accident; it is a consequence of the pro-slavery tilt of the national government created by the Founders' Constitution. The fundamental point to keep in mind about *Dred Scott*, then, is that it is not an aberrational product of "bad apple" Supreme Court justices. It is the natural consequence of the pro-slavery tilt of the Founders' Constitution. *Dred Scott* is not primarily the work of racist individuals; it is the work of systemic racism.

That said, Taney's argument against the Missouri Compromise does seem wrong. It has the form of a syllogism. Laws excluding ordinary property from a territory are so arbitrary that people would never give the government the power to enact them. Slaves are ordinary property. Therefore, the government cannot exclude slavery from a territory. People tend nowadays to attack the second premise, because it is the morally offensive one. And there is a way to do this, consistent with the thinking of the time. The argument against Taney's second premise is that slaves are not in fact ordinary property. There is a natural right to own most kinds of property, but there is not a natural right to property in man. Slavery, some said, is contrary to natural law and can exist only by virtue of positive law. (This was more or less Lord Mansfield's argument in *Somerset*, and US Supreme Court Justice Salmon Chase repeated it, calling slavery "a naked legal right.") Separating slavery from natural right has an important consequence for the Declaration-style argument. Governments are created to secure natural rights, and therefore they would not be given the power to arbitrarily interfere with ownership of property—to the extent that such ownership is a natural right. But to the extent that it is not—and the view that slavery was contrary to natural law was widely held, even by slave owners such as Jefferson—then the Declaration's reasoning does not mean that a government cannot interfere with it.

This argument has the virtue of attacking the premise of Taney's argument that we now find more offensive, and it was broadly accepted in his day. However, it was not universally accepted. The strongest form of the white supremacist arguments for slavery, which focused on purported biological differences between the races, concluded that race-based slavery was in fact consistent with natural law. When the southern states seceded, they wrote this argument into their constitutions and secession documents. So it is not clear that Taney's second premise was wrong, according to the legal understanding of the time—or, as Taney argued, the legal understanding of 1787. (*Dred Scott* is one of the most emphatically originalist opinions of the Supreme Court.)

The flaw in Taney's argument that no one could deny, even at the time, was with the first premise. Laws excluding property from a territory are not so categorically unfair that people would never give the government the power to enact them. In 1774, Taney himself notes, the colony of Connecticut prohibited the importation of slaves as "injurious to the poor, and inconvenient."[10] That barred even the citizens of Connecticut from acquiring slaves in other states and bringing them into the state, even though its laws permitted slavery. By the time of *Dred Scott*, many states banned slavery and provided that slaveholders who voluntarily brought their slaves within those states' borders would lose their ownership rights—even, again, if the slaveholders were state citizens.

Abolition is an even stronger example of why Taney is wrong. Around the time of the Constitution's ratification, northern states were abolishing slavery—Pennsylvania in 1780, Massachusetts in 1783, Connecticut in 1784, New York in 1799. These abolitions typically worked gradually, but they did deprive slave owners of their property—not for taking slaves into some particular territory, but merely for being slave owners. What the *Dred Scott* opinion implies is that those abolitions, even more than the Missouri Compromise, were not "due process of law." According to the logic of *Dred Scott*, the political theory of the Declaration of Independence, codified in the Due Process Clause, tells us that even gradual abolition is unconstitutional. Alexander Smyth made just this argument in Congress when debating the admission of Missouri:

> If you cannot take property even for public use, without just compensation, you certainly have not power to take it away for the purpose of annihilation, without compensation. And if you cannot take away that which is in existence, you cannot take away that which will come into existence hereafter. If you cannot take away the land, you cannot take the future crops; and if you cannot take the slaves, you cannot take their issue, who, by the laws of slavery, will also be slaves. You cannot force the people to give up their property. You cannot force a portion of the people to emancipate their slaves.

Smyth was talking about federal power and the Fifth Amendment's Due Process Clause, and of course at the time there was no federal requirement that states observe due process of law—that comes from the Fourteenth Amendment. But federal courts before the Fourteenth Amendment imposed due-process constraints on states as part of what they called general constitutional law. Equally significant, many state constitutions had due process or "law of the land" clauses. Thus *Dred Scott* implied, for instance, that the Massachusetts Constitution of 1780, far from banning slavery via the provision that all men are born free and equal, entrenched it via its due-process-like provision: "Every individual of the society has a right to be protected by it in the enjoyment of his life, liberty, and property, according to standing laws."

The Founders' Constitution gave us seven Supreme Court justices who signed on to the idea that the Declaration of Independence basically prohibited abolition. But the governments of states that abolished slavery were legitimate, and those laws were accepted as valid. If state governments—created to secure the natural rights of individuals—could deprive their citizens of the right to own slaves, so, too, could the federal government, created for geostrategic reasons and less concerned with the direct protection of natural rights.

The different nature of the federal government means that natural law arguments based on the Declaration should have less force against the federal government than against the states. (A federal law interfering with liberty of contract by imposing maximum hours or a minimum wage, for instance, might be justified by a concern with the competitive pressures labor practices in one state might exert on other states—a geostrategic collective-action justification not available to state governments.) Accommodating the conflicting positions of free and slave states by allowing slavery in some territories and banning it in others is in fact exactly the sort of interstate resolution one would expect the federal government to provide. The power of governments, both state and federal, to take private property was well established at the time of the Founding. It was precisely because of this power that provisions like the federal Takings Clause were inserted into constitutions, ensuring that when the government did take private property, it paid compensation. Even Justice Chase, that early champion of the Declaration-based argument, believed that property rights were not absolute but could be abridged in the public interest.

Dred Scott's appeal to the Declaration as entrenching slavery is ultimately unconvincing. When the Declaration next surfaced in constitutional interpretation, however, it would achieve a more enduring influence—though one now almost as infamous as *Dred Scott*. The basic Declaration argument is that people create governments to secure their natural rights and would therefore not give those governments the power to arbitrarily interfere with those rights. One such arbitrary and oppressive act that is thus categorically impermissible is taking from A and giving to B. Understood narrowly, this does sound like a serious interference with natural rights—though perhaps not beyond the bounds of powers we might want a legislature to have. (The income tax, for instance, takes from some people and then, via government spending, gives to others, yet it is an indispensable feature of modern governments.) It also sounds like a kind of equality: we want the government to treat people equally, not to play favorites. As the idea spread, though, it went beyond the taking of physical property to other kinds of redistribution, and it often worked to prevent the government from promoting equality.

As America industrialized, the employment environment changed. Rather than individuals bargaining for bespoke services or artisans selling their unique goods, workers increasingly operated as fungible factory labor. In such circumstances, workers often lacked bargaining power and ended up laboring in conditions and under terms that were unfair or even dangerous. For example, in 1911, 146 garment workers locked inside the Triangle Shirtwaist Factory died in a fire, succumbing to smoke inhalation or hurling themselves out the windows. Progressive legislatures, in response, tried to protect workers from the imbalance of bargaining power. Legislatures enacted laws, that is, to make workers more equal to employers with whom they were bargaining. And the courts, relying on the theory of the Declaration, struck them down.

The most famous such decision is *Lochner v. New York*. In 1895 New York enacted a law setting maximum hours for bakeshop employees. The law had its origin, most people suspect, in a belief that employers and employees in such establishments were "not on an equal footing," as Justice Harlan's dissenting opinion put it, and that "the necessities of the latter often compelled them to submit to such exactions as unduly taxed their strength." New York was trying to redress this imbalance of bargaining power. It was trying to promote equality. That was an impermissible goal, said the Supreme Court. Restrictions on liberty of contract might be acceptable to protect health—a limit on the working hours of miners, for instance, was upheld in *Holden v. Hardy*—but mere inequality was not a legitimate target of government action. As the court explained in another case, *Coppage v. Kansas*, "No doubt, wherever the right of private property exists, there must and will be inequalities of fortune; and thus it naturally happens that parties negotiating about a contract are not equally unhampered by circumstances." But a state may not, the court continued, decide that the public good will be advanced by "the removal of those inequalities that are but the normal and inevitable result" of private property and liberty of contract.[11] A government created to protect natural rights could never interfere with them simply to promote equality or help out a weaker party.

This was the other major impact of the Declaration on our constitutional jurisprudence: a strong suspicion of redistribution. The natural rights of insiders cannot be abridged to help outsiders, and they often cannot be abridged to help other insiders, either. This Declaration-inspired argument came not in the 1850s, when Lincoln argued with Stephen Douglas and Roger Taney about what it meant to say that all men were created equal, but in 1905, after Lincoln's interpretation had triumphed. If the Civil War cleansed the Declaration of its anti-redistributive principle, the Supreme Court did not get the message. Nor is this an aberration of the early twentieth century. The justice who invokes the Declaration of Independence most often today is Clarence Thomas, and he invokes it consistently to oppose race-based affirmative action, another government attempt to promote equality.

So what does all this suggest? There is broad agreement among legal scholars on the four worst Supreme Court decisions: *Plessy v. Ferguson*, which held that racial segregation was permissible if the races were separate but equal; *Korematsu v. United States*, which upheld the removal of Japanese Americans from the West Coast; *Dred Scott*; and *Lochner*. (Libertarians tend to have a less critical or even positive view of *Lochner*, and they have linked it to the Declaration in precisely the way described here.) These decisions have all been repudiated, of course. Many people argue that they were wrong when decided. Still, if you are trying to tell the standard story, if you are trying to argue that the Constitution should be understood as embodying the principles of the Declaration—our modern values of liberty and equality—this might give you pause. The two most notable successful invocations of the Declaration in American constitutional history led to two of the four worst Supreme Court decisions. And the propositions those invocations established are not our modern values of liberty and equality. They are the polar opposites: the exclusive individualist principles that the government cannot ban slavery and that it cannot attempt to redress inequality.

The standard story misleads us. It is inaccurate in significant ways, and not just because it tends toward a triumphalist version of American history. As the consideration of the impact of the Declaration on constitutional interpretation shows, the standard story gets some important things more or less backward. Why, then, does it have such a grip on our national consciousness?

8

Why We Tell the Standard Story

★

WHY DO WE TELL the standard story? Why, in particular, do we rely on the Declaration of Independence as the source of our modern ideals? This reliance, I suggest, is the heart of the standard story: finding our ideals in the Declaration is what makes the standard story a story of continuity. It is what tells us to identify with and emulate the Founders, what pushes us to consider them great men. And it is what makes the standard story a success story: if we are the same America that was born in 1776, it is because that America survived the challenges it faced.

We have seen several justifications. One is that the standard story is simply objectively true; anything else (even a less triumphalist version) is a verifiable error of fact. I hope this no longer seems persuasive. The second is a retreat to utility: maybe the standard story isn't entirely true, but it brings us together and promotes desirable values. Maybe the Declaration wasn't originally understood as it is now, but it has been a force for good. We have now cast some doubt on these claims. The impact of the Declaration has been much more ambiguous than most people understand. Unity has often come at the cost of justice: we might need to think a little more about whom the standard story brings together, and at what cost.

How did we start thinking that the standard story was useful?

This is in part a product of the historical figures who have appealed to the Declaration at different times. Start with Lincoln and the abolitionists. They rely on the Declaration in large part because they have no alternative. There is no other federal document that speaks of equality. But there is another reason, which is related but distinct: the Declaration looks like a good focal point. As Lincoln used them, the Declaration and the Revolution were sacred moments: an Edenic time when Americans were united behind noble ideals. Lincoln invoked them in support of unity as early as 1838, when he asked Americans to "swear by the blood of the Revolution, never to violate in the least particular, the laws of the country." His concern in that address (to the Young Men's Lyceum) was "the perpetuation of our political institutions," and he made it clear that internal division was what he saw as the threat: any danger "must spring up amongst us. It cannot come from abroad." What he deplores, specifically, is mob violence and "the increasing disregard for law which pervades the country," but slavery is the note played under the paean to order. The mob violence he talks about consists in the murder of slaves "suspected of conspiring to raise an insurrection" and "white men, suspected to be leagued with [them]."

The Lyceum speech invokes the Declaration and the Revolution as moments to swear by; it does not go so far as to say that the ideals of the Declaration support unity. But Lincoln did suggest that in the Gettysburg Address: the Civil War, he said, was a war for the concept of America articulated in the Declaration, a war that would determine whether "any nation so conceived and so dedicated can long endure." In fighting for union, he was fighting for the principles of the Declaration. He invoked the Declaration for union not because it actually supports the idea but because it was something his listeners could agree upon: most people looked back fondly on the Declaration and the Revolution. Not everyone had supported independence at the Founding, but many Loyalists subsequently left (or were driven from) the country, and the population that remained revered the Revolution.

So we can see two reasons motivating Lincoln and the abolitionists. What about after the Civil War? Lincoln's vision won: when we think of the Declaration of Independence now, we think about equality. There is perhaps no better example of this than Martin Luther King's "I Have a Dream" speech, which starts with Lincoln—not Lincoln at Gettysburg, but the Emancipation Proclamation—and then jumps back in time to the Declaration and the Founders' Constitution. By the 1960s, you might think, Lincoln's interpretation was so well established that a crusader for equality would naturally turn to the Declaration.

Except that's not quite what happened. The quest for unity is not a very happy story, because when Americans come together, they seldom do so in support of equality. More often, white Americans come together at the expense of racial equality. Martin Luther King's relationship to the standard story is not an uncritical embrace: he understood the complex interactions between unity and equality.

There is something deeply odd about King's appeals to the Founders' Constitution and the Declaration. They made a promise, he says, that America is dishonoring. He points to segregation. He points to race-based denial of the right to vote. These things are inconsistent with the promise of the Founding, which America must live up to. What's odd about this is twofold. First, King invokes texts that do not support him. Segregation and denying Blacks the vote are perfectly consistent with the Declaration of Independence. At the time of the Declaration, states were free to exclude Black people from their political communities; states were free to enslave them. (All states did, in fact, recognize slavery.) The ideals of the Declaration do not condemn the enslavement of outsiders, and they do not require states to recognize Black people as insiders. Obviously, they do not require integration or voting rights. Similarly, the Founders' Constitution has almost nothing to say about how states treat their own citizens. As far as race is concerned, it gives us an explicit protection of slavery. Segregation and race-based denial of the vote, if that's what states want, are fine in 1776, according to the Declaration. They're fine in 1788, according to the Founders' Constitution, and they were practiced without any serious suggestion that they were unconstitutional. So in one sense, King is in the same position as Lincoln and the abolitionists, making the best he can out of texts that don't support his argument. Yet in another sense, he's in a very different position. The second oddity is what King does not invoke. By 1963, there are other federal documents that speak of equality and that, unlike the Declaration, have the force of law. There's something racist practices are not consistent with, and that something isn't a distant aspiration, it's the Constitution—but not the Founders' Constitution. The Constitution of 1963 is the Reconstruction Constitution, defined principally by the Thirteenth, Fourteenth, and Fifteenth Amendments.

The Fourteenth and Fifteenth Amendments say that states can't segregate or discriminate on racial grounds. The Supreme Court said so about racial segregation of public schools in 1953; in 1957 the president sent the 101st Airborne to Little Rock to enforce a judge's desegregation orders. The words of the Fifteenth Amendment could not be clearer: "The right of citizens of the United States to vote shall not be denied or abridged by the United States or by any State on account of race, color, or previous condition of servitude." So it's strange that King's dream is that the nation will "rise up and live out the true meaning" of "all men are created equal"—something written two hundred years ago and of very dubious relevance—rather than the true meaning of the Fourteenth and Fifteenth Amendments, written considerably more recently and directly on point. There is a promissory note that the nation is dishonoring, certainly, but the note is not the Declaration. It's the Reconstruction Amendments.

Martin Luther King knew that very well—he said so himself. In "The Negro and the Constitution," written when he was a junior in high school, he makes the same argument as in "I Have a Dream": Black Americans are being denied the rights they were promised. But in that earlier essay, he does not invoke the Declaration. Instead, he invokes the Reconstruction Amendments. "The Negro and the Constitution" begins by acknowledging the long history of slavery in America. Starting in 1620, "the institution grew and thrived for about 150 years upon the backs of these black men." Then King jumps forward to the Emancipation Proclamation and the end of slavery, asking: "What was to be the place of [the freed slaves] in the reconstruction of the south?"

What answers the question of how Black Americans deserve to be treated? "I Have a Dream" hops around through time, from text to text, but it never lands on Reconstruction and the Reconstruction Amendments. "The Negro and the Constitution" takes them as its focus. "The nation in 1865 took a new stand," King writes, "freedom for all people. The new order was backed by amendments to the national constitution making it the fundamental law that thenceforth there should be no discrimination anywhere in the 'land of the free' on account of race, color or previous condition of servitude." The young King recognizes that the Reconstruction Amendments—not the Declaration, not the Founders' Constitution—are the promissory note that should be honored. "Today thirteen million black sons and daughters of our forefathers continue the fight for the translation of the 13th, 14th, and 15th amendments from writing on the printed page to an actuality."

What explains the difference between these speeches? In the intervening years, King presumably learned that Reconstruction is divisive, not unifying—like the Civil War. "The Negro and the Constitution" talks about the Civil War, about "conquer[ing] southern armies by the sword." "I Have a Dream" does not mention the war or victory or conquest. It points to the Declaration and the Founding because they are not divisive, because they look like feel-good moments that all Americans can identify with, moments when we can all say our national identity was born. This, I believe, is the fundamental appeal of the standard story, which we can see even in Lincoln's use of it. It is reassuring: nonthreatening, nonconfrontational, nondivisive. It directs our attention to a hallowed and unifying moment in American history: the Revolution and the Founding. More than that, the standard story tells us that we are a good people. America is an anti-racist nation, dedicated from its beginning to equality. Slavery and segregation were anomalies, inconsistent with America's essence. And having defeated them, we can move forward together, united by our love of country and dedication to America's deepest values.

This is the utilitarian justification for telling the standard story instead of a more accurate one. The most effective way to champion the values of Reconstruction, this account tells us, is to locate them in the Founding. Reconstruction is divisive; the Founding is unifying. If we want to get everyone to share our values—if we want to get them to share the value of equality, in particular—we should say that equality has been at America's heart since the beginning, that American history has been a slow but consistent progress toward the full realization of this founding ideal.

Or should we? There are costs associated with the standard story, some obvious and some less so. The standard story, a little reflection shows, is not as inclusive as we would hope; there is something sinister about the unity it produces. It is not as much of a feel-good story as we might like to think—not for everyone, certainly; not for anyone, maybe. Not for anyone who really cares about equality, at least. No matter how you tell the story, it turns out, tying American identity to the Founding is problematic.

The problem, mainly, is slavery. In 1776, slavery is legal in every state. The Founding is a world of pervasive white supremacy. The author of the Declaration of Independence owned slaves. Everyone has always known this, even if some people didn't know until more recently, or didn't admit, that he also carried on a sexual relationship with an enslaved teenager, half-sister to his late wife, and enslaved their children. So in asking modern Americans to see the Founding as an Edenic moment, to see the Founders as role models who stated our deepest ideals, we are asking them to accept that those ideals can coexist with slavery, with rape, with enslaving one's own children because of the color of their skin. That's a big ask, most obviously for Black Americans, but also for anyone who believes in equality. Making the Founding seem more inclusive is a constant struggle for the standard story. The triumphalist version tries to do this by downplaying slavery, portraying it as an aberration contrary to American ideals. This is not very accurate, and it also tends to erase Black people from the story. The whitewashed Founding becomes even whiter.

A different example of this struggle is the musical *Hamilton*, which seems at first like a triumph of inclusion. In a striking novelty of casting, the roles of white Founders Washington, Jefferson, Madison, Hamilton, and more are played by people of color. But *Hamilton* is actually a whitewashing. The cross-racial casting underscores a disturbing feature of the show—while the stage is filled with Black *actors*, there are almost no Black *characters*. Sally Hemings shows up briefly to receive instructions from Jefferson, but that's about it. As a result, the inclusiveness is only skin deep. (In a typical retrojection of modern values into the past, *Hamilton* also exaggerates the anti-slavery and pro-immigrant politics of several characters, including Hamilton himself.)

The other tack in making the standard story inclusive is the one pursued by the 1619 Project: pay more attention to the role and contributions of Black people in American history, highlight Black agency. This is an important improvement in terms of the history. The significance of Black abolitionists has long been underestimated, and work like Manisha Sinha's *The Slave's Cause* is an important corrective. The effect of the pervasive fear of slave rebellions in colonial America has also been neglected, and scholars like Jason Sharples, Alan Taylor, and David Waldstreicher have helped recover its impact on colonial politics.

However, there is only so far you can go with the Founding. I will tell a story in which Black Americans are responsible for the development and realization of modern American values, a story in which we have the rights we cherish today because of their struggles. But it is not a story about Founding America. Jefferson wrote the Declaration of Independence with the enslaved Robert Hemings—the Black son of Jefferson's father-in-law—waiting on him. You cannot take white supremacy out of the Founding. And plenty of people don't want to. In embracing the Founding, we play into their hands.

The standard story cannot do the work we ask of it. It cannot bring Americans together in the pursuit of unity. There are two basic reasons for this. First, in its triumphalist version, the standard story encourages a complacency that is deeply harmful. As the story gets less triumphalist, the complacency is reduced, but the problematic elements grow. Ultimately, the standard story gives us an understanding of American history that is not wrong so much as backward. It misleads us about who the heroes of our history are, and the villains. It misleads us about who *we* are, and who we must be to become the heroes of our story. There is a better way.

9

Why We Shouldn't Tell
the Standard Story

★

THE STANDARD STORY is appealing not because it is historically true but because telling it seems to be a good way to unify America in the pursuit of the values of liberty and equality. Americans are willing to be called on to fulfill the promise of the Revolution and live up to the values of the Founders. They are less willing to be called on to fulfill the promise of Reconstruction and live up to its values. That was what Martin Luther King understood. Locating our deepest values in the Founding is the way we move forward together. (Think again of *The Spirit of '76*, painted in 1876 and celebrated as something that could bring Americans together in support of our shared ideals.)

Yet this argument is not as straightforward as it seems. It is true that Reconstruction is divisive, that significant parts of America view it negatively. But it is not true that the Revolution is a moment all can share. Elevating the Declaration and the Revolution tends to erase Black Americans, perhaps all Americans committed to equality. Even if our American values of liberty and equality were stated in the Declaration and codified in the Founders' Constitution— which they aren't—it would be asking a lot of Black Americans to look to those moments and see the birth of their nation. It is asking

a lot of them to say that Thomas Jefferson articulated their fundamental ideals.

The standard story's defense of Jefferson and the other Founders
is that they held ideals that could not be fully realized in their time.
In some institutional sense, this might be true. Many of the Founders had mixed feelings about slavery. Most realized there was something morally objectionable about it, but they could not have created
a national government opposed to slavery in 1787. So in terms of the
government they created, they were prisoners of their time. But this
is not true of their personal lives. No one forced Washington and
Madison to enslave people. (Washington, at least, provided in his
will that his slaves should be freed upon his wife's death. Madison
did not.) No one forced Jefferson, then in his forties, to pursue a
sexual relationship with a teenager who lacked the ability to grant
or withhold consent—what we would now call at the very least
statutory rape—and to enslave the children he had with her.[1]

So the standard story is not as much of a feel-good story as we
might think. It leaves out, it marginalizes, Black Americans, and
indeed all Americans who would not compromise with slavery.
More broadly, there is a cost to transplanting our modern values
of liberty and equality to the alien soil of the Founding. Put those
values in the Founding and you are putting them in a world of
dominant and pervasive white supremacy. You are suggesting that
white supremacy can coexist with modern ideals. But painting a
multicultural façade onto the Founding does not make it egalitarian. Instead, it compromises our values: it tells us that an acceptance
of slavery might be a sin but is still part of the core American identity we celebrate.

Still, you might think that the standard story is useful. As we
just saw, Martin Luther King thought the most effective way of
pursuing equality was to wrap it in the standard story. He thought
that—for a while. King lived only five years past the "I Have a
Dream" speech, but that was enough time for him to see where the
standard story led. Even before the March on Washington, in his
"Letter from a Birmingham Jail," King had expressed frustration

with those who counseled patience and moderation. His goal was not to put the past behind us and move forward, as the standard story suggests. He hoped for an ultimate future of understanding and brotherhood, but he knew that the path there led through crisis. He wanted conflict—not violence, but "constructive, nonviolent tension which is necessary for growth." Anyway, King argued, those who call attention to racial injustice, who engage in direct action, "are not the creators of tension. We merely bring to the surface the hidden tension that is already alive. We bring it out in the open, where it can be seen and dealt with."

Who is the barrier to growth and racial progress? The avowed racists, surely, and King mentioned them in his "Letter from a Birmingham Jail," citing the "racial injustice" in Birmingham and its "ugly record of brutality." But the "Letter" is more concerned with what King calls "the white moderate." He writes:

> I have almost reached the regrettable conclusion that the Negro's great stumbling block in his stride toward freedom is not the White Citizen's Counciler or the Ku Klux Klanner, but the white moderate, who is more devoted to "order" than to justice; who prefers a negative peace which is the absence of tension to a positive peace which is the presence of justice; who constantly says: "I agree with you in the goal you seek, but I cannot agree with your methods of direct action"; who paternalistically believes he can set the timetable for another man's freedom; who lives by a mythical concept of time and who constantly advises the Negro to wait for a "more convenient season." Shallow understanding from people of good will is more frustrating than absolute misunderstanding from people of ill will. Lukewarm acceptance is much more bewildering than outright rejection.

The people King describes here are the ones who would urge us not to dwell on the admitted injustices of the past but to look forward, in unity. They are those who would tell us that racism is an anomaly in America—contrary to our fundamental, founding ideals—and that our history is a steady progress toward justice and a fuller realization of those ideas. They are the ones, perhaps, who would tell us that racism is slavery, that racism is segregation, and that since those things are no longer enshrined in law, racism is over. Don't be divisive, they say: wait, and we will all move forward together. What King saw was that when America says it is moving forward together, Blacks tend to get left behind. King's "I Have a Dream" speech retreats from this position, at least rhetorically: it calls out the avowed racists but seeks to enlist the white moderates in a vision of unity, where "little black boys and black girls will be able to join hands with little white boys and white girls as brothers and sisters." We will all hold hands and move forward together to realize our shared ideals—that was the dream.

It didn't happen. By 1967, King himself was saying of the "Dream" speech that "some of the old optimism was a little superficial." He noted that the struggle was no longer "merely a struggle against extremist behavior toward Negroes." It was a struggle against systemic racism, against pervasive inequality in jobs, in housing, in education. Those battles were harder because, King said, "many of the very people who supported us in the struggle in the South are not willing to go all the way now." People "who supported morally and even financially what we were doing in Birmingham and Selma" were not willing to acknowledge or struggle against systemic racism and inequality. King had come to see "that racism is still alive in American society. And much more wide-spread than we realized. . . . [H]owever unpleasant it is we must honestly see and admit that racism is still deeply rooted all over America."[2]

King realized that this sort of analysis would be called divisive by white moderates, that some would tell him he was going to inspire backlash. Asked in December 1966 whether King was helping or hurting the cause of civil rights, whites in a national poll chose hurting, 50% to 36%.[3] Eighty-three percent definitely (53%) or probably (30%) agreed that "Negroes would be better off if they would take advantage of the opportunities that have been made available rather than spending so much time protesting." King saw this for what it was. "White backlash," he said, "is merely a new name for an old phenomenon"—namely, white supremacy. Divisive behavior, the calling out of racial injustice, even violent riots, were "the consequences of the white backlash rather than the cause. . . . What it is necessary to see is that there has never been a single solid monistic determined commitment on the part of the vast majority of white Americans on the whole question of Civil Rights and on the whole question of racial equality."

The later King sounds much more like Malcolm X than most people realize. The early King worked hard not to alarm white Americans. But he realized that nonthreatening activism will be condemned anyway by those opposed. (Just ask Colin Kaepernick.) Perhaps worse, it allows those who support equality to indulge in the passive fantasy of steady progress. Without the *active* support of white Americans, there is no progress. There is only the passage of time. And time is not necessarily a meliorative force. In "The Other America," King disparaged "the notion almost that there is something in the very flow of time that will miraculously cure all evils." Rather, King said, "time is neutral. It can be used either constructively or destructively. And I'm absolutely convinced that the forces of ill-will in our nation, the extreme rightists in our nation, have often used time much more effectively than the forces of good will." Then he goes on to a more forceful condemnation of the idea of waiting:

> Somewhere we must come to see that social progress never rolls in on the wheels of inevitability. It comes through the tireless efforts and the persistent work of dedicated individuals. And without this hard work time itself becomes an ally of the primitive forces of social stagnation.

Well, of course. Why would anyone think that time would solve the problem of racial inequality? They might think that if they believed that America was fundamentally a fair place and a land of opportunity for all who work hard enough to grasp it. They might think that if they believed that racism was fundamentally contrary to the American character—a superficial anomaly that could be sliced away like an unsightly mole. They might think that if they believed that racism was only slavery and segregation, and that having ended the overt codification of those practices, we had defeated racism.

This, perhaps, is where the 1619 Project pulls furthest from the standard story. Though it does locate fundamental American ideals in the Declaration, the project does not tell a story of steady or inevitable progress, much less one achieved by whites. The conservative version of the standard story often simply congratulates Americans on fulfilling the ideals of the Founders. That is a recognizable challenge to progress: it tells us that equality has been achieved. The status quo is what things should look like; we should take advantage of our opportunities and stop complaining. But the progressive version may be even worse because it paralyzes those who could be allies. Looking back, white moderates can congratulate themselves on how much their patient and civil work has accomplished for the improvement of the racial problem. To which the 1619 Project says, "No, that wasn't you. That was Black people. We're not the problem; we're the solution. And we're far from done."

It is a useful reminder that revolutionary change typically comes not from the gradual realization of founding principles but from, well, revolution, and that the battle is never won. Ending slavery and segregation does not end white supremacy. Ending explicit racial discrimination—the approach sometimes called colorblindness—does not end white supremacy. There is no more vivid illustration of this than the Supreme Court's notorious decision in *Plessy v. Ferguson*. After the end of Reconstruction, an all-white Louisiana legislature enacted a law that required railroads to "provide equal but separate accommodations for the white, and colored races." Homer Plessy, a railroad passenger, challenged this law as a violation of his rights under the Equal Protection Clause. Infamously, the Supreme Court upheld the segregation requirement. The power of the state legislature, it noted, "extend[s] only to such laws as are enacted in good faith for the promotion of the public good, and not for the annoyance or oppression of a particular class." But to the contention that segregation was enacted to oppress Black people, the court responded:

> We consider the underlying fallacy of the plaintiff's argument to consist in the assumption that the enforced separation of the two races stamps the colored race with a badge of inferiority. If this be so, it is not by reason of anything found in the act, but solely because the colored race choses to put that construction upon it.

That was fatuous, of course. The social meaning of such segregation was obvious: that Blacks were second-class citizens, not good enough to ride with whites. Justice Harlan, dissenting, called out the majority in strong terms. "Everyone knows," he wrote, "that the statute in question had its origin in the purpose, not so much to exclude white persons from railroad cars occupied by blacks, as to exclude colored people from coaches occupied by or assigned to white persons." Its "real meaning" was "that colored citizens are so inferior and degraded that they cannot be allowed to sit in public coaches occupied by white citizens[.] No one would be so wanting in candor as to assert the contrary."

Such discrimination was not permissible under the Constitution, Harlan argued. "But in view of the constitution, in the eye of the law, there is no superior, dominant, ruling class of citizens. There is no caste here. Our constitution is color-blind, and neither knows nor tolerates classes among citizens." What exactly Harlan meant by this has long been debated. Did he mean that that the Constitution prohibited all racial classifications—the position now known as anti-classification, or colorblindness, which would also invalidate race-based affirmative action? (He does use the word "color-blind," although it did not have the same association then that it does now.) Or did he mean that it prohibited only classifications that created classes or castes among citizens—the position now known as anti-subordination?

I find his use of the words "caste" and "classes" telling and tend toward the latter interpretation. But it is hard to be sure. What is much clearer is that for decades, Harlan's dissent has been hailed as visionary and canonical.[4] And justly so. Harlan saw what the other justices could not see, or perhaps would not admit: that state-sponsored segregation was part and parcel of a program of white supremacy. He saw and said something else, too. The passage above about caste and class is the most-quoted part of his dissent. What is less noticed is that it contrasts the claim that the Constitution neither knows nor tolerates classes among citizens with another assertion:

> The white race deems itself to be the dominant race in this country. And so it is, in prestige, in achievements, in education, in wealth, and in power. So, I doubt not, it will continue to be for all time, if it remains true to its great heritage, and holds fast to the principles of constitutional liberty.

What are we to make of *that* passage? Some have pointed to it as evidence that Harlan's views on race may not have been as progressive as we thought. That may well be true. But however the passage reflects on Harlan, it also expresses an important truth.

The white moderates that King complained of tell us that time will improve things, that America is a land of equality where racism is an aberration. This is also the siren song of the standard story. Harlan's dissent tells us the opposite. It tells us that America is a land of white supremacy, and that it will stay that way. It tells us that segregation is not necessary to perpetuate white supremacy—and, conversely, that ending segregation and explicit racial discrimination will not end white supremacy. It tells us that white supremacy and colorblindness can coexist quite happily. A moment's reflection should suggest that this is obviously so. Imagine a country that for over two hundred years enslaved Black people and built a wealthy society at their expense. Imagine that the slaves were freed. Imagine that the government was forbidden to use explicit racial classifications. But imagine that racism persists among the citizenry. What will happen?

The answer is that whites can maintain their privileged position in a host of ways. They can use laws that, although they do not rely explicitly on race, have a disparate impact on Blacks. They can exclude Black people from the benefits of most government programs, by targeting neighborhoods or using other proxies for race, or by administering programs intended to be neutral in a discriminatory way. They can use private discrimination to exclude Black people from economic activity. They can gut social programs that would help Black people. They can pull their children out of public schools and flee from cities to the suburbs. They can rely on advantages built up over two centuries of the exploitation of Black labor.

Disadvantage inflicted by racial discrimination does not go away over time, and this distinguishes it in an important way from discrimination based on sex or sexual orientation. Women have male and female parents, and male and female children; the same is true of LGBTQ+ and heterosexual people. The effect of discrimination against prior generations of women, or LGBTQ+ people, does not fall directly on each new generation: absent continuing discrimination, it diffuses naturally. But Black parents have Black children, and for centuries Black children with a white parent inherited slavery from their Black mothers, and from their white fathers—the original absentee fathers scorning their responsibilities—they inherited nothing. Racial disadvantage persists down the generations; if anything, it compounds over time. In such a country, racial equality is not going to come about on its own. Colorblindness, far from ushering in equality, is likely to protect white supremacy. As Daria Roithmayr describes in *Reproducing Racism*, race-neutral rules work to lock in white advantage. Racial classifications, in the form of affirmative action or reparations, are actually necessary to equality.[5]

Have I described the United States? No, primarily because explicit racial classifications weren't prohibited at the end of slavery—in fact, they generally weren't prohibited until they started being used to help Black people rather than oppress them. Yet I have perhaps come close enough to say something about such a country that will also apply to our own. What I say is what King said: time is obviously not neutral. Heritable disadvantage, disparate impact, private discrimination—all of these things will tend to increase inequality. Time, on its own, tends to help the powerful stay in power. Time—accompanied by private discrimination, by laws with disparate impacts, by policies often chosen deliberately to achieve those impacts—will reinforce status hierarchies.

Lyndon B. Johnson defended affirmative action by analogy to a race:

> Imagine a hundred-yard dash in which one of the two runners has his legs shackled together. He has progressed ten yards, while the unshackled runner has gone fifty yards. At that point the judges decide that the race is unfair. How do they rectify the situation? Do they merely remove the shackles and allow the race to proceed? Then they could say that "equal opportunity" now prevailed. But one of the runners would still be forty yards ahead of the other. Would it not be the better part of justice to allow the previously shackled runner to make up the forty-yard gap, or to start the race all over again? That would be affirmative action toward equality.[6]

If this is so obvious, why would people think otherwise? Why would they think that waiting patiently would bring equality? Some people who say this may be acting in bad faith. They are indifferent to equality, or opposed to it; they do not want to bear the burdens or inconvenience that progress toward equality demands. But many are not. Many genuinely believe that colorblindness is the right road, the morally just path, and that it does lead to true equality. What might make them think that? The standard story. Because that is exactly what it tells us, in both its conservative and progressive versions: that America's ideal of equality is there at the beginning, that the arc of American history bends toward justice, that time will take us to equality.

If that were true, it might be reasonable to say, as the Supreme

Court did in 1883, that it was time for Black people to "take[] the rank of a mere citizen, and cease[] to be the *special favorite of the laws*." It might be reasonable to say, as the Supreme Court did in 2007, that "the way to stop discrimination on the basis of race is to stop discriminating on the basis of race." It might be reasonable to say, as Chief Justice Roberts did in 2013, that racially motivated voter suppression is a problem of the past, that "the Nation is no longer divided" into states with a recent history of voter suppression and those without it. Or as Justice Scalia put it in 1995, "In the eyes of the government, we are just one race here. It is American." It might be reasonable to think that saying "I don't see race" marks one as enlightened rather than delusional or willfully blind. It might be reasonable to suppose that if the hoped-for equality did not arrive, the fault lay not with white America but with Black people—with their culture, or their nature, or their music, or their dress.

It might be reasonable if the standard story is right. But the standard story is wrong, in both its progressive and conservative versions. It is wrong because the truth is that racism is not a superficial aspect of America but a cancer that has metastasized throughout the body. The truth is that it explains much more of American life and American history than we want to admit. That, too, is one of the points of the 1619 Project, that race explains things like traffic patterns in Atlanta.[7] And whatever else may be said about the project, it is responding to a real problem, the whitewashing of American history. In recent disputes over the removal of Confederate statues, some have opposed removal on the grounds that we must be aware of our history, that taking down the statues of men who fought for slavery will prevent us from understanding the truth about our nation. That is exactly backward. The whitewash is keeping up Confederate statues, as though those men fought for a worthy cause, as though the Confederate South was anything other than one of the most unjust and oppressive societies the world has ever seen. ("Our new government," declared Confederate vice president Alexander Stephens in 1861, "is founded . . . upon the great truth that the negro is not equal to the white man; that slavery, subordination to the superior race is his natural and normal condition."[8]) What is true of the Confederate South is also true, in large part, of pre–Civil War America.

Our educational system still does not tell the truth about the history of slavery. We have dislodged the Dunning school, at the university level and among professional historians. But our civic education—what we tell most Americans—lags considerably behind. A survey by the Southern Poverty Law Center in 2017 found that only 8% of high school seniors identified slavery as the central cause of the Civil War. Two-thirds did not know that slavery was ended by constitutional amendment, and less than a quarter could identify the pro-slavery provisions of the Founders' Constitution.[9] In response to the 1619 Project, a number of states enacted laws prohibiting public schools from including its materials in their curriculum. Florida's version mandated the standard story: teachers "may not define American history as something other than the creation of a new nation based largely on universal principles stated in the Declaration of Independence."[10]

And of course how we educate our citizens has consequences for how we understand and govern our nation. Yale professor David Blight, in the introduction to the Southern Poverty Law Center's *Teaching Hard History* report, laments that "ignorance of American history is hardly confined to students and American classrooms; it is vividly on display in high offices today in our government." "The biggest obstacle to teaching slavery effectively in America," he continues, "is the deep, abiding American need to conceive of and understand our history as 'progress,' as the story of a people and a nation that always sought the improvement of mankind, the advancement of liberty and justice, the broadening of pursuits of happiness for all." That is, the biggest obstacle is the standard story and our attachment to it.

This is understandable. As poet Regie Gibson said, "Our problem as Americans is we actually hate history. . . . What we love is nostalgia. We love to remember things exactly the way they didn't happen. History itself is often an indictment. And people? We hate to be indicted."[11] People don't like to feel bad about themselves, or about their country or their ancestors. To those who have grown up imbibing the standard story, where racism is the bad actions of bad people, the idea of systemic racism—that American society is actually pervasively structured to promote white supremacy—sounds like an accusation that everyone is racist. This is why both progressives and conservatives accuse the 1619 Project of trying to define America by its failures. It is why they suggest that it is divisive, that it may make people lose faith in America.

The call of the standard story always takes the same form. Don't be negative, don't dwell on failures, move forward together. The calls for unity often explicitly involve demands to decrease the salience of race—to set aside identity politics, to stop being divisive, to not make things about race. Talking about race may well be divisive: it may divide us into racists and anti-racists. Not talking about race allows solidarity between racists and non-racists—between those who want to maintain white supremacy and those who just don't like thinking about upsetting things. It allows whites to unite, to suggest that racism is a thing of the past, that the status quo of white supremacy is the normal order of things, and that Blacks must cease to be the special favorites of the law. The unity that the standard story offers is the patient and civil coalition formed with the white moderates King identified as the greatest obstacle to progress toward racial equality in his "Letter from a Birmingham Jail." It is the unity of the Founding, celebrated in *The Spirit of '76*, which in 1876 brought together a nation divided by the wounds of the Civil War. It brought the nation together just as the Compromise of 1877 took hold, abandoning the integrated Reconstruction governments to the violence of the Klan. And what it shows us as the true America is three white men marching forward together. When you see the thirteen stars of the Betsy Ross flag, remember that slavery was legal in every one of those thirteen states in 1776. Remember, too, that the first national flag of the Confederacy showed . . . thirteen stars in a circle, each representing a slaveholding state.[12]

The unity of the standard story is a false and partial unity, built upon racial exclusion. It comes with a cost, and it is the same cost every time. "Why do you have to make it about race?" is the question always posed to those who challenge racial hierarchy. Imagine saying this to the enslaved people searching the Declaration of Independence for their liberty, to the drafters of the Constitution writing the Three-Fifths Compromise or the Fugitive Slave Clause. To the later drafters of the Thirteenth Amendment, to the federal troops occupying the South, to the integrated elected governments overthrown by the Klan, to the men and women lynched under Jim Crow, to the civil rights marchers beset with water cannons, billy clubs, and German shepherds. You can only make something about race if it is not about race already. This is the fundamental point we have to understand. For much more of American history and American society than we care to admit, much more than we teach our children, it is already about race. It has been about race from the beginning.

The standard story tells well-meaning white people that their task is to be non-racist, and that if we simply stop thinking about race, all will soon be well. This is bad history and counterproductive advice. We can see this by listening again to Martin Luther King—not the King of the "I Have a Dream" speech, but King at the end of his life, one day before an assassin's bullet struck him down. King's last speech was delivered in Memphis, on April 3, 1968. Called "I've Seen the Promised Land" or "I've Been to the Mountaintop," it is eerie in its prophecy. King seems to know that his time is running short. But most striking is what has happened to his vision of history. Much of the speech is an answer to the question of what age King would like to live in. The answer comes from a tour through world history, in which King considers and rejects historical high points: the Israelites' flight from Egypt, classical Greece and Rome, the Renaissance, the Reformation, the signing of the Emancipation Proclamation, FDR's leadership during the Great Depression. He would choose, he says, the second half of the twentieth century. Not because conditions are good—they are not. "The world is all messed up," King says. "The nation is sick, trouble in the land, confusion all around." Yet in the crisis is potential.

King is thinking, or talking, very differently about America than he did in "I Have a Dream." The idea of the progressive realization of founding ideals is entirely absent. "I've Been to the Mountaintop" never mentions the Declaration or the Founding—King seems to feel a stronger connection to the Hebrew slaves than the Founders. Its reference to Lincoln is far less adulatory: he says that he would stop by 1863 to "watch a vacillating president by the name of Abraham Lincoln finally come to the conclusion that he had to sign the Emancipation Proclamation." But it has one thing that the "Dream" speech lacked: the Civil War. King doesn't mention it explicitly, but it comes in right at the end, with the vision of the promised land. The last line of the last speech Martin Luther King ever delivered is not drawn from the Declaration, or the Constitution, or even the Bible. It is a line that rose around the watchfires of US Army camps, that accompanied the tread of boots as our soldiers marched to bring others freedom, in a war they fought not only for themselves. It is the first line of the "Battle Hymn of the Republic": *Mine eyes have seen the glory of the coming of the Lord.*

10

Magic Tricks and Revolutions

★

THUS FAR, I HAVE focused on problems with the standard story. It is not as accurate as many people suggest. It is not as unifying. It does not promote the cause of equality. Martin Luther King may have embraced it for tactical reasons, but he came to see that this was a mistake. At the end of his life, he set aside the Founding entirely and made his way back to the Civil War.

We need to look at the Civil War and Reconstruction, too, starting with Abraham Lincoln's vision, which was realized by the Reconstruction Congress, of an America that does not fulfill founding ideals but repudiates them. By claiming that he was fulfilling founding ideals, Lincoln obscured the radicalism of the transformation, which to this day has prevented many of us (though not King) from seeing it clearly. Many people, following Lincoln's cue, think of Reconstruction as a process of better realizing founding ideals, through the process of change set out in the Founders' Constitution. We would do better to think of it as a revolution that destroyed Founding America.

That framing has important implications for how we think of ourselves and our relation to the Founding. It means that we can sever that connection. We can hear criticism of the Founding without taking it as criticism of us. The way not to feel blamed for the bad acts of the past is to not identify with the people who committed them. We can discard the standard story entirely, and the hard work has already been done. The unworthy regime we pledge our faith to has already been overthrown, a better one erected in its place. We just need to see that.

I focus on Lincoln because he plays such an outsize role in the creation of our national story. Lincoln did more than anyone else to promote the standard story version of the Declaration. But he did not create that version—abolitionists, including free Blacks like Prince Hall, had been making similar arguments long before Lincoln and the Republican Party made them prominent in national politics.[1] Nor, of course, did Lincoln write the Reconstruction Amendments or win their ratification—credit for that goes to the Reconstruction Congress and the US Army. In interpreting Lincoln's words, I sometimes explain them by reference to the Fourteenth Amendment. I do not mean to say that the Fourteenth Amendment was an exact implementation of Lincoln's aspirations—that sort of patness is seldom accurate, and how Lincoln's views would have evolved had he lived to preside over Reconstruction is deeply uncertain. If we had to pick, though, the Fourteenth Amendment is clearly much closer to Lincoln than to Jefferson. That is my main point: however close or far the Reconstruction Constitution is to the brief statement of ideals that preceded it, that statement is the Gettysburg Address, not the Declaration of Independence.

THE GETTYSBURG ADDRESS AND THE SECOND AMERICAN REVOLUTION

Like the Declaration (or at least its preamble), the Gettysburg Address is a marvel of compression. In 272 words, Lincoln redefined America. Not a union of slaveholders, with a founding document that protected the practice, Lincoln's America was a nation "conceived in liberty, and dedicated to the proposition that all men are created equal." The Gettysburg Address is justly considered one of our founding documents, a statement of the American creed. More precisely, I will argue, it should be seen as *the* founding document of our America, as the Declaration is the founding document of a different America. The impact of the Address can be seen in the grammatical change it made. Before the Civil War—and notably in the Founders' Constitution—"United States" is a plural noun. "After Gettysburg," Garry Wills reports, "it became a singular."[2] (The shift was not necessarily completed immediately or all at once—"United States" remains plural in the Thirteenth Amendment, for instance—but it did occur.) Lincoln had done what the Founders' Constitution did not: make the states into a single nation.

In the Gettysburg Address, Lincoln tells us that the Civil War is a war for America, for the very idea of a nation "conceived in liberty, and dedicated to the proposition that all men are created equal," a war to determine whether any nation so conceived and so dedicated can long endure. America is the Union, he is saying, and if you believe in the principles of the Declaration, you must stand with him. This has some rhetorical force, as an appeal for unity. But just as the Civil War changed from a war for union to a war for freedom, Lincoln's invocation of the Declaration is not just about union. It is about a reinterpretation of the Declaration—a transformation of the document from one concerned with when the governed may throw off allegiance to their governors to one concerned with universal rights the government must respect. Jefferson's equality, remember, is the beginning: it is a pre-political state that cannot survive the transition into political society. Lincoln's equality is very different. It is the end of government—a goal to which a nation can be dedicated, in whose name it can fight a war. Lincoln's version of the Declaration surely does support his side in the Civil War. Lincoln's America is fighting for Lincoln's equality.

But what about Jefferson's America and Jefferson's Declaration? It is a mark of how deeply the standard story has penetrated our self-understanding that we can read Lincoln's invocation of the Declaration without laughing. (Gettysburg Address, shorter version: "In the name of the Declaration of Independence . . . I will use military force to compel you to remain in the Union and remake your society against your will.") In the Civil War, the real Declaration is on the side of the South. Who marched on Washington in '63, in the name of the Declaration? In 1963, it was the civil rights movement, but in 1863, it was Confederate soldiers. The real heirs of the signers of the Declaration of Independence are the southern secessionists. Our list of those independence movements inspired by the Declaration does not often include them,[3] but the southern states overwhelmingly invoked it in their secession documents. South Carolina, for instance, quoted the Declaration extensively— not the language about all men being created equal, but "that whenever any 'form of government becomes destructive of the ends for which it was established, it is the right of the people to alter or abolish it, and to institute new government.'"[4] Other states struck similar echoing notes. "For far less cause than this," Mississippi held, "our fathers separated from the Crown of England."[5] Tennessee's Secession Act stated that its people were "waiving any expression of opinion as to the abstract doctrine of secession, but asserting the right, as a free and independent people, to alter, reform, or abolish our form of government."[6]

The southern states presumably hoped that they were replaying not the Revolution, with its devastating carnage, but the replacement of the Articles of Confederation by the Constitution—the formation of a union with a different degree of central authority, which might not include all the states. In that hope they were wrong, but they were right to invoke the Declaration. (Shorter version of South Carolina's Declaration of Causes: "In the name of the Declaration of Independence . . . we declare our independence." A little more straightforward than Lincoln's argument, isn't it?) The heart of the Declaration is not a moral principle like liberty or equality. It is the political theory that people form governments to protect certain rights and that if, in their judgment, the government threatens those rights, people can rebel. (And no, a nation founded on that principle probably cannot long endure.) The southern states joined the Revolution, and later the Union, to protect some rights they valued, and high on that list was the right to own slaves. They might reasonably have feared that the British would take that right away. And when they started to fear that the federal government would take it away, they left the Union just as they had left the British Empire: they started the Second American Revolution.

This Second American Revolution was, of course, the Civil War.[7] There is a big difference between the First Revolution and the Second, because the rebels won the first war, and they lost the second. But it is important to understand the similarities. These are both wars fought in the name of the Declaration of Independence, under the political theory that people form governments to protect rights and can rebel if the governments threaten those rights. In both cases, the right to own slaves was one of the rights in people's minds.

What rights really were under threat in each case is unclear, and some might distinguish the First from the Second American Revolution on the grounds that the colonists' grievances were more serious. That may be, but the Declaration actually sets a pretty low bar. "Prudence," it says, "will dictate that Governments long established should not be changed for light and transient causes." The invocation of prudence here actually means that the *power* to make the change exists, and the people who want change are the ultimate judge. Mississippi, as noted, said that its grounds were better than those of the colonists. That was not entirely unreasonable. As James Oakes recounts in *The Crooked Path to Abolition*, Lincoln and the Republican Party, while mindful of the limited power of the federal government, worked consistently to undermine slavery where they could.[8] A national government that wants to destroy the institution around which your society is built, even if it lacks the power to do so directly, might well suggest that a different form would more likely effect your safety and happiness.

So the Declaration is on the side of the South. What about the Founders' Constitution? This is not as clear, but the answer again, probably, is the South. There is, for one thing, the argument that the Constitution includes the revolutionary ideal of the Declaration. It is the Declaration that legitimizes the Constitution's breakup of the Articles of Confederation. The Founders did not think that revolution was a onetime event. Jefferson said that "the tree of liberty must be refreshed from time to time with the blood of patriots and tyrants." Madison, remember, wanted to insert as a preface to the Constitution the people's "indubitable, unalienable, and indefeasible right to reform or change their government whenever it be found adverse or inadequate to the purposes of its institution." And an anti-slavery national government is adverse to the purposes of the South.

But set that aside. What is supposed to happen when the states fear the federal government and take arms to fight against it? Who is supposed to win that contest? In the minds of the Founders, the answer is pretty clear. The Founders think that a distant general government might become a threat to liberty. It might start to oppress its citizens. That's what King George and Parliament did. When that happens, the states stand up to defend the rights of their citizens. That's what the state militias did, fighting off the Redcoats. And that war—the Revolutionary War—is the model that's built into the Founders' Constitution. That's what the Second Amendment is about—the well-regulated militia is supposed to protect the security of free states by fighting off the federal army. (Well, that and the suppression of domestic insurrections, i.e., slave revolts.[9]) So along comes the Second American Revolution, when the states stand up for the rights of their citizens. The states—meaning the South—are supposed to win. (The counterargument here is that the Founders were also concerned with the ability of the national government to put down rebellions, like Shays' Rebellion. This just requires us to draw a line between rebellion and secession, which can be done. Daniel Shays never controlled any political unit, did not declare independence, and had perhaps four thousand followers. The Confederacy had eleven to thirteen states, counted almost a third of the free American population, and controlled a territory considerably larger than France, Spain, and Germany combined.)

Abraham Lincoln did many remarkable things, but one of the most remarkable is this sort of magic trick—he makes people think that he's the one fighting for the Declaration and the Founders' Constitution, when in fact he's against them.[10] If you draw a line from the Declaration of Independence through the Founders' Constitution, it doesn't lead to us. It goes to the rebel South, and it stops there. We aren't, as John F. Kennedy said, the heirs of the first Revolution. We aren't the heirs of the Founders. We're the heirs of the people who rejected the theory of the Declaration—who defeated it by force of arms. We also rejected the Founders' Constitution. And we did so, again, by force of arms.

FROM STATUS QUO TO REGIME CHANGE

In the Gettysburg Address, Lincoln invoked the Declaration of Independence to support his position that states could not declare their independence. This is on its face implausible, and much of what Lincoln says about the past is not much better. Founding America is not dedicated to the proposition that all men are created equal. Jefferson's equality is the beginning of an argument, it is not the goal of government. But Lincoln says something about the future that's pretty amazing. He says that this nation shall have a new birth of freedom. And it does. The Reconstruction Amendments—the Thirteenth, Fourteenth, and Fifteenth—give us a new set of founding principles.

So we change things dramatically after the Civil War. If we think of the Civil War as the Second American Revolution, the rebels lost. But in an important sense, the *revolutionaries* won. Here's what I mean by that. You can think of two different kinds of revolutions. One is a regime change revolution: the existing political system is unjust and we're going to change it. That's the French Revolution or the Russian Revolution. The second kind is a status quo revolution: the existing political system is fine, but we're being denied the rights we're owed under it. That's the First American Revolution: the colonists' complaints against King George are basically that he's denied them their rights as Englishmen. The Second American Revolution is the same: the southerners are complaining about threats to their right to own slaves, which they think is their due under the bargain they signed, the Constitution.

One of the most striking things about the Confederate secession acts is that they repudiate union but not the Constitution as they understand it. The Louisiana, Arkansas, Tennessee, and Mississippi secession ordinances provide that rights vested under the Constitution and federal law will remain in force, unless inconsistent with secession. Both Mississippi and Alabama offer to form a union with the other seceding states "upon the basis" or the "principles" "of the . . . Constitution of the . . . United States." The acts that complain about the antebellum system—notably those of Alabama, Arkansas, Kentucky, Missouri, Texas, and Virginia—say not that there is something wrong with the Constitution but that the federal government has distorted it and assumed despotic power.

The United States, at the beginning of the war, is also fighting for the status quo. Lincoln interprets the Constitution as not allowing secession, which I think is at best unclear, but in any case he's trying to restore the status quo ante—which he said in his first inaugural address he had no inclination to disturb. That's why the preliminary Emancipation Proclamation announces reunion as its goal—that's what the letter to Greeley suggests. I don't want to put too much weight on those documents; it may be that Lincoln's views had shifted by September 1862 and he was just not being candid.[11] The important point is that they did shift.

So at some point, things change. As James McPherson describes, Lincoln stops talking so much about the Union and starts talking about the nation.[12] (His shift from "Union" to "nation" is an interesting counterpoint to the common modern tendency to talk about "the United States" outside the Civil War and "the Union" during it.) In the "Fragment on the Constitution and the Union," from 1861, Lincoln is talking, as the title suggests, about the Union. He never uses the word "nation." In his first inaugural address, the word "Union" is everywhere, appearing twenty times. "Nation" is strikingly absent—the adjective "national" appears nine times, and there is one reference to "the Almighty Ruler of Nations," but no reference to the United States as a single nation.

In the Gettysburg Address, something is different. The first sentence says that the Declaration of Independence created "a new nation." The whole address is about that nation, the nation as a singular noun. (The Founders' Constitution, of course, treats "United States" as a plural noun, a collection of states.) There is not a word about the Union, but Lincoln says the nation will have a new birth of freedom.[13] We are going to change the status quo. The existing regime is unjust. Jefferson Davis is leading a rebellion now, and Lincoln is leading a revolution. Karl Marx made exactly this observation. "Up to now," he wrote in 1862, "we have witnessed only the first act of the Civil War—the constitutional waging of war. The second act, the revolutionary waging of war, is at hand."[14] Issuing the Emancipation Proclamation, he continued, was "tantamount to the tearing up of the old American Constitution."[15]

The Gettysburg Address actually tells us most of this. It explains how the new America will differ from the old one, and it suggests a very different political philosophy from that of the Declaration. Essentially, a new nation will be born. This will be accomplished against the will of the states, meaning that the Declaration's criterion of legitimacy for a government is being abandoned. The Declaration maintains that legitimate government authority comes from consent, but America's new government will not be formed by consent. Lincoln is speaking in the middle of a war against people who reject federal authority; consent is obviously not there. Lincoln's revolution cannot be justified by the Declaration. He is not leading a people who wish to separate and govern themselves; he is imposing on some people a form of government they do not want. He is fighting to radically remake the bargains struck in the Founders' Constitution. So what supports the formation of the new government? I think there is no alternative but justice. Lincoln is fighting a war to break the preexisting American order because it is the right thing to do, because slavery is an abomination that can no longer be tolerated.

As a founding principle, justice can be a dangerous one. People differ in their assessments of what is just, and to the Confederates, Lincoln's justice was oppression. However, the Declaration's consent is not perfect, either. In Enlightenment thought experiments, the government gets actual consent from every person who joins the political community, but of course this does not happen in the real world. Most people have no real choice but to accept the society they are born into. (Locke suggested that those who do not consent can leave the country, but that hardly meets the practical concern.) So the Declaration and the Gettysburg Address do not focus solely on legitimacy at the creation of government. They also set out a principle to determine the legitimacy of a government going forward.

For the Declaration, what legitimizes the government is whether it fulfills its purpose of protecting the natural rights of insiders. Any form of government can do this, in theory, including a hereditary monarchy, as long as people consent to it and it protects their natural rights. The government Lincoln describes in the Gettysburg Address, by contrast, is not measured just by the outcomes it delivers but also by its process. It is not just government for the people, which sounds rather like the Declaration. It is government of the people, by the people—it is a democracy. Democracy will be the legitimating principle going forward.

This new America will be different in terms of how its political community is constructed, too. To see this, we need to go beyond the Gettysburg Address to the "Address at a Sanitary Fair," delivered in Baltimore in April 1864, which concerns the changed nature of the war. "When the war began, three years ago," Lincoln notes at the outset, "neither party, nor any man, expected it would last till now. . . . Neither did any anticipate that domestic slavery would be much affected by the war." But, he goes on, "the war has not ended, and slavery has been much affected." The Emancipation Proclamation was issued on January 1, 1863; the Gettysburg Address was given on November 19, 1863. After victories at Gettysburg, Vicksburg, and Chattanooga, it is clear that the Union is going to win the war, and that the war will end slavery.

How to describe this change? The "Address at a Sanitary Fair" shifts, somewhat abruptly, to a discussion of the meaning of liberty. "We all declare for liberty," he says, "but in using the same *word* we do not all mean the same *thing*. With some the word liberty may mean for each man to do as he pleases with himself, and the product of his labor; while with others the same word may mean for some men to do as they please with other men, and the product of other men's labor." Thus, Lincoln continues, "the shepherd drives the wolf from the sheep's throat, for which the sheep thanks the shepherd as a *liberator*, while the wolf denounces him for the same act as the destroyer of liberty, especially as the sheep was a black one." What is Lincoln describing here? The views of abolitionists versus those of slaveholders, certainly, but it can also be described in the more philosophical terms we have developed earlier. The liberty to do what one wants to the limits of one's strength—including the liberty to do as one wills with other people—is the liberty of the state of nature. No one has the right to demand obedience from anyone else, although some have the ability to compel it by force. That is what I have called Jefferson's equality.

Jefferson recognized, of course, that people would not remain in the state of nature. They would come together to form governments to secure their rights. But the job of such a government is to secure the rights *of the people who create it.* The government formed by wolves would protect the rights of wolves against each other, and it would protect their rights to do as they willed with the sheep, too. A government that protects the rights of its citizens, including their right to enslave outsiders, is a Declaration-style government. It is the government that the southern states consistently sought to form and protect—by leaving the British Empire, by joining the Union, and, in the end, by leaving the Union, too. They followed what Lincoln called "the wolf's dictionary," and they saw the federal government—the protective shepherd—as tyrannical. This view is entirely consistent with the Declaration.

Lincoln rejects it. What he contrasts to Jefferson's equality is a very different equality that is not a pre-political starting point but the end goal of government. The government, Lincoln suggests, should intervene to protect individuals from other individuals—to redress the natural consequences of inequalities of power. (This, remember, is what the theory of the Declaration of Independence actually forbids, according to the *Lochner* court.) What kind of government would bear a responsibility to do that, to drive the wolf from the sheep's throat, even if it was, as Lincoln says, a black sheep—an outsider? There are two possible answers here. Neither is consistent with the theory of the Declaration and the Founders' Constitution, but the Reconstruction Constitution ends up making both of them part of our higher law.

A NEW BIRTH OF FREEDOM: THE FOURTEENTH AMENDMENT

The Fourteenth Amendment fundamentally restructured American society. In the same way that the presence of federal troops was a visible testament to the breakdown of the Founders' Constitution, the Fourteenth Amendment provides textual confirmation of a rupture in our constitutional history. The first thing it does is to reverse the *Dred Scott* decision by granting citizenship based on birth in the United States. There will be, its first sentence says, no perpetual outsiders. No hereditary exclusion from our political community. If you're born here, you're one of us. People will not be branded outsiders because of the color of their skin. If anyone will be excluded from this new America, it will be the people who fought against it, the traitors.

That is the first reason that the government might have a duty to protect someone: because that person was born in America and is not an outsider, even if a state would like to exclude them. The focus on birth is a decisive difference from the Declaration's use of "created." The Fourteenth Amendment is not about hypothetical people created in the state of nature, possessing natural rights that may or may not translate into legal rights in society. It is about real people born in the United States and possessing legal rights and citizenship. In this context, it is interesting to consider the contemporary debate over birthright citizenship as applied to the children of undocumented immigrants. Say that birthright citizenship does not apply to them, and what do you have? A class of perpetual hereditary outsiders, doing the work that Americans do not want to . . . it sounds all too familiar.[16]

Birthright citizenship reconstituted the state and national political communities, opening them up in a way the Declaration never contemplated, in a way the Founders' Constitution may well have prohibited. The Declaration does not say anything about how political communities are created or defined, or who controls access to them. It seems to assume that a people may define itself, excluding whomever it wants. Southern states, in particular, jealously guarded their political communities. As Paul Herron documents in *Framing the Solid South*, their secessionist and even Revolutionary constitutions spoke of freemen and whites.[17]

The Founders' Constitution did say something, according to the *Dred Scott* decision: it said (implicitly) that Blacks could never join the American political community. They could never be citizens of the United States. Forcing states to accept as citizens people they do not want violates the most basic political right of the states— the right Jefferson championed in his opposition to the Missouri Compromise, the right to determine who are the members of their political communities. The insider/outsider question is the first and most important question for any state or nation—who are "We the People"? The Founders' Constitution did not answer this clearly, which is why it was left open for *Dred Scott*, but it generally seemed to assume that state citizenship led to federal citizenship—a (state) citizen of one of the United States was a (federal) citizen of the United States. (Think of "the United States" as the name of a collection of states and this seems natural.) The Fourteenth Amendment gives the opposite answer—federal citizenship leads to state citizenship—and with that comes a new society.

Then the Fourteenth Amendment goes on to give people federal constitutional rights—rights to equality, rights to liberty, rights against state governments, which they didn't have before. Some of these rights are for citizens, but others are for all people. No state may "deny to any *person* within its jurisdiction the equal protection of the laws." This is the second reason why the government might have a duty to protect someone: because it has a duty to protect not just citizens but *everyone* within its jurisdiction. This is also not the theory of the Declaration, which limits that duty to insiders. It is a theory of universal human rights in society, as a matter of positive and not natural law.

Section 1 of the Fourteenth Amendment is the section that gets the most attention and has produced the most significant Supreme Court decisions. But there are things to learn from the rest of it, too. Section 2 attempts to respond to a problem the Reconstruction Congress saw would flow from the Thirteenth Amendment. With slavery gone and the Three-Fifths Compromise superseded, the southern states would now be entitled to more representatives in Congress. The Republicans did not want that, so they also provided that if states denied the right to vote to citizens twenty-one or older, "except for participation in rebellion, or other crime," they could not count those people at all in determining the basis for representation. But only male citizens—here, in the amendment designed to protect equality, sex discrimination is explicitly approved.

Section 3 excludes certain people from holding state or federal office: anyone who as a state or federal official had taken an oath to support the Constitution and then participated in the rebellion, unless Congress removed the disability by a two-thirds vote of each house. This section sounds like a punishment for treason—it applies to those who "engaged in insurrection or rebellion" or gave "aid or comfort to the enemies" of the United States, which tracks Article III's definition of treason. (A reduced punishment since treason was typically punished by death.) Rather than punishing all traitors, though, it focuses on those who had taken an oath to support the Constitution. Section 3 rejects the idea later popularized by *The Birth of a Nation* that the Civil War was a breaking apart into two legitimate societies, the North and the South. The Civil War was an insurrection or rebellion. The South was not a legitimate nation: those who formed and supported it betrayed their oath. And it shows that there is an exception to the inclusiveness of the new order promised by Reconstruction. Someone may be marginalized, excluded at least partially from this more open political community. But it will not be Black people—it will be the traitors.

Like the overt sex discrimination of Section 2, Section 3 also shows us a way in which the Fourteenth Amendment fell short of what could have been. As Lisset Pino and John Witt describe, in its original form Section 3 applied to all traitors—anyone who had given aid and comfort to the "late insurrection"—depriving them of the right to vote in federal elections until July 4, 1870.[18] That would unambiguously transfer political power to the loyal southerners, a large percentage of whom were of course freedpeople. Future president James Garfield estimated that the original Section 3 would disenfranchise nine-tenths or "in some instances, ninety-nine hundredths" of the population—presumably meaning the white population.[19] But, as he argued, enforcing such broad disenfranchisement would require "a military force at every ballot-box in eleven States of the Union," and Congress was not willing to commit to that. The narrowed Section 3 did stand as a declaration that secession was illegitimate, and it stopped a small number of former rebels from winning elections as candidates—until the disability was removed, as it often was. Yet it did not stop the mass of former rebels from winning as voters, either in fair elections or those marred by racial violence and voter suppression.

Section 4 carries the same message: the Confederate South was not a real government. It starts by providing that the validity of the public debt of the United States shall not be questioned, including debts incurred to suppress insurrection or rebellion. It says this mostly to establish a contrast with the following sentence, which provides that neither the United States nor any state will pay Confederate debt—or any claim based on the emancipation of any slave. The Confederate governments that took on debt, this says, were not the real state governments.

But were the antebellum laws of slavery not real laws? The denial of compensation for emancipation is more striking than the repudiation of Confederate debt. It is perhaps the sharpest textual indication of a break in our constitutional history. It shows that the Founders' Constitution did not evolve into the Reconstruction Constitution but was displaced by it. Under the Founders' Constitution, of course, slavery was legitimate. Property in slaves was a preferred form of property, given special protection. The federal government lacked the power to end slavery, and while it could, perhaps, under some circumstances free slaves by seizing them from their owners, the Fifth Amendment's Takings Clause ("nor shall private property be taken for public use, without just compensation") would require that the government pay compensation. Notably, the 1862 emancipation of enslaved people in Washington, DC, included compensation.

Uncompensated emancipation suggests not that the Founders' Constitution is being changed but that it is being repudiated—claims based on slavery are as invalid as claims based on rebel debt. Uncompensated emancipation is of course also a feature of the Emancipation Proclamation—and the Takings Clause issue is one of several reasons to think that the Emancipation Proclamation is unconstitutional under the Founders' Constitution. (That the power to seize property generally lies with the legislature and not the executive branch is another.) That is a problem if we want to tell a story of continuity. It is not a problem—it is just supporting evidence—if we want to say that the Civil War broke the Founders' Constitution, not through the actions of the South but through those of the United States.

The Fourteenth Amendment transforms the Founders' Constitution in its substance. It does this specifically with slavery, where it repudiates the earlier order, effectively declaring slavery illegitimate from the beginning. It does so specifically with *Dred Scott*, where it forces open the political communities of the states. But it works more general changes, too. It makes the federal government less geostrategic in its orientation and more of a Declaration-style government. It is more of a Declaration-style government because now the federal government is concerned with protecting the rights of individuals. Indeed, when people talk about how the Constitution is designed to implement the principles of the Declaration, they almost always point to the Fourteenth Amendment—sometimes without noticing that this means they are not talking about the Founders' Constitution. In part due to Supreme Court decisions, however, the federal government ended up protecting individuals primarily from states and secondarily, if at all, from other individuals.[20] Ironically, then, the Fourteenth Amendment, by releasing the southern states from the grasp of war upon ratification, also ended the period in which the federal government truly was a Declaration-style government: the time when federal troops protected the natural rights of freedpeople and Republicans from the former rebels.[21]

Still, this is an inversion, a fundamental reorientation, and it shows in the rhetorical structure, as Akhil Reed Amar has pointed out. The rights that the Founders' Constitution gives individuals are generally rights against Congress, and you can see this in the Bill of Rights, which starts out announcing that prohibition in the first sentence of the First Amendment: "Congress shall make no law . . ." The Fourteenth Amendment, when it announces rights, says something similar, but this time it's about the states: "No State shall . . ." And when it gets to Congress, in Section 5, it says the opposite of the what the First Amendment does: "Congress shall have the power."

I do not mean to ascribe all this substance to Lincoln. At the Sanitary Fair in 1864, Lincoln could not tell his listeners what the Fourteenth Amendment would say. He could not know himself what the future held, and he would never find out. What he could tell them, what is clear from his speeches, is that he is not fighting for the government described in Jefferson's Declaration. He is fighting for a different kind of government, one that does not allow the states to draw racial lines around their political communities, one that imposes obligations on them to give legal rights and protection even to outsiders. Lincoln is promising a political order of inclusive equality rather than exclusive individualism.

That is an enormous difference. People understand, of course, that the Civil War and Reconstruction made drastic changes to America's constitutional order. It is common to refer to Reconstruction as a Second Founding. However, most of the people who say that are still telling a story of continuity. Reconstruction, they contend, is when the ideals of the Declaration entered the Constitution, through the amendment process. The Fourteenth Amendment's ideal of equality, they say, comes from the Declaration.

But it comes from Lincoln's Declaration, not Jefferson's. Jefferson's concept of equality is not our modern ideal; it is a hypothetical truism about the state of nature. The core principle of Jefferson's Declaration has nothing to do with equality: it is independence, the right of a people to define itself and to separate itself from a larger political order. The Civil War and the Fourteenth Amendment rejected that principle as squarely as can be imagined: the war met secession with military force, and the amendment compelled the defeated Confederate states to accept Black people as state citizens. And it is the Fourteenth Amendment and Reconstruction that define our modern Constitution.

One way to see the centrality of Reconstruction to our constitutional regime is to ask which Supreme Court cases are fundamental to our understanding of the Constitution. Which show us how the Constitution is supposed to work? What are the great cases? I ask my law students this, and general audiences too. They tend to come up with roughly the same cases. They say *Brown v. Board of Education*, about the right to integrated schooling. *Loving v. Virginia*, about the right to interracial marriage. *Miranda v. Arizona*, perhaps, the right to remain silent (or, more precisely, to be informed of that right). *Gideon v. Wainwright*, the right to counsel. Maybe *Roe v. Wade*, the right to abortion; or *New York Times v. Sullivan*, the right to comment on matters of public concern. More recently, *Obergefell v. Hodges*, the right to same-sex marriage.

All of these cases have one thing in common: they would have come out the other way under the Founders' Constitution. All of these cases are Fourteenth Amendment cases, where individuals assert constitutional rights against states, not against the federal government. It is a sign of how thoroughly the Reconstruction Constitution has displaced the Founders' Constitution that these are the cases that define our constitutional order. We are not Founding America, and we are not the heirs of that first Republic, either. We are the heirs of the people who destroyed it. We are Reconstruction America.

11

Why, How, and
Who We Are

★

THE AMERICA PROMISED in Lincoln's speeches and delivered
by the Reconstruction Amendments is not a fulfillment of founding
ideals but their repudiation. It is based on inclusive equality, not
exclusive individualism. Its political community is open rather than
closed by race. Its criterion of legitimacy is not whether a government protects the natural rights of insiders—a principle that prohibits redistribution to outsiders and even to other insiders—but
rather whether it represents the will of the people. This principle
allows insiders not just to fight for their own rights but to make
sacrifices for others. The Civil War, far more than the Revolution,
embodies this principle, which the "Battle Hymn of the Republic"
celebrates: Let us die to make men free.

Admittedly, Reconstruction fell short by this metric. It did
not guarantee the vote for women, for instance. But democracy is
a principle that can be more fully realized over time. We sometimes talk about American history as an expansion of the category
of insiders—of who counts as "We the People"—but this is not a
fulfillment of Declaration ideals. Using force to keep states in the
Union and then opening their political communities against their
will is not the triumph of the Declaration but its defeat. So why and
how did this transformation occur at all? What took Lincoln from

suppressing a rebellion to leading a revolution? How was that revolution ultimately accomplished? And what do the answers to these questions mean about our place in the story of America?

WHY THE REGIME CHANGED:
SOLDIERS TO CITIZENS

Lincoln's speeches during the Civil War promised transformation, but he had started out fighting for the status quo, for unity before justice. I do not think it is possible to be completely confident about why he changed, but increasingly I believe that we owe this transformation—and, indeed, the creation of modern America—to Black Americans, in particular to the Black soldiers of the US Army. And I think Lincoln himself tells us this. In the "Address at a Sanitary Fair," after offering the parable of the wolf and the sheep, Lincoln declares, somewhat abruptly, that "the wolf's dictionary, has been repudiated." How could Lincoln be so confident in this assertion? The United States was going to win the war; that was relatively clear. But the Reconstruction Amendments, the instantiation of Lincoln's equality, were still years away. America had not done anything that made its commitment to Lincoln's equality irrevocable. Or had it? After declaring the wolf's dictionary repudiated, Lincoln pivots again, to an apparently unrelated topic: the massacre at Fort Pillow, in which Confederate forces killed some three hundred Black US soldiers after they had surrendered:

> There seems to be some anxiety in the public mind, whether the government is doing its duty to the colored soldier. . . . At the beginning of the war, and for some time, the use of colored troops was not contemplated; and how the change of purpose was wrought, I will not now take time to explain. Upon a clear conviction of duty I resolved to turn that element of strength to account; and I am responsible for it to the American people, to the Christian world, to history, and on my final account to God.

Those are strong words. Though Lincoln had a gift for the telling phrase, he was not prone to overstatement. The inclusion of Black men in the US forces might not, at first glance, seem so significant. Blacks had served in militias in northern states since the earliest days. They fought in the Revolutionary War, on both sides. (Those fighting for the British outnumbered the Patriots four to one.) They had served continuously in the navy, including the War of 1812, where they made up one-quarter of the American forces in the Battle of Lake Erie.

It seems more significant when we recall that military service, especially in combat, has always been a path to citizenship. The Romans awarded citizenship to residents of the empire and even the *barbari* from outside after twenty-five years' service. Today the Immigration and Naturalization Act provides special treatment for naturalization based on military service. The use of Black troops in the Revolution suggested that they could become citizens of their states, as indeed some were, but that did not mean that they would be citizens of a nation that did not yet exist.

Dred Scott, of course, said that the Constitution excluded Blacks from federal citizenship. But in the Civil War, Black men who fought for the nation would become national citizens, with rights that all states would have to respect. As Frederick Douglass put it, "Once let the black man get upon his person the brass letters, U.S., let him get an eagle on his button, and a musket on his shoulder and bullets in his pocket, there is no power on earth that can deny that he has earned the right to citizenship." Participation in the military is a line that people who want to narrow the political community draw for just that reason. When we argue about who should be allowed to serve, we should keep this dimension in mind: Soldiers are full and equal citizens; denial of military service is a way of excluding people from full equality. This is why the choice to include Black soldiers in the national army was so fateful that Lincoln would acknowledge his responsibility to the American people, the Christian world, history, and God. (The massacre, in fact, embodied the South's rejection of this idea: rather than enemy soldiers protected by the laws of war, the Confederates were saying, Blacks remain outsiders, even in the uniform of the US Army. Racist attacks on veterans, after the Civil War and later, responded to the same perceived threat and sent the same message: Black skin trumps blue cloth.)

The process started with the Emancipation Proclamation, issued sixteen months before the Sanitary Fair speech, which made it clear that a Union victory would end slavery. It was a revolutionary moment, as Karl Marx said; it was also probably unconstitutional. Unlike the earlier Confiscation Acts, which freed the slaves of rebels as the British Earl Dunmore and General Clinton had done during the Revolution, the Emancipation Proclamation freed the slaves of loyal southerners. Does the commander-in-chief power extend so far, overriding the Due Process and Takings Clauses? Former Supreme Court justice Benjamin Curtis thought not and wrote a pamphlet arguing as much. Yet Curtis was not a pro-slavery partisan. He dissented in *Dred Scott*, after which he resigned in disgust.

Radical as it was, emancipation was only part of the story—it takes us only to the Thirteenth Amendment. Citizenship is a step beyond—it is the Fourteenth Amendment—and what gets us to that is Black military service. The Emancipation Proclamation explicitly invited Blacks to join the US military, though only for limited purposes. Black men took up the invitation and their roles expanded. Though they had initially been used primarily in noncombat roles, Black troops participated in forty major battles and by the war's end made up 10% of US forces. It is possible, some argue, that just as Black voters can swing elections, Black troops provided the margin of victory in the Civil War. If that is true, Black soldiers gave us our country in one sense: they saved the Union. But even if it is not true, Black soldiers gave us our country in perhaps a deeper and more meaningful way. Black military service led to Black citizenship; Black citizenship necessitated federal protection for individuals against state governments unwilling to accept them as true insiders. And that protection—the Fourteenth Amendment—is the heart of our constitutional identity today.

That Black Americans have been crucial to the development of our ideals is large part of what the 1619 Project is trying to tell us— and perhaps one of the reasons it ruffled feathers. The standard story suggests that our American values are there in the Declaration— and no one would say they are there because of slavery or Black Americans. Slavery—and perhaps by implication Black people—is the problem, what makes it harder to proclaim those values. What I am saying, however, is that our American values come from the Civil War and Reconstruction, and those happened because of slavery and Black Americans. It was the fight against slavery that inspired people to reinterpret the Declaration into the American ideals expressed in the Gettysburg Address. And it was the participation of Black Americans in that fight that made those ideals become law in the Reconstruction Amendments. As Nikole Hannah-Jones writes, Black Americans have never been the problem; they have been the solution.

HOW THE REGIME CHANGED: BREAKING THE FOUNDERS' CONSTITUTION

We have considered *why* America embraced our modern values of liberty and equality. But there is much more to be said about *how* those values entered the Constitution—in particular about how far the process of Reconstruction and the ratification of the Reconstruction Amendments departed from the process of constitutional change set out in Article V of the Founders' Constitution. The Fourteenth Amendment, in particular, was not adopted by that process. If you are faithful to the Founders' Constitution, the Fourteenth Amendment is probably not valid.

Like the idea that the Emancipation Proclamation is unconstitutional or that *Dred Scott* might have been correctly decided, the idea that the Fourteenth Amendment was not validly adopted is heretical in our legal and political culture—and for precisely the same reason: people want to tell a story of continuity. To do that we must believe that the Founders' Constitution would have allowed the

Emancipation Proclamation, that it could not have produced *Dred Scott*, and that the Fourteenth Amendment was added through the normal amendment process. People have gone to extraordinary and somewhat implausible lengths to make all these arguments.

If you do not need to tell a story of continuity, all those difficulties disappear. The Emancipation Proclamation might have been unconstitutional: that is okay because it was part of a repudiation of the preceding order. The Founders' Constitution might have produced *Dred Scott*: that is okay because it is not our Constitution. The Fourteenth Amendment might have been crammed down the throat of an unwilling South: that is okay because Reconstruction America is not based on consent of the governed and the protection of the natural rights of insiders. It is based on justice and democracy, which are better.

Nor is the Fourteenth Amendment based on the niceties of the amendment process set out in a pro-slavery constitution. The two things protected even against amendment, in the Founders' Constitution, were the international slave trade and each state's equal representation in the Senate. We should celebrate, as poetic justice, that the Reconstruction Congress bent the ratification process and excluded senators and representatives from the rebel states in order to force acceptance of the amendment designed to erase the traces of slavery. Let go of the idea of continuity, and the history looks a little different.

To get to the Fourteenth Amendment, we have to start in the closing days of the Civil War—or the closing years. Gregory Downs, who like me describes the Civil War as the death of Founding America, has done pathbreaking work in developing the extent and the significance of the federal military presence in the South, and I rely heavily on his work here.[1] Downs argues that the United States "remained in a state of wartime for three years after surrender in some rebel states and for more than five years in others"—until 1871, when Congress seated members from the former Confederate states.[2] For those years, the South was excluded from the federal government and held under military rule, and it was that military rule that both allowed the transformation of the Founders' Constitution and made the transformation meaningful. Even before peace returned, the new Constitution was violently challenged; when federal troops withdrew, it was eclipsed. But the change had been effected: not through the ordinary amendment process, but by force of arms.

Well before the war was over, though after it was clear that the Union would prevail, Lincoln was thinking about how to reintegrate the states that had seceded. On December 8, 1863, he issued the Proclamation of Amnesty and Reconstruction. This was an accommodationist and conciliatory offer to the secessionists, with a few exceptions for war criminals, high-ranking military officers, and those who had left federal office to aid the rebellion. Accept abolition, swear allegiance to the Constitution, and your treason will be pardoned. Except as to slaves, your property rights will be restored. Once the number of those who had taken the oath and were qualified to vote in 1860 reached 10% of the voters in the 1860 election, they could reestablish a state government that would be recognized as the true government of the state. Louisiana and Arkansas adopted new constitutions in 1864.

The Republican Congress found this too lenient and responded with the Wade-Davis Bill in July 1864. That bill aimed to delay Reconstruction until after the war ended; it required a majority of white men to pledge loyalty, and it required a more elaborate oath—the so-called Ironclad Oath—as a condition of voting in a state constitutional convention. Lincoln pocket-vetoed the bill. How his plans might have evolved, we can only speculate. He spoke of Black suffrage: on April 11, 1865, he expressed a desire to allow some Blacks (those who had fought for the Union and, in a less appealing phrase, the "very intelligent") to vote. Present at that speech was John Wilkes Booth, who fumed in response, "That means n***** citizenship" and "That is the last speech he will ever make." Four days later Lincoln was dead—a martyr not for the cause of Union, but for Black citizenship. Andrew Johnson succeeded to the presidency, and public opinion hardened against the South.

The first stage of Reconstruction turned out to be less reconstitution of the state governments than dissolution, as the federal army
began sweeping away Confederate authority.[3] Rebel governors tried
to resume peacetime operations, calling legislatures into session to
rescind their secession ordinances. The military arrested them. In
Texas, Major General Philip Sheridan pronounced that all the acts
of the Texas government since secession were illegitimate and void.
To fill the vacuum, federal troops spread through the South, eventually occupying more than 630 posts.[4] These military authorities took
over the task of governance—no easy job in a South still simmer-
ing with rebellion and filled with ex-Confederates. Freed slaves first
found their rights not in the words of statutes or the Constitution
but in the willingness of federal troops to stop oppression. They
were "not rights at all in a legal sense but mere claims upon military
power."[5] Toppling slavery required force.

The Emancipation Proclamation, like the Philipsburg Proclamation before it, ended slavery as a practical matter only for enslaved
people who could reach the national forces. (It did not end slavery
at all in the loyal states or the parts of the Confederacy under Union
control.) The Thirteenth Amendment swept more broadly; it was
adopted by Congress in early 1865, but it would not be part of the
Constitution until ratified by three-quarters of state legislatures. As
the US Army moved through the Confederacy, it found "slavery
everywhere" and planters who "understand that slavery will remain
in some form or other."[6]

The crucial question of what freedom meant was settled first by
what rights the military was willing and able to protect. In Virginia, Major General Alfred Terry vacated even the pre-secession
state laws that restricted the rights of free Blacks, announcing:
"People of color will henceforth enjoy the same personal liberty that
other citizens and inhabitants enjoy." In Georgia, Major General
Quincy Adams Gillmore ended Savannah's system of whites-only
public schools.[7] Thus, through the military, the federal government
assumed the role of a Declaration-style government: it protected

the natural rights of freedpeople against other individuals who sought to oppress them.

Meanwhile, the head of the executive branch was trying to reconstitute the civilian governments of the southern states. Andrew Johnson appointed provisional governors, who found themselves vying with the military for authority. Amid that struggle, white southerners "responded violently to this attack on their society," trying to impose their own restrictive understanding of freedom.[8] Through 1865, as Johnson instructed provisional governments to call constitutional conventions and ratify the Thirteenth Amendment, attacks increased—on the military, but more often on freedpeople.

The required twenty-seven ratifications of the Thirteenth Amendment came within a year—from seventeen northern states, joined by eight former Confederate states and the border states of Missouri and Kansas. But Johnson's Reconstruction only transferred power among whites. The conventions he urged selected delegates on the basis of voter qualifications as of 1861—obviously excluding Black men. The South recognized that he was supporting what he himself called "a white man's government."[9] In the fall of 1865, southern states reconstituted their governments and elected federal representatives, with mixed results. The upper South chose federal representatives who mostly had served in the Union army or at least aided the national cause. The lower South chose former Confederates, including perhaps most strikingly former Confederate vice president Alexander Stephens.[10] Congress refused to seat them, with the exception of Tennessee, which had been readmitted by joint resolution on July 24, 1866.

Though the South had not reacquired its voice in the Congress, with state legislatures again in place, the meaning of freedom could now be settled by state law. "With their personal authority over blacks destroyed," writes Foner, "planters turned to the state to reestablish labor discipline."[11] In the lower South, its meaning was settled by the overtly discriminatory Black Codes. These codes, described by Kenneth Stampp as "a twilight zone between slavery and freedom,"[12] restricted Blacks by, for instance, requiring them to sign labor contracts and prohibiting them from taking any job other than farmer or servant without receiving a license and paying a tax.[13] Extensive regulation of the "employment" relationship made it resemble slavery, with "masters" allowed to whip "servants." Breaching or not entering into a contract could trigger the application of vagrancy laws, which took advantage of the Thirteenth Amendment back door: Blacks convicted of vagrancy could be sentenced to work or leased out while prisoners. Blacks were in most states not allowed to possess firearms or other weapons, they were not citizens, and of course they could not vote.

The Republicans in Congress, led by Radicals Charles Sumner and Thaddeus Stevens, found presidential Reconstruction inadequate. In 1866, they pushed back against the Black Codes with the Civil Rights Bill, an attempt to give a federal legislative definition of freedom. It granted citizenship to all persons born in the United States and endowed them with rights of citizenship. It told the southern states that they must open their political communities, like it or not. Johnson vetoed the bill, but Congress overrode the veto. Concerned that a Congress containing southern representatives might repeal it, or that the Supreme Court might invalidate it—among other things, the granting of birthright citizenship to Blacks conflicted with *Dred Scott*—Congress constitutionalized the bill in the Fourteenth Amendment.

Congress passed the Fourteenth Amendment by the required two-thirds majority in June 1866. However, Johnson opposed it, and, with the exception of Tennessee, the former Confederate states rejected it. There was no way to get approval from the required three-fourths of the states. The attempt to make the best of what we had, to transform the United States by law, through the methods set out in the Founders' Constitution, had failed.

And so it went on by other means.

The election of 1866 brought a victory for the Radical Republicans, and in 1867—again over Johnson's veto—Congress adopted the Reconstruction Acts. These acts proclaimed that "no legal State governments or adequate protection for life or property now exists in the rebel states." They dissolved the state governments and made the states "subject to the military authority of the United States." The southern states would not be readmitted to Congress until they met several conditions. They would need new constitutions. Delegates to the constitutional conventions were to be elected by all men—including Blacks but excluding former Confederate officers and leaders. The new constitutions had to provide voting rights to all men, and the new legislatures had to ratify the Fourteenth Amendment.

This is, quite simply, a destruction of the states and a reconstitution of their governments with a different political community. It is revolution from above. Congress wiped out the rebel states and created new ones, identical in their geography but little else. And it did all of this by military force. In *We the People: Transformations*, Bruce Ackerman masterfully describes the difficulties of trying to explain Reconstruction within the Article V framework, concluding that the conditions placed on southern representation in Congress are "naked violations of Article V." Ackerman embeds his account of the dubious legality of the Fourteenth Amendment in a complex and creative model of constitutional change that ties it to the Founding and the New Deal.[14] My point here is different and in some ways simpler. Reconstruction is a revolution not just because it is a dramatic change, but because it breaks and sets aside the prior legal regime.

RECONSTRUCTION TO REDEMPTION

The southern whites were no more enthusiastic about the Fourteenth Amendment after the Reconstruction Acts than before them. But stripped of their governments and controlled by the US Army, they had no power to stop it. The southern states held new conventions, wrote new constitutions, and ratified the Fourteenth Amendment. The southern constitutional conventions of 1867–69 showed a transformation. These were no longer the states that had formed the Confederacy.[15] There was a substantial Black presence—majorities in Louisiana and South Carolina. And the constitutions that resulted were strikingly progressive. They invoked the Declaration of Independence—not for the right to revolution or Jefferson's equality but for Lincoln's. They created free public education, which in Louisiana and South Carolina was integrated. They granted Blacks equal civil and political rights. They reformed divorce laws to protect women and offered public services on a scale never before seen in the American South: free medical care, free education, publicly funded hospitals, jails, and orphan asylums.[16] Where they fell short of Radical aims, it was largely the failure to broadly redistribute land.

Still, crucially, and just like the Fourteenth Amendment, they depended for their ratification and their implementation on military force, on the tens of thousands of soldiers still occupying the defeated South. The white response to this expansion of public support was "a carnival of violence."[17] The former rebels opposed redistribution. They did not want these public services going to support Black people, and they did not want to share them with Blacks, either. Public support for Black people marked them as insiders; public support shared with Black people marked them as equals. This same dynamic makes modern whites reject state support, even at the cost of their lives. As Jon Metzl puts it, they are dying of whiteness.[18]

During Reconstruction, they were killing for it. Rebels attacked Republicans and freedpeople. In Georgia, fifty white men wearing disguises murdered the leader of the constitutional convention.[19] A Democratic newspaper wrote that "these constitutions and governments will last just as long as the bayonets which ushered them in existence, and not one day longer."[20]

The 1868 presidential election was a referendum on Reconstruction. The Republicans ran Ulysses S. Grant, the highest-ranking Union general from the Civil War. The Democrats ran Horatio Seymour, a former governor of New York who had referred to the whites who murdered Blacks in the draft riot of 1863 as "my friends."[21] Grant won a dominating Electoral College victory, 214–80. He won the popular vote by over 5%, but the margin was still only a few hundred thousand—less than the number of Black votes cast, suggesting that Seymour might have won the white vote. Voter suppression and other irregularities occurred in the South, particularly in Georgia; in two majority-Black Georgia counties, not a single vote for Grant was recorded.

The interference with Black voting owed much to the Ku Klux Klan, which from its 1866 founding spread rapidly through the South. Southern Republican governments had to contend with constant violence. The ratification of the Fifteenth Amendment in 1870 did little to prevent Democratic attempts at disenfranchisement. By 1871, former rebels had regained control of the legislatures in Virginia, North Carolina, Georgia, and Tennessee—sometimes because white voters constituted a sufficient majority to win a fair election, and sometimes by other means. Where Democrats took control, legal discrimination and Klan violence followed. Even in areas under nominal Republican government, Republican leaders were attacked. Despite some successes, local authorities were unable to muster sufficient force to stop the Klan. When they tried, the results were often disastrous. In 1872, disputed elections in Louisiana resulted in both Democrats and Republicans claiming victories. In Grant Parish, Republicans trying to prevent a Democratic seizure of the government erected defenses around the county seat of Colfax. After a three-week siege, whites overpowered and massacred the defenders.

Congress passed Enforcement Acts in 1870 and 1871. While the Fourteenth Amendment banned the states from infringing on individual rights, these made some rights violations by private individuals a federal crime. They showed that Reconstruction had made the federal government into more of a Declaration-style government. (Ultimately, the Supreme Court would reject this expansion of federal authority and hold that Congress could generally not protect citizens from other individuals, just as later it would reject civil rights acts that protected individuals from racial discrimination by other individuals.[22]) Federal troops were able to restore order where they were used. Sustained military pressure and federal prosecutions largely broke the Klan. But northern endurance broke, too. The financial panic and a depression in 1873 led to Democrats taking the House of Representatives in the election of 1874. In 1875, Grant refused to aid Republicans in Mississippi against white violence, resulting in a Democratic landslide in the elections. In 1876, the presidential election contest between Rutherford B. Hayes and Samuel Tilden ended in a stalemate. In an informal compromise, Democrats accepted the Republican Hayes as president with the understanding that military oversight of the former Confederate states would end.[23] It did. And Redemption swept the South.

Massacres and lynchings followed as whites and Democrats overthrew the remaining Reconstruction governments: Hamburg, South Carolina, 1876; Thibodaux, Louisiana, 1887; Wilmington, North Carolina, 1898.[24] The last Black representative, George Henry White of North Carolina, left office in 1901. Even after the transfer of power was complete, violence persisted as a means of maintaining racial hierarchy: Atlanta, Georgia, 1906. Elaine, Arkansas, 1919. Tulsa, Oklahoma, 1921. Rosewood, Florida, 1923. It took longer than a day, but in the end, the Reconstruction governments could not be sustained without the bayonets that brought them into existence. The ballot, supposedly guaranteed by the Fifteenth Amendment, was not enough without the bullet to protect it—not when Redeemers used both votes and violence to bring Reconstruction down. The voting rights of Black people were empty words through much of the South until the Second Reconstruction brought the Voting Rights Act of 1965.

Reconstruction accomplished a lot, particularly with regard to Black politics. But Reconstruction's greatest achievement was the destruction of Founding America—at least on paper. The exclusivity of the Founding obviously persisted in practice. The meaning of Redemption was that Blacks were not, in fact, full and equal citizens. That exclusivity persists to this day, helped on by the standard story. The battle for America's identity is ongoing. Now let's think a little more carefully about who are the heroes and the villains of that battle.

WE ARE THE BAD GUYS: THE WORLD TURNED UPSIDE DOWN

One way to get a more accurate picture of our relation to the Founders' vision is to look at founding-era discussions of the Constitution—in particular, the *Federalist Papers*. *Federalist* no. 46, which discusses the relationship between the nation and the states, is particularly illuminating. In it, Madison is basically trying to reassure people that the states will remain the primary sovereigns in the American system. People worried that a single national government might become an oppressive tyrant, and many features of the Constitution the Framers wrote are designed to make that less likely. Several of the *Federalist Papers* aim to allay people's fears on that score. Madison here is saying, don't worry.

First, don't worry because the federal government isn't so scary and dangerous. It is just another representative of the people. The people are the ultimate sovereign, so the federal and state governments actually aren't opposed to each other. They're both agents of the people. But which will receive greater trust and support? The states, Madison answers. "Many considerations, besides those suggested on a former occasion, seem to place it beyond doubt that the first and most natural attachment of the people will be to the governments of their respective States." The state governments will employ more people; they'll pay out more money. They'll enact the more significant regulations. And, he says, members of the federal government will still feel an attachment to their states. They're unlikely to try to expand federal power at the expense of the states.

And what if they should? What if the federal government tried to extend its power beyond the due limits? Well, says Madison, the states have the advantage in the means of defeating such encroachments. If several adjoining states objected to some federal measure, their concerted action "would present obstructions which the federal government would hardly be willing to encounter." In fact, he suggests, all the states would unite to resist. "Every government would espouse the common cause. A correspondence would be opened. Plans of resistance would be concerted. One spirit would animate and conduct the whole. The same combinations, in short, would result from an apprehension of the federal, as was produced by the dread of a foreign, yoke." It would be like the Revolution. But, Madison goes on, that wouldn't happen. "What degree of madness could ever drive the federal government to such an extremity. . . . [W]hat would be the contest in the case we are supposing? Who would be the parties? A few representatives of the people would be opposed to the people themselves; or rather one set of representatives would be contending against thirteen sets of representatives, with the whole body of their common constituents on the side of the latter."

Even if that happened, the states would win the fight. "Let a regular army, fully equal to the resources of the country, be formed; and let it be entirely at the devotion of the federal government; still it would not be going too far to say, that the State governments, with the people on their side, would be able to repel the danger." The US Army, he estimates, couldn't muster more than 25,000 or 30,000 men. "To these would be opposed a militia amounting to near half a million of citizens with arms in their hands, officered by men chosen from among themselves, fighting for their common liberties, and united and conducted by governments possessing their affections and confidence." The Revolution shows us that the federal government will never be able to defeat the states.

Today, we can say that things have not worked out the way Madison predicted. Are people more attached to their states or their nation? There's regional variation on this—unsurprisingly, state identity is stronger in the former Confederate states—but most modern Americans put the nation first. People often move from state to state and thereby change their state citizenship without thinking much of it—less than they would if they moved to a different country and changed their national citizenship. State and local governments do employ more people than the federal government, but the federal government spends more. And about a third of state and local spending is actually of federal funds. What about the army? The standing US armed forces are about 1.2 million service members, with another 800,000 reserves. The state militias . . . don't really exist anymore. There's the National Guard, numbering about 350,000, but that's actually a federal force that can be called into federal service. Some states do have their own self-defense forces that can't be summoned into the federal army—Georgia, Mississippi, Missouri, and Texas, for instance—but most don't. The state capacity to offer military resistance to the federal government is entirely gone.

Reading *Federalist* no. 46 is like reading speculative science fiction from a long time ago. It's describing and predicting a world that didn't come to pass. Of course, people don't read the *Federalist Papers* to marvel at how the past imagined the future. People read the *Federalist Papers* to learn how to resolve modern controversies. That's how the Supreme Court reads them, as a guide to how to understand the Constitution—how to understand, in a sense, who we are.

From that perspective, reading the *Federalist Papers* is a bit like the plot of Isaac Asimov's science fiction Foundation series. Asimov's conceit was that sometime thousands of years in the future, a field of study called psychohistory develops. It uses psychological techniques to predict the future, the idea being that individuals are unpredictable but people in the aggregate are not, and therefore from looking at current conditions it's possible to forecast what will happen on a global or even galactic scale. The foremost practitioner of psychohistory, a man named Hari Seldon, runs his predictions and sees that the current galactic empire, decadent and polarized, will collapse. So he starts a plan that will allow a successor civilization to arise much faster than it normally would, thereby reducing the human suffering that will occur during the intervening dark ages. He leaves messages and instructions for the leaders of this civilization, which he calls the Foundation, to consult at the appropriate times. He predicts the problems the Foundation will encounter, and he tells them the solutions.

Most people nowadays, if they know about Hari Seldon, associate him with big data—as a speculative forerunner of modern mapping and predictive techniques. Another parallel, maybe a more striking one, is with a particular way of thinking about the Constitution and the *Federalist Papers*. According to this view, the Framers of the Constitution were demigods—they were the Hari Seldons of their day. They saw the path America would take and the challenges it would face, and they put the answers in the Constitution. We don't have recorded messages from them to open at particular moments of crisis, but the answers to our current problems are there if we look hard enough, if we understand well enough. If we can be enough like them, maybe.

But here's what happens in the Foundation trilogy. Hari Seldon's first few recordings are spot-on, and they resolve the crises that they're addressing. Then there's a terrible crisis and everyone gathers to listen to the recording to hear how Hari Seldon has solved this problem, and he's talking about something totally different. And that's maybe a better description of the experience of reading the *Federalist Papers* now, if you're reading them for guidance through a modern crisis. The predictions of the Framers of the Constitution were accurate for a time, but history diverged from their path a while back. If you're worried now that the federal government has grown too powerful or is doing too much—and plenty of people do worry about that—and you look to the *Federalist Papers* for guidance, it's as though you turned on the Hari Seldon recording and got something totally irrelevant. Don't worry, people will consider their state citizenship primary? States will outspend the federal government? State militias will defeat the federal army? No. Again, *Federalist* no. 46 is describing a world that didn't come to pass.

Except that in part it did. In one very important way, what Madison wrote about in *Federalist* no. 46 did happen. Just not the way he predicted. The federal government, he said, would never fight a war against the states. But it did, and it won.

Here's the moment where reading the *Federalist Papers* is like *being* in a science fiction story. There's a common plot device in science fiction where the hero is hunting some enemy. A clone, an android replicant, something that looks human but really isn't. It's not one of us; it's alien, different, the enemy. The hero goes through the various trials and adventures and finally kills the enemy and examines the body only to find that . . . it's human. And realization slowly dawns. *If that's the human, then I'm the robot. I'm the clone. I'm the enemy.*

This is the moment that you should have when you realize how backward the standard story is. When you look down at the corpse of the Confederacy—and you might want to double tap to be sure it's dead—you are not seeing the deviant outsider that was properly vanquished by the principles of the Declaration. You are seeing the body of Founding America. You are seeing the death of the central principle of the Declaration, the death of the Founders' Constitution. (Thurgood Marshall: "While the Union survived the Civil War, the Constitution did not."[25]) That's what you see so vividly in *Federalist* no. 46. Madison—who of course is a slave owner from Virginia—is describing the Civil War and telling us not to worry, the South will win. From the perspective of the Declaration and the Founders' Constitution, we are the robot. We are the enemy. That is the terrible contradiction at the heart of the standard story—not that slave owners wrote a document promising equality to all men (they didn't), but that it gives us a story within which we are not the heroes at all. We are the bad guys.

Yet there's another twist. The bad guys—the national government—turned out to be good. The Reconstruction Constitution is better than the Founding Constitution. Lincoln's equality is better than Jefferson's equality. To give Madison credit, he did see this possibility. Toward the end of *Federalist* no. 46, he says that if by some chance the federal government does attain ascendancy over the states, there can be only one reason. "If, therefore, as has been elsewhere remarked, the people should in future become more partial to the federal than to the State governments, the change can only result from such manifest and irresistible proofs of a better administration, as will overcome all their antecedent propensities."

That was a valid prediction. Nowadays, we have a greater attachment to the federal government and a lesser one to the states. But that's because the national side was ultimately the side of freedom, of equality, of justice—and it took that side in Reconstruction.

12

Redemption Songs

*Inclusive Equality and Exclusive
Individualism in Modern America*

★

IN CRITICIZING THE standard story to this point, I have largely
focused on ways it misleads us about the past. But it leads us astray
in the present, too. The triumphalist standard story encourages
complacency, while more accurate versions ask us to accept that racism and slave owning can coexist with our modern value of equality.
All versions have the potential to support exclusive individualism.
If you look at modern America, including the very recent past, you
can see inclusive equality and exclusive individualism at war. We
are met, you could say, on a great battlefield of that war, testing
whether a nation dedicated to inclusive egalitarian ideals can long
endure. And just as the ideology of the Declaration, properly understood, worked against the United States in the Civil War, so, too,
it works today against the ideals of the Gettysburg Address and
Reconstruction.

The differences between inclusive equality and exclusive individualism can be described in several ways, but there are just two
main themes. The first has to do with attitudes toward outsiders.
An exclusive political community is closed, viewing outsiders as
fundamentally different, objects of fear and suspicion. An inclusive
political community is open, viewing outsiders as fundamentally

similar, potentially valuable members of the community. The second has to do with relations inside the community. An individualist community understands the government as existing for the benefit of individuals. Redistribution from one individual to another, even from insider to insider, is suspect. The criterion of legitimacy that expresses this principle is protection of the natural rights of individual insiders. Political outcomes are legitimate if they do not interfere with the rights of insiders; the form of government does not matter. By contrast, an egalitarian community understands the government as existing for the benefit of the community. Redistribution may be acceptable if it makes the community as a whole better off—if, perhaps, it promotes equality. The criterion of legitimacy that expresses this principle is democracy. Political outcomes are legitimate if they make society better off when every individual's interest is weighed equally and accurately, and the way to do that is to give every individual an equal voice in the political process. You could say that both themes have to do with the appropriate degree of care for other people: inclusion vs. exclusion is about care for outsiders and equality vs. individualism is about care for fellow insiders.

As we've seen, exclusive individualism is the theory of the Declaration of Independence and the Founders' Constitution, while inclusive equality is the theory of the Gettysburg Address and the Reconstruction Constitution. The exclusive individualist political regime is born in war against an (allegedly) oppressive national government, the inclusive equality one in a war against subnational units trying to destroy the nation. But how do these principles appear in the modern world? How do the stories we tell about the past translate into the present? We are not the heirs of the Founders; the Confederates are. And the Confederates have their own heirs today.

The best way to see the modern battle is to ask: What would happen if you took the exclusive individualist regime created by the Founding and made it inclusive and egalitarian with Reconstruction? What if you forced some states to accept as insiders people they wanted to exclude and gave those people an equal voice in the democratic process?

You might expect two primary reactions from those who wanted to hold on to founding ideals. First, you would expect resistance to the conferral of equal insider status. You would expect attempts to brand these people as, if not complete outsiders, inferiors. Less obviously, you might expect reduced support for government services in general, but especially to the extent that those services go to the new insiders. Providing government services to people marks them as insiders; sharing services with them marks people as equals. Second, you would expect resistance to the idea of equal voice. You would expect attempts to undermine the ability of the new insiders to participate in the political process. Failing that, you might see a fallback to the argument of the Declaration that the criterion of legitimacy for political outcomes is one of substance, not process. Democracy is not the test: protecting the natural rights of insiders is.

We see all of this today. What I've said here about insiders and outsiders is, in American history, mostly about whites and Blacks. (Not completely: white Republicans and civil rights activists get lynched, too, and racial discrimination takes many forms and falls on many groups.) We see it in the racial politics of America—in the attempts to construct a racial hierarchy and to brand Black people as inferior. That is the social meaning of the Black Codes, segregation, Jim Crow, Confederate iconography, and the Dunning school of history. We see reduced support for government services: the closing of public pools and schools in the wake of desegregation decisions, the opposition to Medicaid expansion and the Affordable Care Act. We see denial of equal voice with successive generations of voter suppression tactics, aided recently by the Supreme Court. We even see rejection of democracy.

The struggle continues. There are different ways to describe the divide. It is in part regional—North vs. South, coasts vs. interior, urban vs. rural. It is in part racial, white vs. nonwhite. It is in part generational: old vs. young. But it is also, to some extent, partisan.

Our major political parties are consistently on different sides of these issues—although they have shifted positions over the past century and a half.

The 1852 presidential election began a long period of solid Democratic control over the South. The first fissure appeared in 1948, when southern Dixiecrats walked out of the Democratic convention in protest of its pro–civil rights platform. Instead of Harry Truman, they nominated Strom Thurmond, whose States' Rights ticket carried four former Confederate states and received over a million votes. The civil rights legislation of the 1960s completed the break. When Democratic President Lyndon Johnson signed the Civil Rights Act of 1964, he famously lamented, "I think we just delivered the South to the Republican Party for a long time to come." Johnson was largely correct, though not immediately. In 1968, the states that had voted for Strom Thurmond went for George Wallace and the American Independent Party, and Democrat Hubert Humphrey won Texas. Democrat George McGovern won only Massachusetts and DC in 1972, making Republican Richard Nixon's sweep of the South somewhat less probative. And in 1976, Democrat Jimmy Carter won almost all the former Confederacy. But since Carter, no Democrat has won Alabama, Mississippi, South Carolina, or Texas, and Democratic inroads into the rest of the South have been relatively rare. George W. Bush carried all the former Confederate states in his two wins. Barack Obama won Florida and Virginia twice and North Carolina once. Hillary Clinton in 2016 and Joe Biden in 2020 both carried Virginia, and Biden picked up Georgia as well.

Overall, though, there is a clear and consistent pattern. The party of Lincoln has taken over the former Confederacy—not, like Lincoln, by military force, but by adopting its ideology. Modern Republicans often portray themselves as fighting for founding values in an America that has turned its back on them. There is, I believe, a lot of truth to that claim. But founding values have a lot in common with Confederate values, and America turned its back on them in Reconstruction. We have seen the fight for founding values in Reconstruction America before. It is Redemption.

Redemption won the first time. It ended Reconstruction and restored white supremacy. It took away Black voting rights and erected Confederate monuments. It retold with the noose the same story written with the lash: America is a white man's country. The Second Reconstruction restored many of the gains of the first—integration, voting rights. It, too, met opposition. As Ian Haney López describes in *Dog Whistle Politics*, Republican political rhetoric both responded to and activated white racial anxieties, warning that the Black outsiders southern states had been forced to accept were now taking the things that properly belonged to white insiders.

Richard Nixon's 1968 campaign promised law and order rather than the protests and riots then wracking America. Nixon criticized the Warren Court and promised to appoint justices who would strictly construe the Constitution. Each of these themes, neutral on its face, tapped into racial concerns. The riots were a reaction to racial inequality. The Warren Court's "activism" typically consisted of decisions supporting the rights of politically weak groups, notably racial minorities. Nixon expressed support for the court's decision in *Brown* but also said it was wrong for the federal government to impose its views on local communities.

In 1980, Redemption themes sounded even more clearly in Reagan's campaign. Reagan told stories about Black people receiving government support: the "strapping young bucks" buying T-bone steaks with welfare stamps, the "welfare queens" driving Cadillacs. The language could have come from the fight against Reconstruction: in 1874, opposing a civil rights bill, a Democratic newspaper editor warned whites that under the anti-discrimination provisions, "your children at school must sit on the back seats and in the cold, whilst the negro's children sit near the stove and on the front seats, and enjoy in every instance the money you toil for, whilst Sambo is sleeping and stealing." When Reagan praised states' rights in Philadelphia, Mississippi, his audience knew who threatened those rights: the federal government that defeated the states in the Civil War, the civil rights workers who were murdered there sixteen years before. When Reagan spoke about the Constitution, he promised originalism: an approach to judicial interpretation that would restore the Founding and erase the Second Reconstruction of the Warren Court.

The pattern continues. In 2012, the Supreme Court, under the leadership of Reagan administration veteran John Roberts, struck down key parts of central Second Reconstruction legislation, the Voting Rights Act. Newly liberated from federal oversight, former Confederate states enacted numerous measures that made voting more difficult—particularly for urban voters, particularly for people of color. (In 2020, for instance, the Republican governor of Texas decreed that each county would get one drop-off location for mail-in ballots: one for the 169 people of rural Loving County, 89% white, one for the 4.7 million people of urban Harris County, 31.4% white.)

In 2016, America elected Donald Trump as president. Sociologist Arlie Hochschild, interviewing Trump voters, found a common concern. As she reports in *Strangers in Their Own Land,* Trump voters felt that undeserving others—Blacks and immigrants—were taking things that belonged to insiders: they were "cutting in line" for the American dream.[1] One reaction is to vote for someone who will strike back against the others. (When the fight over Trump's border wall led to a government shutdown, a Trump voter lamented the suffering imposed on some of his supporters: "He's not hurting the people he needs to be hurting.") Another reaction is to reject the government services entirely. Jonathan Metzl's *Dying of Whiteness* describes how poor whites turn against government programs that would help them, because they do not want to share them with the others. "Ain't no way I would ever support Obamacare or sign up for it," Metzl reports an interview subject saying, "no way I want my tax dollars paying for Mexicans and welfare queens."[2] This man—Trevor, a forty-one-year-old uninsured Tennessean—did in fact die from liver damage and knew he was dying at the time of the interview. Yet he not only supported Tennessee's refusal to expand Medicaid coverage; he even suggested that he would decline coverage if it was available.

Heather McGhee has expanded on this point in *The Sum of Us*. If government services are provided in a nondiscriminatory way, whites have to share them with nonwhites, with people they do not accept as full insiders. This may involve intermingling, as with integrated swimming pools or public schools, or it may not, as with Medicaid. In either case, it sends a message that these others are in fact insiders, and that they are equals. To avoid that message, some people would rather eliminate the service entirely: drain the pool, shut down the school, reject the billions of dollars the federal government offered for Medicaid expansion. Racial resentment is mobilized to cut government support: as McGhee says, this is why we can't have nice things.[3] One of the consistent American political dynamics is that racial anxiety is used as a wedge issue to divide the working class, to prevent class solidarity. Racists benefit psychologically from withdrawal of government services, maybe—the absence of shared government support makes it easier to believe that Blacks are not truly insiders and equals. However, rich people benefit in a more tangible way: the way to prevent the government from offering services is by cutting taxes. Racial and economic inequality form an unholy alliance.

The Founding tells us to consider taxation—the means by which the government provides services and takes care of the vulnerable—as cause for revolution. (Technically taxation without representation, but that subtlety gets lost in translation. And a broader rejection of federal tax is consistent with the Founding: the Founders' Constitution did not clearly give the federal government the power to tax income, which is why the Sixteenth Amendment was necessary.) The Tea Party, which (again, not coincidentally) sprang up in response to our first Black president, invoked the Patriots of the Boston Tea Party but was also using an acronym: Taxed Enough Already. Taxes are the basic means of redistribution, so the Declaration's anti-redistribution theory of politics supports tax resistance as well as opposition to government services. More generally, pitching in to help out others on a national scale is pretty clearly not a founding value. One of the big early constitutional debates was about whether the federal government was allowed to spend money to aid victims of natural disasters such as a fire that devastated Savannah, Georgia. Hamilton was in favor, Madison opposed. The Fourth Congress decided it lacked the power to help. Madison's last act as president was to veto an infrastructure bill on the grounds that Congress could not spend money to promote the general welfare.

And what about democracy? In recent years, the Republican Party has benefited from the structural features of the Constitution that allow a minority to control every branch of the federal government. Because of the Electoral College, a candidate can win the presidency while losing the popular vote. Because of equal state representation, a party representing a minority of the population can control the Senate, where the fewer than two million people of the Dakotas outweigh the nearly forty million Californians. (Because of partisan gerrymanders, a minority of voters can control the House of Representatives, too.) A minority-elected president can nominate judges to be confirmed by senators representing a minority of the population, giving the minority control over the judicial branch, too.

Perhaps in response to these features, the Republican Party has tended to disfavor policies that make voting easier, and to support various forms of restrictions, which is anti-democratic in a certain sense. But the more extreme anti-democratic principle has surfaced, too. In the face of Democratic victories in the 2020 presidential election, the Trump campaign sought to have courts nullify some state elections, leaving the choice of electors, perhaps, to the state legislatures. Other Republicans suggested that the state legislatures should themselves nullify the elections and certify their own slate of electors. Trump and Senate ally Lindsey Graham both called Georgia secretary of state Brad Raffensperger, asking him to find some way to change the results. Most directly, Utah senator Mike Lee tweeted: "Democracy isn't the objective; liberty, peace, and prospefity [*sic*] are. We want the human condition to flourish. Rank democracy can thwart that." The *National Review*, echoing William F. Buckley's support of disenfranchising Blacks, asked candidly whether we might be better off with fewer voters.[4] We are back to the Declaration, where the test of political legitimacy is outcomes, not process.

And then, the strongest echo of Redemption: On January 6, 2021, Donald Trump addressed a rally near the White House. A mile and a half down Pennsylvania Avenue, in the US Capitol, Congress had assembled to certify Joe Biden as the winner of the presidential election. Trump praised the crowd as patriots. "Our country has had enough," he said. He rattled off a long list of alleged Democratic fraud. "We're not going to let it happen. . . . Our country will be destroyed, and we're not going to stand for that. . . . We're going to walk down Pennsylvania Avenue . . . and we're going to the Capitol. . . . [W]e're going to try and give our Republicans . . . the kind of pride and boldness that they need to take back our country."

What did it all mean? Reading the transcript, it's hard to know—but the audience thought they understood. When Trump finished, the crowd marched to the Capitol, where they confronted a small number of Capitol police and movable barricades. Some police grappled with the crowd as they pushed against the barricades. Others moved the barricades aside and posed for selfies. Rioters breached police lines on the west side of the Capitol. Others scaled the walls, broke windows, and forced doors. Some seemed aimless, while others wore military gear and acted with purpose. As the crowd flowed into the building, Secret Service agents evacuated Vice President Mike Pence from the Senate Chamber. Some lawmakers and staff hid in offices. Police pushed furniture in front of the doors to the House Chamber and waited inside with drawn guns. Someone fired shots through the door into the chamber. Air Force veteran Ashli Babbit tried to climb through a broken window into the Speaker's Lobby, where representatives were sheltering, and a police officer shot her dead. Other rioters forced their way into the Senate Chamber, from which lawmakers had been evacuated.

They rifled through papers the senators had left behind and took pictures of themselves. Overall, some eight hundred people entered the Capitol building, where they roamed for hours, looting offices and assaulting police and reporters. Some carried Confederate battle flags.

A mob attacking the seat of government to overturn the results of a democratic election: even without the Confederate flag, you can't find much in American history to compare that to other than Redemption. But Redemption was regional, and this was national. The Confederate battle flag was raised again throughout the South, but it had never before entered the US Capitol. That makes the question of where we go from here a little more pointed. One region of the country cannot abandon another to this Second Redemption. If it wins this time, it wins everywhere.

What can help defeat it? We need a better national story, because in just about every way, the standard story supports the Second Redemption against the ideals of the First and Second Reconstruction. In its triumphalist version, the standard story encourages complacency. A vision of inevitable progress, of an America in which racism is an aberration and a thing of the past, allows non-racists to join with racists in defense of the status quo. (In response to the 1619 Project, the Trump administration produced the 1776 Report, a version of the standard story that is triumphalist to the point of absurdity. "The American people," it says, "have ever pursued freedom and justice," and "wrongs have always met resistance from the clear principles of the nation." Thus we triumphed over slavery, listed as one of the "challenges to America's principles" and may hope to similarly defeat progressivism and identity politics, two of the other listed challenges.) The standard story supports those who call the 1619 Project ideology, who were aghast when NFL players kneeled during the national anthem, who condemn the Black Lives Matter protests as disruptive and divisive. But neither civility nor time reduce racial inequality. Instead, they tend to exacerbate it.

In its less triumphalist versions, the standard story shows us a world of white supremacy and tells us that this is the source of our deepest ideals. Racists are very comfortable with that. They are very comfortable extolling the virtues of the great Founders while acknowledging that those men owned slaves. Racism and white supremacy can, for some people, become a feature of the standard story rather than a bug.

No matter how you tell it, the standard story translates poorly into the modern world. The heroes of the Founding are state militias and quasi-private paramilitary groups like the Sons of Liberty fighting the oppressive national government, and also defending Americans from the dangerous outsiders described in the Declaration: Native Americans and enslaved people. Fast-forward two hundred fifty years and ask who plays those roles now. We don't have state militias defending us against the national government anymore, but we have highly militarized state police deploying excessive force against Black people. (Against whites as well—features of American society that grow out of attempts to maintain racial hierarchy often end up hurting many more people than their initial targets.) We do have quasi-private paramilitary organizations. They were leading the attack on the Capitol; they are the Proud Boys, the Oath Keepers, the Three Percenters. We had them in the fight against Reconstruction, too: the Ku Klux Klan and the White League. These are not our heroes.

The Declaration tells us to focus on infringements on our own rights, to judge their seriousness ourselves, and not to think about what we might be doing to others. To insist rather hysterically on one's own rights ("They're trying to make us slaves!") and ignore the harm one inflicts on others is the Declaration in action. When Americans were driven to frenzy by requests that they wear masks to avoid exposing others to COVID-19, they were acting out the founding script. (And it was no coincidence that the others they might expose, front-line workers in service industries, were disproportionately people of color.)

The deep ideology of the Declaration and the Founding, which is encoded in the standard story, turns out to work very poorly in the modern world. It supports racism and inequality, selfishness and vigilantism. It opposes redistribution and taxation, which Supreme Court Justice Oliver Wendell Holmes once called "what we pay for civilized society." (Holmes fought for the United States in the Civil War and dissented from *Lochner*. His will left his estate to the federal government.) It is no surprise that people carrying Confederate flags identify themselves as patriots, that they walk happily alongside people dressed in Revolutionary garb, that together these people storm the seat of the national government. The standard story tells us just that: Treason against the national government in defense of your view of your rights is American patriotism.

13

The Better Story

★

I HOPE THAT THE standard story now seems less desirable. However, we should take a moment to remember why it can be appealing to people of goodwill. It is nice to think that America starts with a statement of laudable values, liberty and equality, that we still honor today. It is nice to think that the war that made America was a war for those values, maybe even a war that ended slavery. And it is nice to think that the Constitution we wrote after that war was a device for implementing those values, and that fidelity to that Constitution can guide us even now.

It is nice, but it is not very plausible, and it turns out to have a significant downside, too. At least, that is so if we are talking about the Declaration of Independence, the Revolutionary War, and the Founders' Constitution. But does that mean that we must root our identity in a Declaration that was actually about independence, a Revolution that overall strengthened the institution of slavery, and a Constitution that protected slavery and was largely indifferent to individual rights? Not at all. What is so amazing about our history is that all of the standard story makes sense . . . if we simply shift our focus. The Gettysburg Address does contain our modern values of liberty and equality. The Civil War was a war for those values, and it ended slavery. The Reconstruction Constitution was a method of making the ideals of the Gettysburg Address into real law.

What happens if we understand that we are not Founding America, nor the political heirs of that first Republic? We get a very different story. It's a story about getting better, like the standard story is. Except it doesn't look back. It's not about getting better by getting closer to some mythical past. It's about getting better by making a better future. Making a nation that is more just. It's not a success story, because we only move forward when we realize that we have failed—and sometimes that takes a hundred years. And it's not a story of continuity. It's a story of rupture, of breaks with the past.

The America born in 1776 is flawed, according to this story. It's flawed of necessity, because compromise was required to win independence from Britain, and it's a step forward from the monarchical regime it replaces: new ideas are in the air. But it's deeply flawed, most notably by its embrace of slavery. The Revolutionaries who declare their independence overstate the injustices inflicted on them and ignore the injustices they inflict on others. The America they create fails—the Articles of Confederation are a disaster, lasting less than ten years. Americans work within them as long as they can, hoping for improvement, but in the end they have to break the existing order.

The Founders' Constitution shatters the Articles—and not by the method the Articles set out. It, too, is a step forward, an attempt to move closer to the ideal of a single nation with shared values and common goals. It, too, is flawed, and for the same reason: It protects slavery; it ignores oppression. It is at best equivocal on the issue of redistribution, of bearing burdens to protect others. The federal government's taxing power and ability to respond to natural disasters are both highly contentious topics. The Supreme Court brings out the worst in it through several pro-slavery decisions, announcing that the political community is closed according to race. And it, too, fails. Measured according to the goals set out in the preamble, the Founders' Constitution is a worse disaster than the Articles. It does not create a more perfect union: eleven states secede, thirteen if you accept the Confederate claims to Missouri and Kentucky. It does not insure domestic tranquility: Americans kill more Americans than any foreign enemy ever has, some three-quarters of a million dead. It brings the blessings of liberty to the Founders, but to their posterity the curse of war.

As the war goes on, the United States (not "the North") realizes why this catastrophe happened and what needs to be done. Anti-slavery Republicans were willing to work within the system, but the secessionists were not. Rather than try to restore what had been, the Reconstruction Congress decides to build something new. There will be no more compromises with slavery, no more deals with the devil. The Black soldiers who fought for the United States in its war against traitors will be citizens, and as citizens they will have rights.

Reconstruction destroys the Founders' Constitution—and not by the method the Founders' Constitution sets out. It is not a fulfillment of the Founders' vision, but a rejection of it, a recognition of its failure. The Reconstruction Constitution is better—vastly better. It bans slavery; it bans racial discrimination in voting; it gives individuals rights against states. It creates a political community that is not walled off by a racial line but open to every person born on American soil. It justifies this new nation not with fictitious consent and a fetish for natural rights but with justice and democracy.

The new America is also flawed. In the very same sentence that penalizes states for racial discrimination in voting, the Fourteenth Amendment licenses sex discrimination. The Reconstruction Amendments move the federal government closer to the role of a Declaration-style government, but not all the way—not as far as the US Army went in protecting the freedpeople. The Supreme Court brings out the worst in it, too, narrowing rights under the Fourteenth Amendment, limiting congressional power to protect individuals from other individuals, and scorning the idea that the amendment protects women's rights. ("The paramount destiny and mission of woman are to fulfill the noble and benign offices of wife and mother," wrote Justice Bradley.) When it reads the Fourteenth Amendment generously, it is to include the theory of the Declaration—that the government is forbidden to act to promote equality.

Reconstruction fails, too, almost as quickly as the Articles of Confederation—though less because of flaws within it than attacks from without. There is no change in the words of the Constitution, no written trace in our higher law—certainly no change by the method the Constitution sets out—but a violent revolution sweeps away the Republican governments of the South. It all but erases the Fifteenth Amendment, and much of the Fourteenth as well. Systems of peonage and convict leasing undermine the Thirteenth. This is the work of bad people doing bad things, and also of good, or indifferent, people who will not bear the discomfort necessary for lasting change. The racists are willing to fight, the non-racists are not, and the anti-racists are too few to hold on to their gains. A new regime takes hold, and this one is far worse. American history takes steps backward as well as steps forward.

But we do go forward. Inspired, once again, by military service and a war against a racist enemy—this time Nazi Germany—Black Americans press their calls for equality. The Supreme Court invalidates government racial segregation, in public schools and elsewhere. President Johnson, introducing the Voting Rights Act, links Lexington and Concord to Appomattox and Selma. "The real hero of this struggle," he says, is the Black American "whose demonstrations have been designed to call attention to injustice, designed to provoke change, designed to stir reform." Congress passes the Voting Rights Act and other civil rights laws—some of them just like the Reconstruction laws the Supreme Court struck down— and now the court upholds them. For just about the only time in American history, the court is on the side of progress. It brings out the best in the Reconstruction Constitution—not just in the ways the drafters expected, but as a source of rights for women and later for LGBTQ people. Again, it's a revolution, again without written change in our Constitution, but this time nonviolent.

And then what? Now what? Our Constitution is still flawed. We have the Electoral College, a legacy of slavery, which seems increasingly likely to stop a majority of Americans from electing the candidate of their choice. We have equal representation of the states in the Senate, which gets worse as the population gaps between states grow more extreme. The six senators from the three largest states represent roughly the same number of people as the sixty-two senators from the smallest thirty-one. Ideological cohesion among less-populous states, which is real though not complete, makes this worse, because it leads to actual and not theoretical minority rule. There is also a racial effect: the ten least-populated states are rural and overwhelmingly white.

We Americans are not perfect, either. Some of us are bad. Some are indifferent and unwilling to sacrifice for others. Some are easily distracted, misled, manipulated. We go forward and we go back. We elect Reagan, we elect Obama, we elect Trump. But what makes us American—our deepest ideal—is that we keep trying. America is born in an attempt to find a new and better way, to escape the stale and oppressive monarchies of Europe. We don't get it right immediately. Yet we keep going. We're looking for America, and we know that the America we're looking for isn't something that's given to us by Founding Fathers. It's something we make, something we find inside ourselves. The true America is not handed down from the past but created anew by each generation, created a little better, and what we can give the future is the opportunity to get just a little closer than we did ourselves. That's the promise that makes us American. That's the promise we have to keep.

Well, that's the optimistic version, anyway. You could tell a sadder story—about how the Second Reconstruction of the Warren Court era met the Second Redemption of the Reagan Revolution, how the Supreme Court—relying on cases from the First Redemption—invalidated key parts of the Voting Rights Act and the Violence Against Women Act, how it converted the Equal Protection Clause from a shield against oppression of Blacks to a sword that aggrieved whites could wield to cut down attempts to promote equality, notably affirmative action. How the actual governance of our country moved further and further away from majority rule, how increasing inequality led to increasing reliance on racial division, how one of our political parties all but explicitly embraced voter suppression as its means to retain power. (Maybe the real problem with *The Birth of a Nation* was just that it said the quiet part loud.) About how Americans can no longer hear each other across a partisan divide, how the two halves of the country paddle furiously in opposite directions as we all plunge together over a waterfall.

But my whole argument is that this need not be our fate. We don't have to follow the sadder story all the way down that road. A better story can do real work to overcome this divide, to bring us together in a productive way.

How do you change someone's mind on an issue that relates to their sense of self? People who feel threatened or attacked become defensive and resistant to change. They are unwilling to listen to someone on the other side. Research suggests that the key is to be non-adversarial, to emphasize agreement and shared values, and then let others reach the desired conclusions on their own.[1] All of this makes sense intuitively. People trust members of their group; they are mistrustful of outsiders. Starting out with an attempt to find agreement makes you look less like an outsider. Starting out with an affirmation—something that supports the other person or their view—gives them a reserve of positive feelings that helps mitigate the discomfort of a different perspective. Both these things can also help suggest that people on the other side are not so different after all.

The biggest surprise I've had in discussions with people across the political spectrum is how much of their hostility is rooted in fear. Fear on one side probably seems reasonable to you—I confess that the fears of one side seem more reasonable to me than those of the other—but the important point is that the fear on all sides is equally real. Research suggests that even limited interpersonal interaction can have a significant effect in reducing ungrounded or hyperbolic fears.

Last, people tend to believe things they figure out for themselves. As a negative method—a method of combating beliefs—this consists in asking questions, rather than attacking the beliefs. Effective questioning can lead a listener to disassemble their own mental constructs when they would not have accepted a direct challenge. As a positive method, it consists in letting the listener reach conclusions on their own—even if they are conclusions you have in mind. You can see this technique in fiction, particularly scary stories or urban legends. A common form of these kinds of fiction is designed to end with a terrifying conclusion—but the story almost always stops short of the ultimate revelation, closing with a fact that is one inferential step away. (The sweater on the grave means that the hitchhiker was a ghost; the hook in the car door means that the scratching was the crazed killer; the writing on the wall means that the murderer was there when the girl got home . . .) The point of this is to allow the reader to reach the last step on their own, which makes it credible—something they came up with—rather than something presented by someone else.

How can we communicate in this way? The better story I have suggested fits a lot of these criteria. It is non-accusatory. It can start out with an affirmation and points of agreement—the greatness of America, our shared values. It can develop through a process of questioning the standard story—that is in part what I have tried to do here. And if it is accepted as a story, it leads to conclusions about America and our duty as Americans that are a lot more productive than the complacency and inaction the standard story encourages. The better story is in fact better in so many ways.

Its first advantage, though certainly not a sufficient one, is that it is more accurate. The Gettysburg Address and the Reconstruction Constitution do contain our modern values of liberty and equality, or at least statements from which those values might plausibly be derived. The Declaration of Independence and the Founders' Constitution do not. Relatedly, giving up on the identification with the Founding lets us avoid many of the problematic aspects of the standard story. We do not have to whitewash the Founding—we do not need to downplay the sins of the Founders, we do not need to distort the Revolution, we do not need to insist that *Dred Scott* is a mistaken interpretation of the Founders' Constitution—because judgments of the Founding are no longer implicit judgments about us. We can look to Abraham Lincoln as the father of our country, not George Washington; we can look to Lincoln, not Thomas Jefferson, as the author of our creed.

This is generally an improvement. The political heroes of the Founding are the drafters of the Declaration and the Founders' Constitution: Washington, the father of our country; Jefferson, who stated our ideals; Madison, who had so much influence over the Constitution; Hamilton, who has become much more popular recently; and some others like Benjamin Franklin. The political heroes of Reconstruction are the Republican Congress and Lincoln. Thaddeus Stevens, Charles Sumner, and John Bingham can replace Madison, Hamilton, and Franklin.

Franklin is a loss, but otherwise we're getting an upgrade. Jefferson wrote that all men were created equal but enslaved his children; as death approached, he decided to free some of them but not their mother. Stevens, as death approached, directed that he be buried in an integrated graveyard, with the epitaph explaining: "I have chosen this that I might illustrate in my death the principles which I advocated through a long life, equality of man before the Creator." Madison may have argued against admitting in the Constitution the idea that there can be property in man, but the Founders' Constitution protected slavery. Sumner gave a speech entitled "No Property in Man" to propose an amendment abolishing slavery. Thirty-four of the signers of the Declaration of Independence owned slaves; so did about twenty-five of the fifty-five delegates to the Constitutional Convention. With a few exceptions, the Radical Republicans of the Reconstruction Congress never had slaves—and if they did, they freed them.

The Civil War is a better war than the Revolutionary War. Each is a war fought by states that allowed slavery, seeking independence from a nation that had at least in part abandoned it, a war where that nation offered freedom to slaves who would join its forces, using emancipation as a military measure. The difference there, of course, is that the Founders were the slaveholding states and the Union was the nation. But the Civil War was something else, too. Unlike the Revolution, which was based on boilerplate Enlightenment beliefs about the rights of insiders, it was a war where Americans fought in the name of new ideals, unheard of in the world, and wrote a constitution to make those ideals a reality and give them the force of law. Immediate abolition, uncompensated emancipation. Fundamental rights for all. The equality of people in society, not the state of nature. Lincoln and Grant resisted pressure to drop abolition as a condition of peace. The Revolution and the Founders' Constitution chose unity over justice, but the Civil War and Reconstruction put justice ahead of unity.

The heroes and villains are different. The Founding reveres paramilitary organizations like the Sons of Liberty. The army of the national government is viewed suspiciously—the Founders did not want a standing army. In Reconstruction, US Army troops, including many Black soldiers, are the heroes, and paramilitary organizations like the Klan and the White League are the villains. The presence of a standing army within a civilian population, dreaded by the Revolutionaries, is what protects the freedpeople. Reconstruction shows us that the villains are those who want to restrict the political community, who would tell you that people born here are not real Americans, that there is some ineffable Americanness that they can never have. They told us that about the Founders' Constitution in *Dred Scott*. By Americanness, they meant whiteness, and they might have been right. So we beat them in war and we broke their Constitution, and we made them accept a new one at the point of a bayonet.

Reconstruction isn't perfect—it leaves out women. But the principle there—that democracy is what legitimates a political regime—pushes us in the right direction. The legitimating principle of the Declaration—protection of the natural rights of insiders—

doesn't have the same expansive force. The goal of this story is not to live up to the past but to be better, even if that means breaking with the past. And that means hope for all groups.

The heroes of the better story, like Lincoln and the Reconstruction Congress, are not perfect, either, but we do not need to whitewash them or to incorporate their flaws in our self-understanding. Again, the point of the better story is not that we should strive to be like the past—it is that we should strive to be better. If there's no way to do that within the system, what do Americans do? We tear things down and start again. American history, in this story, is not steady success and continuity; it is a series of failures and reinventions. That sets us the basic dilemma. Our world is not perfect. What should we do? Strive for gradual improvement, like Lincoln before the Civil War, or demand revolution, like Garrison and the Reconstruction Congress? Either option may be right in a given situation, but having made the revolutionary choice, we should own it.

The better story is more inclusive of Black Americans. Like the 1619 Project, it recognizes their role in the founding of the country and the realization of our ideals. Our ideal of equality is not present in Jefferson's Declaration. It is there in Lincoln's version of the Declaration, which is today's. But how does it get there? Through the work of abolitionists, including free Blacks and ex-slaves like Frederick Douglass and Prince Hall. And how does that value enter the Constitution? Through the Fourteenth Amendment, which is a necessary consequence of Black military service: those who fought for the United States will be citizens, and as citizens they will need the protection of the federal government against those who would return them to slavery.

Some free Blacks participated in the conventions that ratified the Founders' Constitution, but none held federal office. Far larger numbers of Blacks participated in the Reconstruction constitutional conventions, and many Blacks held federal office during Reconstruction. These were extraordinary men. South Carolina representative Robert Smalls, born into slavery, won freedom by commandeering a Confederate ship and helped convince Lincoln to allow Black men to enter the army. Representative James Rapier of Alabama, educated in Scotland, returned to America and helped enact the Civil Rights of 1875. He tried to get Congress to fund southern public schools and to distribute western land to freedpeople. Hiram Revels of Mississippi, the first Black senator, served as a chaplain during the Civil War and helped recruit and organize two Black regiments. Blanche Bruce, also a senator from Mississippi, was born into slavery but ended up a social luminary in Washington, DC.

Some people do not like a story that centers Reconstruction, because they find it hard to see themselves in Reconstruction. But no story is perfectly inclusive. There are people who find it hard to see themselves in the Founding, too. The people who are uncomfortable with Reconstruction are those who identify with the secessionists instead of the United States. The people who are uncomfortable with the Founding are those who think that writing "all men are created equal" doesn't make up for enslaving your children. If someone has to be left out, I think we should marginalize the traitors. That, too, is the lesson of the better story: it is what Section 3 of the Fourteenth Amendment did.

Thinking about Reconstruction gives us a better vision of what we must do. The Founders felt that they were being oppressed. With some exceptions, they did not notice, or did not care, that they were oppressing others. They fought for their own rights. That is not a very inspiring vision in general, but it is particularly poorly suited to this moment. Some of the heroes of the Civil War and Reconstruction, particularly the Black ones, fought for their own rights, but many recognized that injustice was being inflicted on others and fought against it—even though they themselves might have profited from that injustice. That is the attitude we need today. That is the "Battle Hymn of the Republic": the soldiers who sang that they would die to make men free.

The "Battle Hymn of the Republic," incidentally, would make a better national anthem than "The Star-Spangled Banner." Far from professing a willingness to die for the freedom of others, "The Star-Spangled Banner" boasts of American victory over "the hireling and slave." That reference is to the five thousand or so American slaves who, as in the Revolution, escaped to British forces and assisted in the fight against their American enslavers in the War of 1812. Enslaved men fought for the Americans, too, some conscripted and others promised freedom. While the British did give freedom to enslaved people who joined their ranks, refusing to honor a provision in the Treaty of Ghent that promised return of their "slaves or other private property," the Americans betrayed that promise.

If we are connected to the Founding, we should think of slavery as our original sin. This is not actually a productive attitude. If slavery is the original sin, the message to take from it is that slavery is bad, and to be good one should not be an enslaver. That message is accurate, and it is one that Founding America should have heeded. Founding America's inability to hear and act on that message is what led to its destruction at the hands of people who did both those things. But precisely because our America is born with the destruction of slavery, thinking about slavery as our original sin is not helpful to us going forward. Slavery is Founding America's original sin, and it is over. In the standard story, that is part of the self-congratulation that can encourage complacency: we fixed it, we have atoned, we are done. It is also part of the resistance to the idea that change is needed: *I'm not enslaving anyone*, the response goes. *I never did. I have done nothing wrong.*

The original sin of Reconstruction America is Redemption. Redemption is bad in part because it's white supremacist terrorism, and of course that's a lesson. Even more important—because, as with slavery, there are not that many people nowadays who defend white supremacist terrorism—Redemption is bad because it marks a failure of will by people who are not necessarily white supremacists, but who are too tired of division, of tension, of being uncomfortable, to follow through in the struggle for equality. This is a sin that people might recognize in themselves: *I did not perpetrate injustice myself, but, yes, maybe I did stand by, maybe I did not fight against it as hard I could have.* The message of the better story is that we must bear discomfort to fight for justice; we must be willing to endure conflict, even with those we think of as our team, our fellow insiders. Justice must sometimes come before unity—that is the lesson we must learn or, like Founding America, face a revolution from those who learn it without us.

Putting unity ahead of justice is the sin that echoes through our America—in Redemption, of course, in the Jim Crow era, and more recently in the 1960s, when civil rights protests and race riots across the country thrust forward the question of racial inequality. Americans at the time took a very dim view of those protests. The summer of 1967, or more precisely the issuance of the *Kerner Report* analyzing its violence, provides a good pivot from a list of the attractions of the better story to a more focused analysis of the present day. The riots of 1967 had different instigating events, but concerns about excessive policing were a common thread. In *America on Fire*, Elizabeth Hinton argues that "the so-called urban riots from the 1960s to the present can only be properly understood as *rebellions*" and notes that "the violence was in response to moments of tangible racism . . . almost always taking the form of a police encounter."[2]

In Cincinnati, a resident protests what he thought was the wrongful conviction of his cousin. Police arrest him for blocking the sidewalk. A meeting held to protest that arrest spirals out of hand, and looting breaks out. In Newark, a march against police brutality turns into looting. In Detroit, a police raid on an unlicensed drinking club provides the spark. In Milwaukee, it is the rumor of police brutality against a young boy. In several cities, the National Guard is called up. In Detroit, President Johnson invokes the Insurrection Act to send in federal troops. By the end of the summer, in cities across the country, almost a hundred people have died, whole neighborhoods have burned, and tens of millions of dollars of property has been destroyed.

Johnson creates a bipartisan commission to investigate and report on the cause of the riots. The *Kerner Report* is issued in 1968. The riots, it concludes, involved Blacks "acting against local symbols of white American society, authority, and property in Negro neighborhoods—rather than against white persons." Why did it happen? "White racism," the report concludes, "is essentially responsible for the explosive mixture which has been accumulating in our cities since the end of World War II." Discrimination and segregation—both by operation of law and through the choices of individuals—concentrated Blacks in poverty. "Our nation is moving toward two societies," the report warns, "one black, one white—separate and unequal."[3]

Black people have been promised equality; they have heard it announced by courts and legislatures, but they have not seen results. "Frustrated hopes are the residue of the unfulfilled expectations aroused by the great judicial and legislative victories of the civil rights movement and the dramatic struggle for equal rights in the South." Violence has become more accepted because of anti-government rhetoric and "white terrorism directed against nonviolent protestors." And Blacks distrust the police. "To some Negroes," the report says, "police have come to symbolize white power, white racism, and white repression. And the fact is that many police do reflect and express these white attitudes."[4]

What is to be done? "To pursue our present course will involve the continuing polarization of the American community and, ultimately, the destruction of basic democratic values." The alternative is a real attempt to complete "the major unfinished business of this Nation"—to finally "make good the promises of American democracy to all citizens, urban and rural, white and black, Spanish-surname, American Indian, and every minority group." The report recommends massive investment targeted for high impact "to close the gap between promise and performance." "The realization of common opportunities for all," the report says, "will require a commitment to national action—compassionate, massive, and sustained, backed by the resources of the most powerful and the richest nation on earth. From every American it will require new attitudes, new understanding, and, above all, new will."[5]

The will was not there. Johnson ignored its recommendations. One month after the *Kerner Report* was released, Martin Luther King was assassinated. Riots broke out in over a hundred cities.

In the 1968 election, Richard Nixon's law-and-order platform triumphed. As the years went by, Nikole Hannah-Jones writes, they brought "increased police militarization, law-enforcement spending and mass incarceration of Black Americans."[6] Those trends have continued right up to the present moment. And of course they did not start in 1968. Like so many other distinctive features of American society, our unusual police forces have a racial origin. How did they get so big, so fast, asks Jill Lepore. "The reason is, mainly, slavery."[7] From the first slave patrols, to the later enforcers of Jim Crow laws, from the shield against urban unrest, to a gear in the machine of mass incarceration, the work of police in America has always had a racial dimension that required massive force.

We should ask ourselves now, as the Kerner Commission did, where do we go from here? How do we avoid the failures of will that doomed attempts to promote racial equality in the past? Part of the answer is to change Americans' self-conception—to change it in a way that makes Americans more willing to see pervasive injustice, and less willing to see it continue. That is the main goal of our better story, reorienting the American story around Reconstruction. Let go of the Founding, cut the connection between Mo'ne Davis and Roger Taney. This is not as radical or unprecedented as it might seem. The Founders were not even thought of as such until Lincoln's day.

We also need to let go of the Confederacy. Rethinking the standard story will help because founding values are in many ways Confederate values. Part of the reason attachment to the Confederacy endures is that our standard story is there telling us that fighting for your rights against the oppressive national government is the essence of America. But the standard story also presents itself as based on a commitment to equality and unity. That is false, but it is seductive, and it allows well-meaning people to believe that their Confederate values are actually on the side of equality. Thus, for instance, in the hands of Ronald Reagan, the standard story was used to promote a very Confederate vision—a narrowed political community, a distrust of the federal government—but it did so in optimistic and uplifting trappings. Reagan's most famous campaign ad proclaimed that it was "Morning in America."

What is different about this moment is that the Confederate vision is not presented as warm and unifying. Donald Trump had a vision similar to that of Reagan—outsiders cutting in line, undeserving others taking what belongs to real Americans, a distrust of government—but it was presented in dark and divisive tones. (Hillary Clinton, accepting the Democratic nomination in 2016, said exactly this: "He's taken the Republican Party a long way, from 'Morning in America' to 'Midnight in America.' He wants us to fear the future and fear each other."[8]) Storming the Capitol was the logical endpoint. With the Confederate vision presented more starkly, by the government and by white supremacists rallying around Confederate statues and iconography, well-meaning whites—the non-racist adherents to the standard story—find white unity harder, because it becomes more apparent to them that they are uniting with racists. When the lines are clearly drawn, the non-racist category disappears: you can be racist, or you can be anti-racist.[9] You cannot defend white supremacists storming the Capitol in the name of colorblindness and civility.

That is where we are now with the Confederacy. It has become clearer—in part because of our government, in part because of the actions of white supremacists, and in part because of a mass protest movement calling them out—that what seemed to some like a benign veneration of a mythic Lost Cause is in fact part of a system that symbolizes and perpetuates racial hierarchy. And faced with the choice, well-meaning whites are largely taking the anti-racist side. Mississippi is removing the Confederate battle emblem from its flag; around the nation, Confederate statues are coming down. Even some descendants of the men depicted agree. "Why are we protecting statues that symbolize oppression instead of protecting the people that were oppressed?" asks Robert Lee III, great-great-grandnephew of the Confederate general.[10] "The removal of the [Richmond] Jackson statue and others," wrote two great-great-grandsons of Stonewall Jackson, "will necessarily further difficult conversations about racial justice. It will begin to tell the truth of us all coming to our senses."[11]

We cannot choose from whom we are descended, but we can choose with whom we identify. And before we say that it is too much to ask white Americans to accept that their ancestors were flawed, we should consider that Black Americans have had to do it for generations, and in a more difficult way.[12] Many Black Americans are descended from slave owners—and the lack of choice there has a whole other dimension. "I have rape-colored skin," writes the poet Caroline Williams in the *New York Times*. "I am more than half white, and none of it was consensual."[13]

So it is possible to change our perspective. And it will make a difference. The standard story tells us that we should look for injustices inflicted on ourselves and fight against those. It tells us that racism is the bad actions of bad people, and all we must do to promote equality is not be racist and wait for America's values to be realized. Don't enslave people and you're good. And maybe you *can* enslave people—maybe you can rape your slaves and enslave your children—if you write elegantly enough about equality.

The better story tells us that we should recognize injustices against anyone, even if we ourselves profit from them. It tells us that racism may be all around us, but that does not mean we made it, and that the existence of injustices that benefit us does not make us unjust—not if we oppose them. The heroes of the better story are people born into a world they did not make, into a system that is not their fault. They are heroes because they recognized that changing it was their responsibility, and they turned a war for union into a war for freedom.

So how do we change it now, in this world we did not make? I said before that colorblindness and time—the nostrums of the standard story—are not enough. Colorblindness and time entrench white supremacy. What is needed are conscious remedies, things like reparations and affirmative action. The Supreme Court, in what could plausibly be called Second Redemption decisions, has cut back affirmative action essentially to the context of admissions to universities and graduate schools, and there it hangs by a thread. While I support affirmative action, it might in some ways be counterproductive. Affirmative action has some practical effect in promoting racial equality, but its symbolic or cosmetic effect may be stronger than its practical one. And that may be harmful to the cause of equality.

Saying anything coherent about affirmative action is difficult—thanks again to the Supreme Court, arguments about it tend to circle around the concept of diversity that enhances the educational experience.[14] This is a nebulous concept that is probably not the real reason the champions of affirmative action support it. Writing in *Grutter v. Bollinger*, the Supreme Court decision that upheld the affirmative action program at the University of Michigan Law School, Justice Sandra Day O'Connor came somewhat closer to what I think is the real justification: American ideals are inconsistent with a racially stratified society. "Effective participation by members of all racial and ethnic groups in the civic life of our Nation is essential if the dream of one Nation, indivisible, is to be realized."[15] So far, so good. Yet what does affirmative action really do? Does it create an environment in which members of all racial and ethnic groups can succeed? No—if that environment existed, there would be no need for it. O'Connor went on to say that "in order to cultivate a set of leaders with legitimacy in the eyes of the citizenry, it is necessary that the path to leadership be visibly open to talented and qualified individuals of every race and ethnicity." Again, so far, so good. But is that what affirmative action really does? No—again, if the path were truly open, there would be no need for affirmative action. What affirmative action does is to make it *look like* the path is open when in fact it is not. And what this does is to lull people—well-meaning whites in particular—into overestimating the degree of racial equality that has been achieved.

Affirmative action is not enough. Like the standard story, it may even make real change harder by allowing whites to feel that they have done enough. If you are trying to change people who fundamentally disagree with you, it helps to start by making them feel good about themselves. But if you are trying to get action from people who fundamentally agree with you, it is important not to let them feel good about themselves while doing nothing. Which brings us to reparations. The standard story asks us to think about racism as the anomalous and un-American bad acts of bad people, and this leads to an understanding of reparations as payments that bad people make to those they have wronged. Of course, if you think about it that way, the idea of reparations is too bitter a pill for white America to swallow. *I am not racist,* the reaction goes. *I have done nothing wrong. I am not going to make payments based on guilt I don't have to people I didn't harm, especially since slavery and segregation are so far in the past.*

That reaction is understandable, and I do not think there is any way to accept it on its own terms and defeat it. The only way past it is to change the framing. *You are not a bad person,* we should say. *You are not racist. But society is. Society has been racist since the beginning. That is not your fault. What makes an American hero is seeing the injustice in the world you were born into, a world you did not make, and working to change it.* The fact is that racial disadvantage is heritable, and the fact is that the infliction of racial disadvantage did not end in 1865, or 1954, or 1963. Part of what went on for years and years was active economic predation of Black people. Mortgage lenders steered Black homebuyers into mortgages they could not afford. The city of Ferguson, Missouri, according to the Department of Justice Report, used its police and courts to generate revenue from its Black citizens. "When we think of white supremacy," wrote Ta-Nehisi Coates, "we picture Colored Only signs, but we should picture pirate flags."[16]

Another part of what persisted was backlash to Black success. The racial terrorism of the Jim Crow era was designed to reinforce racial hierarchy, and one way it did that was to target Black accumulations of wealth. As Carol Anderson writes in *White Rage*, "The trigger for white rage, inevitably, is Black advancement."[17] And still another part—perhaps the most consequential—was the exclusion of Blacks from opportunities for economic advancement and government support. At the state level, discriminatory laws for many years excluded Black people from the education and professions that facilitated white wealth accumulation. At the federal level, starting with the New Deal, and through the rest of the twentieth century, the government poured out financial assistance to the American people. But these programs were often designed to exclude Blacks, and when they were not designed that way, they were usually administered by local authorities, which created the opportunity for discriminatory implementation. As Ira Katznelson describes in *When Affirmative Action Was White*, government benefit programs "were crafted and administered in a deeply discriminatory manner."[18] The initial rollout of the Social Security Act excluded domestic and farm laborers. Whatever the motivation, the result was that nationwide, 65% of Blacks were excluded, 70–80% in parts of the South.[19] Other New Deal laws, like the Fair Labor Standards Act, had similar exclusions: southern Democrats were willing to support them "provided these statutes did not threaten Jim Crow."[20] Implementation of the Serviceman's Readjustment Act (the GI Bill) notoriously excluded Blacks from most of the $95 billion expended between 1944 and 1971. "Written under southern auspices," Katznelson says, "the law was deliberately designed to accommodate Jim Crow. Its administration widened the country's racial gap."[21] Federal support for homeownership, through the GI Bill and the Federal Housing authority, was administered unequally, impeding Black homeownership and producing residential segregation.[22] The segregation of our neighborhoods is not simply the product of private choice: it, too, is systemic. In *The Color of Law*, Richard Rothstein lays out in detail how federal, state, and local governments used all the tools at their disposal to produce and support segregation.

For decade after decade, the federal government actively assisted the development of the middle class, pumping out money to support education, skills training, homeownership. But either explicitly or implicitly, these programs directed their benefits overwhelmingly to whites and not Blacks. What is the outcome? "Imagine two countries," Katznelson writes, "one the richest in the world, the other among its most destitute. Then suppose that a global program of foreign aid transferred well over $100 billion, but to the rich nation, not the poor."[23] That is the story of US domestic spending since the 1930s. Predictably, it has produced a vast and durable wealth gap.[24] In 2016, the Brookings Institute reports, the median net worth of a white family was nearly ten times that of a Black family.[25]

The wealth gap is one reason that Blacks and whites in many ways simply live in different worlds in terms of their experience of America. Pervasive discrimination and disparate treatment is another, but wealth matters. Wealth, far more than income, shapes the pattern of a person's life: the schools and homes they can afford, the ability to weather setbacks, the ability to support their children while alive and enrich them through inheritance after death. On almost every indicator of well-being, Blacks fare worse. Black people live in poorer neighborhoods—even those who are high earning. Black families at the $75,000 income level live in poorer neighborhoods than white families below the $40,000 level.[26] Seventy-two percent of white families owned their primary residence in 2016, compared to 42% of Black families—a wider gap than in 1960.[27] Black life expectancy consistently lags that of whites, Black infant mortality exceeds white, and Black women are two to three times more likely to die from pregnancy-related causes.[28] Residential racial segregation leads to educational segregation, and both private schools and majority-white public schools tend to outperform majority-minority public schools, which typically have a concentration of students from poor families. (Recent studies suggest that poverty segregation, rather than racial segregation, drives the achievement gap.[29]) We are still facing what the *Kerner Report* identified, what it warned against: two nations, separate and unequal.

The *Kerner Report* also echoes our present moment for another reason. In the summer of 2020, protests against police brutality and economic injustice swept the nation. Some, again, degenerated into looting. Some turned violent after unprovoked police attacks—something cell phone videos now establish beyond doubt, beyond the dueling accounts of protesters and police reports. But there are signs that it may be different this time. Perhaps because of the COVID-19 pandemic, perhaps because of the years of video evidence of racial injustice, Americans seem to be thinking differently about race. In recent years, the number of white Americans who think that racial discrimination is a big problem has soared in polling—from barely over 50% in 2015 to over 70%.[30] Ninety percent agree that racism and police violence are problems in America.[31] Majorities across all racial groups expressed support for the Black Lives Matter movement and peaceful protests of George Floyd's murder.[32] The bottom line, a Brookings report concludes, is that "it's not 1968 anymore. A large share of white Americans now endorse views on race relations once confined largely to African Americans."[33]

If we can take this moment, we can make a real and lasting change. It need not—and it should not—involve any individuals being singled out as wrongdoers. It need not involve payments from any person or to any person by reason of past conduct or events. It simply involves the decision that as the government for decades deliberately excluded Blacks and other minorities from wealth-building programs, it should now deliberately include them. That means investment intended to reduce the racial wealth gap. Studies have been done estimating the effects of different interventions: a report published in 2016 analyzed the effect of eliminating different disparities.[34] Homeownership was the most significant; labor market interventions such as job-creation programs and minimum-wage hikes also looked promising.

It is not my purpose here to argue for particular policies—simply that what we need now is a large-scale federal spending program deliberately aimed in the opposite direction from that of large federal spending programs of the past nine decades, one designed to reduce rather than increase the racial wealth gap. We need this in part because it is the right thing to do. Many white Americans resist reparations because they understand the idea as payments from wrongdoers to those they have injured, they feel accused, and they protest their innocence. That sort of reparations plan understandably strikes some people as unfair. Targeted investment is different. It is a systemic response to a systemic problem, which does not attempt to identify specific wrongdoers or injured parties but simply addresses the massive and undeniable inequality that exists. Targeting investment to poorer communities is a reasonable policy in terms of promoting equality, no matter how the inequality came about. And targeting investment to Black and minority communities is fairer than what we did for the past ninety years, to say nothing of the two hundred before that. It is fairer than pretending that we didn't do what we did, or that it had no lasting consequences. Strikingly, in July 2020, the city council of Asheville, North Carolina, voted to approve just such a targeted investment plan. Evanston, Illinois, has adopted a similar program to promote homeownership.

We also need it because of the consequences it could have. It offers the possibility of a real transformation. Many of the pathologies of American society we most feel most acutely now—our economic inequality, our tattered social safety net, our underfunded schools, our militarized police, our over-incarceration, our distrust of government authority, our brutal economic system, our neurotic insistence on individual liberty—have their roots in racism. Our undemocratic Electoral College, our dysfunctional voting system, our overabundance of guns, our outsize belief that individuals get the lives they deserve—all of this is tied to racial inequality.[35] This is a large part of what the 1619 Project tries to tell us. These pathologies are reinforced by the standard story that encourages us to look to the Founding for our sense of self, to focus on our own rights, and to fight whatever we think infringes them. The politics of racial resentment is not just killing the heartland—it is poisoning the country.

Attacking racial inequality is not the same thing as attacking racism, at least not directly. But the relationship between those two things is complex and multidirectional. Racism, of course, produces racial inequality through discrimination. Yet racial inequality also calls forth racism because racial inequality, if it is not to be seen as unfair, requires a justification that racism can provide. If we could reduce racial inequality, we might well find we have reduced racism. (In addition, reducing racial inequality would reduce segregation, and greater contact generally reduces bias.) And that would weaken one of the strongest forces that maintains our pathological exceptionalism, that prevents us from joining other modern industrialized democracies on issues from health care to drug laws to parental leave. One of the strongest, and one of the most difficult to see, one of the hardest to confront directly.

Martin Luther King, in his last speech, saw transformative potential in the convulsions around him. "The nation is sick, trouble is in the land, confusion all around." But "only when it is dark enough can you see the stars." The moment he was looking toward did not come in 1968. However, it may be approaching now. If we can meet this moment—if we can rise to the challenge of making a better America—we can still be the heroes of our story.

That is what American ideals demand of us—not the ideals of Founding America, which was a different country and not one we should aspire to emulate, but Reconstruction America, which for all its failures was born from the belief that we fight not only for ourselves, that we should lift up even those we did not push down, and that the future can be better than the past. Making a more just nation is not about returning to our origins or making America (anything) again. It is about making America.

That is all.

That is everything.

Bibliographical Essay

IT HAS BEEN over a decade since I wrote a review of a pair of books by Jack Balkin, *Living Originalism* and *Constitutional Redemption*, the project that started to give the ideas of this book shape in my mind. Since then, I have been in a continuous process of learning, researching, and refining the ideas. It is hard to list everyone who has helped me in that process, but I make an effort in the acknowledgments. Here, I try to list the works that proved the most helpful, or challenging, as I wrote the book. The sources are organized by the topic for which I found them most useful, as they occur in the book.

The standard story: Jack Balkin, *Living Originalism* and *Constitutional Redemption*; Mark Graber, *Trumping the Declaration: Presidents and the Declaration of Independence in the Twentieth and Twenty-First Centuries*; Jill Lepore, *This America: The Case for the Nation*; Rogers Smith, *That Is Not Who We Are!: Populism and Peoplehood.*

Lincoln and his foils: *The Speeches and Writings of Abraham Lincoln*, edited by Don Fehrenbacher; Harry Jaffa, *Crisis of the House Divided: An Interpretation of the Issues in the Lincoln-Douglas Debates*; Ibram X. Kendi, *Stamped from the Beginning: The Definitive History of Racist Ideas in America*; James Oakes, *The Radical and the Republican: Frederick Douglass, Abraham Lincoln, and the Triumph of*

Antislavery Politics and *Freedom National: The Destruction of Slavery in the United States, 1861–1865.*

Malcom X and Martin Luther King: *The Autobiography of Malcolm X: As Told to Alex Haley*; James H. Cone, *Martin & Malcolm & America: A Dream or a Nightmare*; David J. Garrow, *Bearing the Cross: Martin Luther King, Jr., and the Southern Christian Leadership Conference*; Walter Dean Myers, *Malcolm X: By Any Means Necessary.*

The Declaration of Independence: Danielle Allen, *Our Declaration: A Reading of the Declaration of Independence in Defense of Equality*; David Armitage, *The Declaration of Independence: A Global History*; Carl Becker, *The Declaration of Independence: A Study in the History of Political Ideas*; Joseph J. Ellis, *Writing the Declaration of Independence*; Pauline Maier, *American Scripture: Making the Declaration of Independence*; Daniel Rodgers, *Contested Truths: Keywords in American Politics since Independence*; Alexander Tsesis, *For Liberty and Equality: The Life and Times of the Declaration of Independence*; Garry Wills, *Inventing America: Jefferson's Declaration of Independence.*

Slavery and the Revolution: Bernard Bailyn, *The Ideological Origins of the American Revolution*; Patricia Bradley, *Slavery, Propaganda, and the American Revolution*; Christopher Leslie Brown, *Moral Capital: Foundations of British Abolitionism*; David Brion Davis, *Slavery and Human Progress, Inhuman Bondage: The Rise and Fall of Slavery in the New World, The Problem of Slavery in the Age of Revolution, 1770–1823,* and *The Problem of Slavery in Western Culture*; Paul Finkelman, *Slavery and the Founders: Race and Liberty in the Age of Jefferson* and *Defending Slavery: Proslavery Thought in the Old South*; George Sydney Fisher, *The True History of the American Revolution*; Woody Holton, *Forced Founders: Indians, Debtors, Slaves, and the Making of the American Revolution in Virginia*; Gerald Horne, *The Counter-Revolution of 1776: Slave Resistance and the Origins of the United States of America*; Matthew Mason, *North American Calm, West Indian Storm: The Politics of the Somerset Decision in the British Atlantic*; J. R. Oldfield, *Popular Politics and British Anti-Slavery: The Mobilisation of Public Opinion Against the Slave Trade, 1787–1807*;

Robert Parkinson, *The Common Cause: Creating Race and Nation in the American Revolution*; Manisha Sinha, *The Slave's Cause: A History of Abolition*; Alan Taylor, *The Internal Enemy: Slavery and War in Virginia, 1772–1832*; Larry E. Tise, *Proslavery: A History of the Defense of Slavery in America, 1701–1840*; George William Van Cleve, *A Slaveholders' Union: Slavery, Politics, and the Constitution in the Early American Republic*; William Wiecek, *The Sources of Antislavery Constitutionalism in America, 1760–1848*; Gordon Wood, *The Radicalism of the American Revolution*.

The Founders' Constitution: Akhil Reed Amar, *America's Constitution: A Biography*, *The Bill of Rights: Creation and Reconstruction* and *America's Unwritten Constitution*; Douglas Bradburn, *The Citizenship Revolution: Politics and the Creation of the American Union, 1774–1804*; Michael J. Klarman, *The Framers' Coup: The Making of the United States Constitution*; Gerard N. Magliocca, *The Heart of the Constitution: How the Bill of Rights Became the Bill of Rights*; Jack Rakove, *Original Meanings: Politics and Ideas in the Making of the Constitution*; David Waldstreicher, *Slavery's Constitution: From Revolution to Ratification*; Sean Wilentz, *No Property in Man: Slavery and Antislavery at the Nation's Founding*.

Dred Scott and antebellum America: Paul Finkelman, *An Imperfect Union: Slavery, Federalism, and Comity*; Mark A. Graber, *Dred Scott and the Problem of Constitutional Evil*; Martha Jones, *Birthright Citizens: A History of Race and Rights in Antebellum America*; James H. Kettner, *The Development of American Citizenship, 1608–1870*; Michael O'Brien, *Intellectual Life and the American South, 1810–1860*.

The Gettysburg Address: James M. McPherson, *The War That Forged a Nation: Why the Civil War Still Matters* and *Abraham Lincoln and the Second American Revolution*; Garry Wills, *Lincoln at Gettysburg: The Words That Remade America*.

Reconstruction: David W. Blight, *Race and Reunion: The Civil War in American Memory*; Pamela Brandwein, *Rethinking the Judicial Settlement of Reconstruction*; Gregory P. Downs, *After Appomattox: Military Occupation and the Ends of War* and *The Second*

American Revolution: The Civil War–Era Struggle over Cuba and the Rebirth of the American Republic; W. E. B. Du Bois, *Black Reconstruction in America*; Garrett Epps, *Democracy Reborn: The Fourteenth Amendment and the Fight for Equal Rights in Post–Civil War America*; Eric Foner, *A Short History of Reconstruction, The Second Founding: How the Civil War and Reconstruction Remade the Constitution, The Fiery Trial: Abraham Lincoln and Slavery*, and *Reconstruction: America's Unfinished Revolution*; Henry Louis Gates Jr., *Stony the Road: Reconstruction, White Supremacy, and the Rise of Jim Crow*; Steven Hahn, *A Nation Under Our Feet: Black Political Struggles in the Rural South from Slavery to the Great Migration*; Paul E. Herron, *Framing the Solid South: The State Constitutional Conventions of Secession, Reconstruction, and Redemption, 1860–1902*; Gerard N. Magliocca, *American Founding Son: John Bingham and the Invention of the Fourteenth Amendment*; James Oakes, *Freedom National: The Destruction of Slavery in the United States, 1861–1865*; Lisset Pino and John Fabian Witt, "The Fourteenth Amendment as an Ending: From Bayonet Justice to Paper Rights"; Charles Postel, *Equality: An American Dilemma, 1866–1896*.

Race relations over time: Carol Anderson, *White Rage: The Unspoken Truth of Our Racial Divide*; Edward E. Baptist, *The Half Has Never Been Told: Slavery and the Making of American Capitalism*; Mehrsa Baradaran, *The Color of Money: Black Banks and the Racial Wealth Gap*; Douglas A Blackmon, *Slavery by Another Name: The Re-Enslavement of Black Americans from the Civil War to World War II*; Elizabeth Hinton, *America on Fire: The Untold History of Political Violence and Black Rebellion since the 1960s*; Noel Ignatiev, *How the Irish Became White*; Ira Katznelson, *When Affirmative Action Was White: An Untold History of Racial Inequality in Twentieth-Century America*; Michael J. Klarman, *Unfinished Business: Racial Equality in American History*; Philip A. Klinkner and Rogers Smith, *The Unsteady March: The Rise and Decline of Racial Equality in America*; Manning Marable, *How Capitalism Underdeveloped Black America*; Cedric J. Robinson, *Black Marxism: The Making of the Black Radical Tradition*; Richard Rothstein, *The Color of Law: A Forgotten History* *of How Our Government Segregated America*; Rogers M. Smith, *Civic Ideals: Conflicting Visions of Citizenship in U.S. History*; C. Vann Woodward, *The Strange Career of Jim Crow*.

Racial equality in modern America: Michelle Alexander, *The New Jim Crow: Mass Incarceration in the Age of Colorblindness*; James Baldwin, *The Fire Next Time*; Eduardo Bonilla-Silva, *Racism without Racists: Color-Blind Racism and the Persistence of Racial Inequality in America*; Paul Butler, *Chokehold: Policing Black Men*; Ta-Nehisi Coates, *Between the World and Me* and *We Were Eight Years in Power: An American Tragedy*; Jacob Hacker and Paul Pierson, *Let Them Eat Tweets: How the Right Rules in an Age of Extreme Inequality*; Arlie Hochschild, *Strangers in Their Own Land: Anger and Mourning on the American Right*; Issa Kohler-Hausman, *Misdemeanorland: Criminal Courts and Social Control in an Age of Broken Windows Policing*; Ian Haney López, *Dog Whistle Politics: How Coded Racial Appeals Have Reinvented Racism and Wrecked the Middle Class*; Heather McGhee, *The Sum of Us: What Racism Costs Everyone and How We Can Prosper Together*; Jonathan Metzl, *Dying of Whiteness: How the Politics of Racial Resentment Is Killing America's Heartland*; Daria Roithmayr, *Reproducing Racism: How Everyday Choices Lock in White Advantage*.

Acknowledgments

RATHER THAN A narrowly focused analysis, this book aspires to present a big-picture assessment, or reassessment, of American constitutional history. One of the first things I realized when trying to put the big picture together was how much I was still influenced, even while trying to present something novel, by my teachers. Bruce Ackerman, Akhil Amar, Jack Balkin, and Robert Burt all had powerful effects on my thinking about the Constitution, and their generosity in correspondence and conversation has made the impact continuing.

As I worked on the project, over the course of almost a decade, I benefited from the assistance of a series of extremely helpful research assistants. Paul Cozzi, Conor Ferrall, Benjamin Gilberg, Julie Girard, Ellyn Jameson, Max Kaufman, Brenna Stewart, Francisco Torres, and Catherine Yun all helped develop and refine the arguments.

A number of friends and colleagues gave me helpful input, talking over the ideas and reading the manuscript in its different drafts. Melissa Bortnick, Taylor Davis, Noah Feldman, Larry Hardesty, Lauren Havens, Tom Lincoln, Sandy Mayson, Kellen McCoy, Ryan Paillet, Richard Primus, Emily Turner, Liangzhen Tan, Rebecca Tushnet, and Bill Weber all provided comments and critiques that strengthened the book. I owe special gratitude to the historians Greg Downs, Paul Finkelman, Mark Graber, Carlton Larson, and Gerard Magliocca, who lent me their expertise.

Victoria Skurnick, at Levine Greenberg Rostan Literary Agency, helped me turn the idea into a book proposal, and Tim Mennel at the University of Chicago Press helped turn the manuscript into a readable book. Without their efforts, you wouldn't be reading this.

Last, I thank my family. Long ago, my parents taught me that sometimes justice must come before unity. More recently, they read drafts of the book. It's been both a joy and a privilege to help my own children, Rana and Maron, grow up into a world where different versions of the American story are being heard. And in that venture, and so much else, I'm lucky and grateful to have the support and companionship of my wife, Felicia Lewis.

Notes

INTRODUCTION

1. Ryan Briggs, "Taking Back Taney: All-Star Little Leaguers Make Good a Sullied Name," *Hidden City*, August 20, 2014, https://hiddencityphila.org/2014/08/taking-back-taney-all-star-little-leaguers-make-good-a-sullied-name/.
2. Ximena Conde, "Philly's Taney Dragons to Drop the Controversial Name, a Reminder of the Dred Scott Decision," WHYY PBS, June 25, 2020, https://whyy.org/articles/phillys-taney-dragons-to-drop-the-controversial-name-a-reminder-of-the-dred-scott-decision/.

CHAPTER ONE

1. For a survey of presidential uses of the Declaration, see Mark A. Graber, *Trumping the Declaration: Presidents and the Declaration of Independence in the Twentieth and Twenty-First Centuries* (forthcoming). Graber reveals, among other things, that references were much rarer before the twentieth century, that Lincoln was the first president to quote the phrase "all men are created equal," and that Trump is an outlier in terms of how nonsubstantive his references to the Declaration are. Also important, he notes that the Declaration has changed from a challenge to a congratulation: after the 1970s, it became the symbol not of work to be done but "of America's triumph over a racist past."

CHAPTER TWO

1. Tom Mackaman, "An Interview with Historian Gordon Wood on the New York Times' 1619 Project," World Socialist Web Site, November 27, 2019,

https://www.wsws.org/en/articles/2019/11/28/wood-n28.html. See also Wesley Frank Craven, *The Legend of the Founding Fathers* (Ithaca, NY: Cornell University Press, 1956).

2. Frederick Douglass, "The Constitution of the United States: Is It Pro-Slavery or Anti-Slavery?," speech, Glasgow, March 26, 1860. Scholars generally agree that Douglass's shift was tactical: he believed that the Republican strategy was more likely to lead to abolition than the Garrisonian one. See Paul Finkelman, "Frederick Douglass's Constitution: From Garrisonian Abolitionist to Lincoln Republican," *Missouri Law Review* 81, no. 1 (2016): 68. "Douglass was not interested in history, logic, or law, and he had openly and forthrightly renounced his previous constitutional analysis. He was interested in political action that would undercut the Fugitive Slave Act of 1850 and slavery itself."

3. Malcolm X, "The Ballot or the Bullet," April 12, 1964, available at http://malcolmxfiles.blogspot.com/2013/06/the-ballot-or-bullet-april-12-1964.html. Although Malcolm X didn't make the point explicitly, the presidents he notes here are the first and last presidents to preside over a slaveholding America. His complaint, we could say, was that the March on Washington never got to Reconstruction. Whatever we think of his general disdain for the March, he was right that white liberals watered down its militancy. John Lewis had drafted a speech that spoke of revolution and threatened "a Sherman's march" to "destroy segregation." Washington Archbishop Patrick O'Boyle insisted that the words be taken out, and they were. See Charles Euchner, *Nobody Turn Me Around: A People's History of the 1963 March on Washington* (Boston: Beacon Press, 2010).

4. Malcolm X, Speech at Queens College, May 5, 1960, available at http://malcolmxfiles.blogspot.com/2013/05/queens-college-speech-may-5-1960.html.

5. Malcolm X, "The Ballot or the Bullet."

6. Malcolm X, "The Black Revolution," April 8, 1964, available at http://malcolmxfiles.blogspot.com/2013/07/the-black-revolution-april-8-1964.html.

7. Malcolm X, "The Black Revolution."

8. Malcolm X, "The Ballot or the Bullet."

9. My goal in this book is not to discuss existing scholarship so much as to offer an alternate perspective. *Our Declaration* is an interesting book well worth reading. As a general matter, though, I believe it makes the same mistake that many readers of the Declaration do, which is to confuse arguments that *could be made* based on the Enlightenment social contract theory that underlies the Declaration with the arguments the Declaration *actually makes*, which are quite different. Danielle Allen, *Our Declaration: A Reading of the Declaration of Independence in Defense of Equality* (New York: Norton, 2014).

10. Under fire, the 1619 Project seems to have backed off the claim that 1619 is the true birth year of the nation, removing those words and asserting that the claim was always metaphorical. That seems reasonable. Centering slavery and the contributions of Black Americans in our national narrative is a worthy

goal, and it requires us to rethink a number of things, but it does not really suggest that an American nation came into being in 1619. However, I will argue that 1776 is not our nation's birth year, and I mean that very literally.

11. Jake Silverstein, "Why We Published The 1619 Project," *New York Times Magazine*, December 20, 2019, https://www.nytimes.com/interactive/2019/12/20/magazine/1619-intro.html.

12. Adam Serwer, "The Fight Over the 1619 Project Is Not about the Facts," *Atlantic*, December 23, 2019, https://www.theatlantic.com/ideas/archive/2019/12/historians-clash-1619-project/604093/.

13. George F. Will, "Opinion: The '1619 Project' Is Filled with Slovenliness and Ideological Ax-Grinding," *Washington Post*, May 6, 2020.

14. "From the Editor's Desk: 1619 and All That," *American Historical Review* 125, no. 1 (February 2020).

15. Sean Wilentz, "American Slavery and 'the Relentless Unforeseen,'" *New York Review*, November 19, 2019, https://www.nybooks.com/daily/2019/11/19/american-slavery-and-the-relentless-unforeseen/. Wilentz also argues that "the fight for black freedom is a universal fight; it's a fight for everyone. In the end, it affected the fight for women's rights—everything. That's the glory of it. To minimize that in any way is, I think, bad for understanding the radical tradition in America." Serwer, "The Fight Over the 1619 Project." But as this is exactly what Nikole Hannah-Jones already said ("not only for ourselves—black rights struggles paved the way for every other rights struggle, including women's and gay rights . . ."), it is not clear whom he thinks he is arguing with. Hannah-Jones, "Our Democracy's Founding Ideals Were False When They Were Written: Black Americans Have Fought to Make Them True," *New York Times Magazine*, August 14, 2019, https://www.nytimes.com/interactive/2019/08/14/magazine/black-history-american-democracy.html.

CHAPTER THREE

1. See Pauline Maier, "The Strange History of 'All Men Are Created Equal,'" *Washington & Lee Law Review* 56 (1999), noting that "many knowledgeable, intelligent people" believe that the Declaration and the Constitution are "basically all the same thing" (873) and the common belief that interpretation of the Declaration has not changed over time (874).

2. See Maier, 876. Jefferson said as much himself. See his letter to Henry Lee from May 8, 1825, stating his goal as "to justify ourselves in the independent stand we are compelled to take." *Founders Online*, National Archives, https://founders.archives.gov/documents/Jefferson/98-01-02-5212.

3. See, for example, Susan B. Anthony et al., Declaration of the Rights of the Women of the United States (July 4, 1876), arguing for female suffrage and equal rights for women. For a survey of the movements that have invoked

this understanding of the Declaration, see Alexander Tsesis, *For Liberty and Equality: The Life and Times of the Declaration of Independence* (New York: Oxford University Press, 2012); and David Armitage, *The Declaration of Independence: A Global History* (Cambridge, MA: Harvard University Press, 2007).

4. Jefferson, letter to Henry Lee, May 8, 1825.

5. Jefferson's contemporaries agreed that the Declaration was neither novel nor radical. "There is not an idea in it," John Adams wrote, "but what had been hackneyed in Congress for two years before." Joseph Ellis, *What Did the Declaration Declare?* (New York: Bedford, 1999), 44. Ellis also writes, "In the late eighteenth century [the philosophy of the Declaration] was widely accepted as commonplace" (44).

6. Abraham Lincoln, Speech on Dred Scott Decision, Springfield, June 26, 1857.

7. Thomas Jefferson, "Notes of Proceedings in the Continental Congress June 7–August 1, 1776," *Founders Online*, National Archives, https://founders .archives.gov/documents/Jefferson/01-01-02-0160.

8. See Maier, "Strange History," 877; and Ellis, *What Did the Declaration Declare?*, 18.

9. Akhil Amar first opened my eyes to this very important point.

10. Jefferson to Roger Weightman, June 24, 1826, Library of Congress, https:// www.loc.gov/exhibits/jefferson/214.html. This letter confirms several important points: Jefferson is concerned with a pre-political starting point (birth, or in the Declaration, creation), he is concerned with legitimate authority ("legitimately"), and he is concerned specifically with the divine right of kings ("by the grace of God").

11. Locke's statement of the right to revolution is that "all *Power given with trust* for the attaining an *end*, being limited by that end, whenever that *end* is manifestly neglected, or opposed, the *trust* must necessarily be *forfeited*, and the Power devolve into the hands of those that gave it, who may place it anew where they shall think best for their safety and security." John Locke, "Second Treatise," in *Two Treatises of Government*, ed. Peter Laslett (Cambridge: Cambridge University Press, 1964), §149, p. 385.

12. Maier, "Strange History," 877.

13. The analysis of Jefferson's equality is as follows: "What did it mean to say all men were 'created equal' in 1776? . . . [T]hat all men were originally free of subjection, and so were all on the same level, because nobody had a title from God or nature to rule others. All legitimate authority, as the Declaration of Independence went on to say, was founded upon consent." Maier, 883. See also Garry Wills, *Lincoln at Gettysburg: The Words That Remade America* (New York: Simon & Schuster, 1992), 100: "Put the claims of the Declaration as mildly as possible, and it still cannot be reconciled with slavery."

14. Jefferson to John Adams, January 22, 1821. *Founders Online*, National Archives, https://founders.archives.gov/documents/Jefferson/98-01-02-1789. In *Notes on the State of Virginia* (1785), Jefferson expressed beliefs in the racial inferiority of Blacks and concerns about violence attendant to emancipation. See also

Jefferson to John Holmes, April 22, 1820: "We have the wolf by the ear, and we can neither hold him nor safely let him go. Justice is in one scale, and self-preservation in the other." He began a translation of Condorcet's anti-slavery pamphlet but never finished it, perhaps, the National Archives speculates, because he did not believe Condorcet's claims about racial equality. Library of Congress, https://www.loc.gov/exhibits/jefferson/159.html.

15. This is a common reading of "unalienable." See, for example, Danielle Allen, *Our Declaration: A Reading of the Declaration of Independence in Defense of Equality* (New York: Norton, 2014), 173, glossing inalienability as meaning that "nobody should take this [right] away from us."

16. See Guido Calabresi and A. Douglas Melamed, "Property Rules, Liability Rules, and Inalienability: One View of the Cathedral," *Harvard Law Review* 85 (1972): 1089.

17. See Edward L. Rubin, "Rethinking Human Rights," *International Legal Theory* 9, no. 5 (2003): 17–20, describing views on alienability of liberty. Thomas Hobbes, *Leviathan; or, The Matter, Forme and Power of a Commonwealth Ecclesiasticall and Civil*, ed. M. Oakeshott (Oxford: Basil Blackwell, 1957), §§ 13–15.

18. See, for example, Randy E. Barnett, *Our Republican Constitution: Securing the Liberty and Sovereignty of We the People* (New York: HarperCollins, 2016) I.1: "What are inalienable or 'unalienable' rights? They are those you cannot give up even if you want to and consent to do so, unlike other rights that you can agree to transfer or waive. Why the claim that these rights are inalienable? The Founders want to counter England's claim that, by accepting the colonial governance, the colonists had waived or alienated their rights. The Framers claimed that with inalienable rights, you always retain the ability to take back any right that has been given up."

19. *Annals of Congress* 35, no. 999 (1820): 1005. See Ian Bartrum, "The Constitutional Canon as Argumentative Metonymy," *William & Mary Bill of Rights Journal* 18, no. 327 (2009): 378–79.

CHAPTER FOUR

1. This estimate, offered by documentary filmmaker Arlen Parsa, is hard to verify but seems accurate according to Tom Kertscher, "Fact-Check: They Signed the Declaration of Independence—but Nearly Three-Quarters Owned Slaves," *Chicago Sun-Times*, September 10, 2019, https://chicago.suntimes.com/2019/9/10/20859458/fact-check-declaration-independence-slaves-trumbull-painting-arlen-parsa. Eighth-grade students in Ohio, doing their own research, concluded that forty-one did: http://www.mrheintz.com/how-many-signers-of-the-declaration-of-independence-owned-slaves.html.

2. See George William Van Cleve, *A Slaveholders' Union: Slavery, Politics, and the Constitution in the Early American Republic* (Chicago: University of Chicago Press, 2010), 3: "The Revolution itself ultimately strengthened slavery."

3. Tom Mackaman, "An Interview with Historian Gordon Wood on the New York Times' 1619 Project," World Socialist Web Site, November 27, 2019, https://www.wsws.org/en/articles/2019/11/28/wood-n28.html. Wood acknowledges in this interview both that plantation slavery (hereditary and racial) was different from the practice of enslaving defeated enemies, and that slavery had generally been abolished in western Europe by the thirteenth century. Those propositions are hard to square with his claims that slavery existed everywhere without substantial criticism until the Revolution.

4. Sean Wilentz, *No Property in Man: Slavery and Antislavery at the Nation's Founding* (Cambridge, MA: Harvard University Press, 2018), 25.

5. David Brion Davis, *The Problem of Slavery in Western Culture* (Oxford: Oxford University Press, 1966), 60. Davis also notes that "the legal and moral validity of slavery was a troublesome question in European thought from the time of Aristotle to the time of Locke" (13).

6. Van Cleve, *Slaveholders' Union*, 41.

7. Thomas Clarkson, *The History of the Abolition of the African Slave-Trade*, vol. 1 (1808), 259, 261.

8. How widely the *Somerset* case was known, and how important it was seen to be, is disputed. For a useful primer on the debate, and in particular the role of Sean Wilentz, see Joseph M. Adelman, "The 1619 Project and the Work of the Historian," *The Junto*, January 23, 2020, https://earlyamericanists.com /2020/01/23/the-1619-project-and-the-work-of-the-historian/#more-23076; and William Hogeland, "Against the Consensus Approach to History," *New Republic*, January 25, 2021, https://newrepublic.com/article/160995/consensus -approach-history.

9. Matthew Mason, "North American Calm, West Indian Storm: The Politics of the Somerset Decision in the British Atlantic," *Slavery & Abolition* 41, no. 4 (2020). Mason offers a useful survey and the argument that "the politics of slavery and those of the imperial crisis of the 1770s interlinked, but in ways that tamped down rather than encouraged protest against the decision among North American Patriots. Staking a position in defense of slavery would . . . have split the Patriot movement."

10. David Hartley to Ben Franklin, November 14, 1775. The letters are available at https://founders.archives.gov/documents/Franklin/01-22-02-0153. Hartley's proposal in the House of Commons may be found in William Cobbett, *The Parliamentary History of England, from the Earliest Period to the Year 1803* (1813), 1049 (Debate on Mr. Hartley's Propositions for Conciliation with America, December 7, 1775).

11. Richard Henry Lee to Catherine Macaulay, Philadelphia, November 29, 1775, *Lee Family Digital Archive,* http://leefamilyarchive.org/papers/letters /transcripts-gw%20delegates/DIV0248.html.

12. Thomas Jefferson to John Randolph, November 29, 1775, *Founders Online,* National Archives, https://founders.archives.gov/documents/Jefferson/01-01 -02-0141.

13. See Van Cleve, *Slaveholders' Union*, 43: "Many South Carolinians were fighting the Revolution to protect their slave property."

14. See Robert Parkinson, *The Common Cause: Creating Race and Nation in the American Revolution* (Williamsburg, VA: Omohundro Institute of Early American History and Culture, 2016), 251–52.

15. See Christopher Leslie Brown, *Moral Capital: Foundations of British Abolitionism* (Williamsburg, VA: Omohundro Institute of Early American History and Culture, 2012), 13.

16. Clarkson, *History of the Abolition*, chap. 11.

17. Brown, *Moral Capital*, 27. See also J. R. Oldfield, *Popular Politics and British Anti-Slavery* (Oxon: Routledge, 1998), 53: "increasingly after 1790 the societies in the United States began to look to Britain for inspiration and not vice versa."

CHAPTER FIVE

1. Fragment on the Constitution and the Union. Similarly, the Republican Party platform in (1860 and 1864) announced its devotion to "the principles promulgated in the Declaration of Independence and codified in the Constitution."

2. Jack M. Balkin, *Constitutional Redemption: Political Faith in an Unjust World* (Cambridge, MA: Harvard University Press, 2011), 20.

3. See Akhil Reed Amar, *America's Constitution: A Biography* (New York: Random House, 2005), 43–51.

4. Amar, 43.

5. See Gerard N. Magliocca, *The Heart of the Constitution: How the Bill of Rights Became the Bill of Rights* (Oxford: Oxford University Press, 2018), 9.

6. Magliocca, 17.

7. See Barron v. Baltimore, 32 U.S. (7 Pet.) 243, 248 (1832) (§ 9); Fletcher v. Peck, 10 U.S. (6 Cranch) 87, 138 (1810) (§ 10).

8. Akhil Reed Amar, *The Bill of Rights: Creation and Reconstruction* (New Haven, CT: Yale University Press, 1998).

9. The exceptions are bills of attainder and ex post facto laws, banned by Article I, Section 10.

10. See William M. Wiecek, *The Sources of Antislavery Constitutionalism in America, 1760–1848* (Ithaca, NY: Cornell University Press, 1977). Neither, of course, did the Constitution as generally understood. See James Oakes, "Making Freedom National: Salmon P. Chase and the Abolition of Slavery," *Georgetown Journal of Law and Public Policy* 13 (2016), noting "the presumption, accepted by nearly all Americans from the Revolution to the Civil War, that abolition was something *states* did" (409); and "Abolition could only be accomplished state by state because central government established by the Constitution could *not* interfere with slavery in the states" (410).

11. See Paul Finkelman, *Slavery and the Founders: Race and Liberty in the Age of Jefferson*, 3rd ed. (Abingdon, UK: Routledge, 2014).

12. Don E. Fehrenbacher, *The Slaveholding Republic: An Account of the United States Government's Relations to Slavery* (New York: Oxford University Press, 2001), 40.

13. Amar, *America's Constitution*, 98.

14. Frederick Douglass, "The Constitution and Slavery," *The North Star*, March 16, 1849.

15. See Amar, 158–59.

16. As discussed below, not even the most ardent abolitionists maintained that the federal government could actually ban slavery in the states where it existed.

17. See Paul Finkelman, "The American Suppression of the African Slave Trade: Lessons on Legal Change," *Akron Law Review* 42 (2009), noting that "many slave owners in Virginia and Maryland opposed the African trade for narrowly economic reasons: they had more slaves than they needed, and knew that if the trade ended their surplus slaves would become more valuable" (442).

18. See Sean Wilentz, *No Property in Man: Slavery and Antislavery at the Nation's Founding* (Cambridge, MA: Harvard University Press, 2018), 73.

19. See Noah Feldman, *The Three Lives of James Madison: Genius, Partisan, President* (New York: Farrar, Straus and Giroux, 2017), 163.

20. 1860 U.S. Census.

21. See Walter Johnson, *Soul by Soul: Life Inside the Antebellum Slave Market* (Cambridge, MA: Harvard University Press, 2001), 5: "Approximately one million enslaved people were relocated from the upper South to the lower South." This was two and a half times the number transported to America from Africa. See Henry Louis Gates Jr., "Slavery, by the Numbers," *The Root*, February 10, 2014, https://www.theroot.com/slavery-by-the-numbers-1790874492.

22. Different states followed different rules, giving rise to a number of court cases, including *Scott v. Emerson* and its federal sequel, *Scott v. Sandford*.

23. Wendell Phillips, *Review of Lysander Spooner's Essay on the Unconstitutionality of Slavery* (Boston: Andrews & Prentiss, 1847), 4.

24. Sean Wilentz, "Constitutionally, Slavery Is No National Institution," *New York Times*, September 16, 2015.

25. A number of scholars, with different themes and emphases, make this argument. See, for instance, Charles Beard, *An Economic Interpretation of the Constitution of the United States* (New York: Macmillan, 1913) and Michael Klarman, *The Framers' Coup: The Making of the United States Constitution* (Oxford: Oxford University Press 2016). My argument is quite different. The ideals of the Declaration are not what we think—its main value is protection of the rights of insiders, not equality. The Founders' Constitution is not con-

cerned with either of these things; it is focused on geostrategic issues. And if we look for the influence of the Declaration on the Constitution, as I do in chapter 7, it is lamentable.

26. Wilentz, *No Property in Man*, 10–11, 6.

27. See Guido Calabresi and A. Douglas Melamed, "Property Rules, Liability Rules, and Inalienability: One View of the Cathedral," *Harvard Law Review* 85 (1972): 1092.

28. Wilentz, *No Property in Man*, xi.

29. Dred Scott v. Sandford, 60 U.S. 393, 45 (1856): 2.

30. John Quincy Adams, Speech at Bridgewater, November 6, 1844.

31. See, for example, Wilentz, *No Property in Man*, 23: "the paradox fitfully fell apart." But paradoxes don't fall apart; compromises do. The point, presumably, is that a paradox retains the possibility of purity. A compromise accepts its impurity: it is compromised. Wilentz wants to suggest that modern American ideals were present at the Founding—in the Declaration, in the Founders' Constitution—and that American history has been a halting progress toward fuller realization of those values. I think this view is aptly described as the most destructive falsehood in all of American history.

CHAPTER SIX

1. By way of example, in 1856 UNC chemistry professor Benjamin Hedrick supported the Republican candidate, John C. Frémont. For this he was fired by the university and driven from the state by the threat of mob violence. See Michael Kent Curtis, "St. George Tucker and the Legacy of Slavery," *William & Mary Law Review* 47, no. 1157 (2009): 1195.

2. Eric Foner, *Forever Free: The Story of Emancipation and Reconstruction* (New York: Vintage Books, 2005), xxii.

3. W. E. B. Du Bois, *Black Reconstruction in America, 1860–1880* (New York: Harcourt, Brace, and Co., 1935), 713.

4. See, for example, Kenneth Stampp, *The Era of Reconstruction, 1865–1877* (New York: Vintage Books, 1965); and John Hope Franklin, *Reconstruction after the Civil War* (Chicago: University of Chicago Press, 1961).

5. Andrew Kohut, "From the Archives: Fifty Years Ago: Mixed Reviews about Civil Rights but Support for Selma Demonstrators," Pew Research Center, January 16, 2020, https://www.pewresearch.org/fact-tank/2020/01/16/50-years-ago-mixed-views-about-civil-rights-but-support-for-selma-demonstrators/.

6. The objection was made by a state representative. See Mike Tipping, "New State Ballad Honors 20th Maine, Despite Pro-Confederate Objections," *Maine Beacon*, June 7, 2019, http://mainebeacon.com/new-state-ballad-honors-20th-maine-despite-pro-confederate-objections/. It is a perfect encapsulation of the view that the Civil War was a war between the states, which separated into North and South and then rejoined. That view is rejected by the Fourteenth Amendment.

7. I am not saying here that opponents of slavery were necessarily in favor of racial equality—there is an enormous difference between banning slavery and creating equality. My point is just that when we choose unity, we accept offenses against equality—first slavery, then Redemption.

8. As W. E. B. Du Bois wrote, "Labor class unity failed in the South because the theory of race was supplemented by a carefully planned and slowly evolved method, which drove such a wedge between white and black workers that there probably are not today in the world two groups of workers with practically identical interests who hate and fear each other so deeply and persistently and who are kept so far apart that neither sees anything of common interests. It must be remembered that the white group of laborers, while they received a low wage, were compensated in part by a sort of public and psychological wage." Du Bois, *Black Reconstruction in America*, 700. Or as President Lyndon B. Johnson said, "If you can convince the lowest white man he's better than the best colored man, he won't notice you're picking his pocket. Hell, give him somebody to look down on, and he'll empty his pockets for you."

9. See Philip A. Klinkner and Rogers M. Smith, *The Unsteady March: The Rise and Decline of Racial Equality in America* (Chicago: University of Chicago Press, 1999).

CHAPTER SEVEN

1. Pauline Maier, "The Strange History of 'All Men Are Created Equal,'" *Washington & Lee Law Review* 56 (1999): 882.

2. Maier, 883.

3. Cong. Globe, 38th Cong., 1st Sess. 1319 (1864).

4. The 1952 Democratic Party platform, available at https://www.presidency.ucsb.edu/documents/1952-democratic-party-platform.

5. Lyndon B. Johnson, "Remarks upon Signing the Civil Rights Bill," July 2, 1964, available at https://millercenter.org/the-presidency/presidential-speeches/july-2-1964-remarks-upon-signing-civil-rights-bill.

6. Lyndon B. Johnson, "Special Message to the Congress: The American Promise," March 15, 1965, available at http://www.lbjlibrary.org/lyndon-baines-johnson/speeches-films/president-johnsons-special-message-to-the-congress-the-american-promise/.

7. 378 U.S. 226, 286 (1964).

8. America's Founding Documents, National Archives, https://www.archives.gov/founding-docs/declaration.

9. In *For Liberty and Equality: The Life and Times of the Declaration of Indepen-*

dence (New York: Oxford University Press, 2012), Alexander Tsesis provides a valuable survey of the different groups that have appealed to the Declaration for support.

10. Dred Scott v. Sandford, 60 U.S. 393, 414 (1856).

11. 236 U.S. 1, 17–18 (1915). The idea that the rights of property and contract lead inevitably to inequality is a standard Enlightenment trope. See, for example, Jean-Jacques Rousseau, *Discourse on the Origin and Basis of Inequality among Men*. And unsurprisingly, the Declaration, that statement of generally accepted Enlightenment principles, was celebrated during the *Lochner* era. "The celebration of the Declaration in Dred Scott was followed by similarly fulsome praise in the decisions of the Lochner era." Carlton F. W. Larson, "The Declaration of Independence: A 225th Anniversary Re-Interpretation," *Washington Law Review* 76 (2001): 708.

CHAPTER NINE

1. Statutory rape occurs when one party is incapable of consent. Sally Hemings was incapable—not because she was fourteen when she joined Jefferson in Paris (the age of consent in America then tended to be between ten and twelve, and was set at eleven in France by the Napoleonic Code of 1791) but because she had no rights he was bound to respect when she was in America. In Paris, Sally Hemings was free and received a wage, which complicates the situation; Annette Gordon-Reed notes that Hemings threatened to stay in France rather than return to Monticello. See Annette Gordon-Reed, *The Hemingses of Monticello: An American Family* (New York: Norton, 2008), 352.

2. Andrew K. Franklin, "King in 1967: My Dream Has 'Turned into a Nightmare,'" *NBC News*, https://www.nbcnews.com/nightly-news/king-1967-my-dream-has-turned-nightmare-flna8C11013179.

3. Public Opinion Polls on Civil Rights Movement, 1961–1969, https://www.crmvet.org/docs/60s_crm_public-opinion.pdf.

4. See Richard A. Primus, "Canon, Anti-Canon, and Judicial Dissent," *Duke Law Journal* 48 (1998): 243.

5. Daria Roithmayr, *Reproducing Racism: How Everyday Choices Lock in White Advantage* (New York: NYU Press, 2014).

6. Lyndon B. Johnson, speech at Howard University, June 4, 1965.

7. Kevin M. Kruse's essay in the 1619 Project describes how "interstates were regularly used to destroy black neighborhoods [and] to keep black and white neighborhoods apart." Kruse, "What Does a Traffic Jam in Atlanta Have to Do with Segregation?," *New York Times Magazine*, August 14, 2019.

8. Alexander H. Stephens, Cornerstone speech, March 21, 1861.

9. *Teaching Hard History*, Southern Poverty Law Center, January 31, 2018, https://www.splcenter.org/20180131/teaching-hard-history.

10. Emily Bloch, "Florida Restricts How US History Is Taught, Seen as a Way to Get Critical Race Theory Out of Classroom," *USA Today*, June 11, 2021, https://www.usatoday.com/story/news/education/2021/06/11 /florida-education-board-strict-guidelines-us-history-critical-race-theory /7652613002/.

11. Regie Gibson, quoted in "'The Mere Distinction of Colour': Telling the Story of Slavery at Montpelier," National Trust for Historic Preservation, November 1, 2017, https://savingplaces.org/stories/the-mere-distinction-of-colour -tells-story-slavery-montpelier#.YOit9ehKiUk.

12. Indeed, the design committee was reportedly "overwhelmed by requests not to abandon the 'old flag' of the United States." John M. Coski, *The Confederate Battle Flag: America's Most Embattled Emblem* (Cambridge, MA: Harvard University Press, 2005).

CHAPTER TEN

1. Danielle Allen, "A Forgotten Black Founding Father: Why I've Made It My Mission to Teach Others about Prince Hall," *Atlantic*, March 2021, https:// www.theatlantic.com/magazine/archive/2021/03/prince-hall-forgotten -founder/617791/.

2. Garry Wills, *Lincoln at Gettysburg: The Words That Remade America* (New York: Simon & Schuster, 1992), 145.

3. Alexander Tsesis has a valuable discussion of different readings of the Declaration at the time of secession, noting that many in the South and elsewhere relied on the Declaration to justify secession. See Tsesis, *For Liberty and Equality: The Life and Times of the Declaration of Independence* (New York: Oxford University Press, 2012), 161–69.

4. "Confederate States of America—Declaration of the Immediate Causes Which Induce and Justify the Secession of South Carolina from the Federal Union," Avalon Project, Yale Law School, https://avalon.law.yale.edu/19th _century/csa_scarsec.asp.

5. "A Declaration of the Immediate Causes Which Induce and Justify the Secession of the State of Mississippi from the Federal Union," Avalon Project, Yale Law School, https://avalon.law.yale.edu/19th_century/csa _missec.asp.

6. "Secession Acts of the Thirteen Confederate States," American Battlefield Trust, https://www.battlefields.org/learn/primary-sources/secession-acts -thirteen-confederate-states.

7. As long ago as 1927, Charles and Mary Beard characterized the Civil War as a Second American Revolution. They meant that it was a transfer of power from southern planters to northern capitalists. Other historians after them have used the same phrase. For instance, see Gregory P. Downs, *Second Amer-*

ican Revolution: The Civil War–Era Struggle Over Cuba and the Rebirth of the American Republic (Chapel Hill: University of North Carolina Press, 2019); and James M. McPherson, *Abraham Lincoln and the Second American Revolution* (New York: Oxford University Press, 1991). I use "Second American Revolution" in two different senses here. First, the secession of the southern states was what I will call a status quo revolution that mirrored the First Revolution. Second, the transformation of American society with Reconstruction was what I will call a regime change revolution.

8. James Oakes, *The Crooked Path to Abolition: Abraham Lincoln and the Antislavery Constitution* (New York: Norton, 2021).

9. See Carl T. Bogus, "The Hidden History of the Second Amendment," *U.C. Davis Law Review* 31 (1998): 309.

10. Garry Wills makes a similar observation, although he does not say that the real Declaration supported the South. See Garry Wills, *Lincoln at Gettysburg: The Words That Remade America* (New York: Simon & Schuster, 1992), 38: "[Lincoln] performed one of the most daring acts of open-air sleight of hand ever witnessed by the unsuspecting."

11. Oakes's *The Crooked Path to Abolition* has a sophisticated discussion of the complexities and changes in Lincoln's thought; so does Eric Foner's *The Fiery Trial: Abraham Lincoln and Slavery* (New York: Norton, 2010).

12. James M. McPherson, *The War That Forged a Nation: Why the Civil War Still Matters* (New York: Oxford University Press, 2015), 6.

13. In the second inaugural address, both "Union" and "nation" appear, but "Union" refers each time to the country in the past. Speaking of the present, Lincoln uses only "nation."

14. Karl Marx, article in *Die Presse*, August 9, 1862; reprinted in Karl Marx and Frederick Engels, *Collected Works*, vol. 19 (New York: International Publishers, 2009), 226.

15. Karl Marx, article in *Die Presse*, October 12, 1862; reprinted in Marx and Engels, *Collected Works*, 19: 249–50. See, generally, Donny Schraffenberger, "Karl Marx and the American Civil War," *International Socialist Review* 80, https://isreview.org/issue/80/karl-marx-and-american-civil-war.

16. Manning Marable notes that "for generations, many white American workers refused certain menial jobs on the principle that they refused to 'do n***** work.'" Marable, *How Capitalism Underdeveloped Black America*, rev. ed. (Cambridge, MA: SouthEnd Press, 2000), 45.

17. Paul E. Herron, *Framing the Solid South: The State Constitutional Conventions of Secession, Reconstruction, and Redemption, 1860–1902* (Lawrence: University Press of Kansas, 2017).

18. Lisset Pino and John Fabian Witt, "The Fourteenth Amendment as an Ending: From Bayonet Justice to Paper Rights," *Journal of the Civil War Era* 10, no. 1 (March 2020).

19. Pino and Witt, citing Cong. Globe, 39th Cong., 1st sess. (1866), 2463.

20. I'm not going to talk much about these decisions, which are a little technical.

21. See Pino and Witt, "The Fourteenth Amendment as an Ending."

CHAPTER ELEVEN

1. For the account of Reconstruction more generally, I rely primarily on Eric Foner.

2. Gregory P. Downs, *After Appomattox: Military Occupation and the Ends of War* (Cambridge, MA: Harvard University Press, 2015), 3.

3. Downs, 20.

4. Downs, 25.

5. Downs, 40.

6. Downs, 42, quoting the letters of Colonel Charles Bentzoni.

7. Downs, 53, 54.

8. Downs, 55–56.

9. Andrew Johnson speech of January 21, 1864.

10. Eric Foner, *A Short History of Reconstruction* (New York: HarperCollins, 2010), 92.

11. Foner, 93.

12. Kenneth Stampp, *The Era of Reconstruction, 1865–1877* (New York: Vintage, 1965), 80.

13. See Foner, *A Short History of Reconstruction*, 93. W. E. B. Du Bois, *Black Reconstruction in America, 1860–1880* (New York: Harcourt, Brace, and Co., 1935), 167–80.

14. Bruce Ackerman, *We the People: Transformations* (Cambridge, MA: Harvard University Press, 1998).

15. Foner, *A Short History of Reconstruction*, 137.

16. Downs, *After Appomattox*, 231.

17. Downs, 231.

18. Jonathan M. Metzl, *Dying of Whiteness: How the Politics of Racial Resentment Is Killing America's Heartland* (New York: Basic Books, 2019).

19. Downs, *After Appomattox*, 196.

20. Foner, *A Short History of Reconstruction*, 142.

21. Foner, 145.

22. Cruikshank, 92 U.S. 542 (1876), comes from the Colfax massacre.

23. See C. Vann Woodward, *Reunion and Reaction: The Compromise of 1877 and the End of Reconstruction* (New York: Oxford University Press, 1966).

24. See Allen W. Trelease, *White Terror: The Ku Klux Klan Conspiracy and Southern Reconstruction* (Westport, CT: Greenwood Press, 1979); and Carol Anderson, *White Rage: The Unspoked Truth of Our Racial Divide* (New York: Bloomsbury, 2016).

25. See also, for example, Downs, *The Second American Revolution*, noting that "in some ways the [civil] war represented not the salvation of the republic but its death" and that the Founders "were fathers of a country that died" (4, 15).

CHAPTER TWELVE

1. Arlie Russell Hochschild, *Strangers in Their Own Land: Anger and Mourning on the American Right* (New York: New Press, 2016).
2. Jonathan M. Metzl, *Dying of Whiteness: How the Politics of Racial Resentment Is Killing America's Heartland* (New York: Basic Books, 2019), 3–6.
3. Heather McGhee, *The Sum of Us: What Racism Costs Us and How We Can Prosper Together* (New York: One World, 2021).
4. Kevin D. Williamson, "Why Not Fewer Voters?," *National Review*, April 6, 2021, https://www.nationalreview.com/2021/04/why-not-fewer-voters/. In 1957, in the same magazine, Buckley wrote an editorial entitled "Why the South Must Prevail." He asked "whether the White community in the South is entitled to take such measures as are necessary to prevail, politically and culturally, in areas in which it does not predominate numerically?" and concluded: "The sobering answer is *Yes*. . . . because, for the time being, it is the advanced race." William F. Buckley, "Why the South Must Prevail," *National Review*, August 24, 1957, available at https://adamgomez.files.wordpress.com/2012/03/whythesouthmustprevail-1957.pdf.

CHAPTER THIRTEEN

1. For discussions of this, the work of Dan Kahan and the Cultural Cognition project at Yale Law School is important, as is that of Kathleen Hall Jamieson at the Annenberg Center of the University of Pennsylvania. Relevant books include Peter Boghossian and James Lindsay, *How to Have Impossible Conversations: A Very Practical Guide* (New York: Hachette, 2019), and the classic study of the persistence of belief: Leon Festinger, Henry W. Riecken, and Stanley Schachter, *When Prophecy Fails* (Minneapolis: University of Minnesota Press, 1956).
2. Elizabeth Hinton, *America on Fire: The Untold History of Political Violence and Black Rebellion since the 1960s* (New York: Liveright, 2021), 7.
3. National Advisory Commission on Civil Disorders, *Kerner Commission Report on the Causes, Events, and Aftermaths of the Civil Disorders of 1967*, 5, 1.
4. *Kerner Report*, 5.
5. *Kerner Report*, 1.
6. Nikole Hannah-Jones, "What Is Owed," *New York Times Magazine*, June 30, 2020, https://www.nytimes.com/interactive/2020/06/24/magazine/reparations-slavery.html. Incarceration increased dramatically toward the

end of Reconstruction, as some states saw the possibility of using the Thirteenth Amendment "except as punishment for crime" loophole as a way to continue to extract forced labor. The Mississippi prison population went from 272 in 1872 to 1,072 in 1877. Over the same period, Georgia's grew from 432 to 1,441. Manning Marable, *How Capitalism Underdeveloped Black America*, rev. ed. (Cambridge, MA: SouthEnd Press, 2000), 111–12. More recently we have seen mass incarceration and even the use of misdemeanors as a form of social control. See Michelle Alexander, *The New Jim Crow: Mass Incarceration in the Age of Colorblindness* (New York: New Press, 2012); and Issa Kohler-Hausman, *Misdemeanorland: Criminal Courts and Social Control in an Age of Broken Windows Policing* (Princeton, NJ: Princeton University Press, 2019).

7. Jill Lepore, "The Invention of the Police," *New Yorker*, July 20, 2020.

8. Pamela Engel, "Clinton Jabs Trump," *Business Insider*, July 28, 2016, https://www.businessinsider.com/clinton-trump-dnc-speech-2016-7.

9. This is a theme of Ibram X. Kendi's *How to Be an Antiracist* (New York: One World, 2019).

10. Dana Schaeffer, "Descendants Weigh in on Confederate Statue Debate," *ABC News*, July 7, 2020, https://abcnews.go.com/US/descendants-weight-debate-confederate-symbols/story?id=71642026.

11. Jack Christian and Warren Christian, "The Monuments Must Go," *Slate*, August 16, 2017, https://slate.com/news-and-politics/2017/08/stonewall-jacksons-grandsons-the-monuments-must-go.html.

12. From the colonists charging King George with making them into slaves, to university applicants complaining about the "racism" of affirmative action, to parents demanding that schoolchildren not be exposed to material that might make them feel bad about themselves or their ancestors, it often seems that what upsets white Americans the most is experiencing a fraction of what Black Americans routinely endure.

13. Caroline Randall Williams, "You Want a Confederate Monument? My Body Is a Confederate Monument," *New York Times*, June 26, 2020, https://www.nytimes.com/2020/06/26/opinion/confederate-monuments-racism.html.

14. See Kermit Roosevelt III, "The Ironies of Affirmative Action," *University of Pennsylvania Journal of Constitutional Law* 17 (2015).

15. 539 U.S. 306, 332 (2003).

16. Ta-Nehisi Coates, *We Were Eight Years in Power: An American Tragedy* (New York: One World, 2017), 201.

17. Carol Anderson, *White Rage: The Unspoked Truth of Our Racial Divide* (New York: Bloomsbury, 2016), 3.

18. Ira Katznelson, *When Affirmative Action Was White: An Untold History of Racial Inequality in Twentieth-Century America* (New York: Norton, 2005), 38–39.

19. Katznelson, 43.

20. Katznelson, 55. See also Marc Linder, "Farm Workers and the Fair Labor Standards Act: Racial Discrimination in the New Deal," *Texas Law Review* 65 (1987), noting that by 1938 the farmworkers exclusion "had become routine in New Deal legislation" (1336).

21. Katznelson, *When Affirmative Action Was White*, 113, 114.

22. See Richard Rothstein, *The Color of Law: A Forgotten History of How Our Government Segregated America* (New York: Norton, 2017).

23. Katznelson, *When Affirmative Action Was White*, 142.

24. See William Darity Jr. et al., *What We Get Wrong about Closing the Racial Wealth Gap* (Samuel Dubois Cook Center on Social Equity, 2018), https:// socialequity.duke.edu/wp-content/uploads/2020/01/what-we-get-wrong.pdf.

25. Kriston McIntosh et al., "Examining the Black-White Wealth Gap," Brookings, February 27, 2020, https://www.brookings.edu/blog/up-front/2020/02 /27/examining-the-black-white-wealth-gap/.

26. Hannah-Jones, "What Is Owed."

27. "Reducing the Racial Homeownership Gap," Urban Institute, https://www .urban.org/policy-centers/housing-finance-policy-center/projects/reducing -racial-homeownership-gap.

28. "Racial and Ethnic Disparities Continue in Pregnancy-Related Deaths," CDC Newsroom, September 5, 2019, https://www.cdc.gov/media/releases /2019/p0905-racial-ethnic-disparities-pregnancy-deaths.html.

29. Dick Startz, "The Achievement Gap in Education: Racial Segregation versus Segregation by Poverty," Brookings, January 20, 2020, https://www.brookings .edu/blog/brown-center-chalkboard/2020/01/20/the-achievement-gap-in -education-racial-segregation-versus-segregation-by-poverty/.

30. "Poll: Majority of Americans Say Racial Discrimination Is a 'Big Problem,'" *All Things Considered*, June 21, 2020, https://www.npr.org/2020/06/21/881477657 /poll-majority-of-americans-say-racial-discrimination-is-a-big-problem.

31. "Nine Out of Ten Americans Say Racism and Police Brutality Are Problems," *Guardian*, July 8, 2020, https://www.theguardian.com/us-news/2020 /jul/08/americans-racism-police-brutality-problems-poll.

32. Kim Parker, Juliana Menasce Horowitz, and Monica Anderson, "Amid Protests, Majorities Across Racial and Ethnic Groups Express Support for the Black Lives Matter Movement," Pew Research Center, June 12, 2020, https:// www.pewsocialtrends.org/2020/06/12/amid-protests-majorities-across-racial -and-ethnic-groups-express-support-for-the-black-lives-matter-movement/.

33. William A. Galston, "When It Comes to Public Opinion on Race, It's Not 1968 Anymore," Brookings, June 22, 2020, https://www.brookings.edu/blog /fixgov/2020/06/22/when-it-comes-to-public-opinion-on-race-its-not-1968 -anymore/.

34. Amy Traub et al., "The Racial Wealth Gap: Why Policy Matters," Dēmos, June 21, 2016, https://www.demos.org/research/racial-wealth-gap-why-policy -matters.

35. For the Electoral College, see Alexander Keyssar, *Why Do We Still Have the Electoral College?* (Cambridge, MA: Harvard University Press, 2020); and Jesse Wegman, *Let the People Pick the President: The Case for Abolishing the Electoral College* (New York: Macmillan, 2020). For the effect of belief in a just world, see Hsin-Ya Liao, Ying-Yi Hong, and James Rounds, "Perception of Subtle Racism: The Role of Group Status and Legitimizing Ideologies," *Counseling Psychologist* 44 (2016): 238.